Understanding Research
Becoming a Competent and Critical Consumer

W. Paul Jones
University of Nevada, Las Vegas

Jeffrey A. Kottler
California State University, Fullerton

PEARSON
Merrill
Prentice Hall

Upper Saddle River, New Jersey
Columbus, Ohio

Library of Congress Cataloging-in-Publication Data
Jones, W. Paul.
  Understanding research : becoming a competent and critical consumer / W. Paul Jones, Jeffrey A. Kottler.
    p. cm.
  Includes index.
  ISBN 0-13-119844-0
  1. Research—Study and teaching (Higher) 2. Reading comprehension—Study and teaching (Higher) 3. Critical thinking—Study and teaching (Higher) I. Kottler, Jeffrey A. II. Title.

LB2326.3.J66 2006
78.1'70281--dc23   2004061619

Vice President and Publisher: Jeffery W. Johnston
Executive Editor: Kevin M. Davis
Development Editor: Autumn Benson
Production Editor: Mary Harlan
Production Coordination: Linda Zuk, WordCrafters Editorial Services, Inc.
Design Coordinator: Diane C. Lorenzo
Photo Coordinator: Monica Merkel
Text Design and Illustrations: Pine Tree Composition, Inc.
Cover Designer: Jason Moore
Cover Image: Superstock
Production Manager: Laura Messerly
Director of Marketing: Ann Castel Davis
Marketing Manager: Autumn Purdy
Marketing Coordinator: Tyra Poole

This book was set in Palatino by Pine Tree Composition, Inc. It was printed and bound by Courier Kendallville, Inc. The cover was printed by Coral Graphic Services, Inc.

Photo Credits: p. 2: Laura Bolesta/Merrill; p. 18: Terry Vine/Getty Images Inc.–Stone Allstock; p. 48: Bob Thomas/Getty Images Inc. Stone–Allstock; p. 76: Ryan McVay/Getty Images Inc.–Photodisc; p. 100: Jesse Boswell. Le Tre Finestre, 1924. Torino, Galleria d'Art Moderna/Art Resource, N.Y.; p. 112: Bruce Ayres/Getty Images Inc.–Stone Allstock; p. 146: John Beatty/Getty Images Inc.–Stone Allstock.

Pearson Education Ltd.
Pearson Education Singapore, Pte. Ltd.
Pearson Education Canada, Ltd.
Pearson Education—Japan

Pearson Education Australia PTY, Limited
Pearson Education North Asia Ltd.
Pearson Educacion de Mexico, S.A. de C.V.
Pearson Education Malaysia, Pte. Ltd.

10 9 8 7 6 5 4 3 2 1
ISBN 0-13-119844-0

Preface

This text is intended as a non-traditional, student-centered introduction to reading and making sense of published research. Perhaps much to your surprise, it is designed to make the subject fun, exciting, and meaningful. In this introduction and in the next chapter, we want to talk to you about what to expect, what you will learn, some of the concerns you may have about this content, and most important, why this course is going to be so important to your career—and to your life. Skeptical? That is one trait of a good researcher.

LET'S BE HONEST

Most research texts are boring and irrelevant. Students at both the undergraduate and graduate levels often dread and fear their research courses. They don't see a direct connection between their desire to help people, their need for practical skills, and their required coursework in research. Unfortunately, most of the texts available for these classes only make things worse. They are typically huge tomes—heavy, dense, loaded with useful stuff that is largely buried in the turgid prose.

Let's face it: There are basically three reasons why you are taking this course:

1. You want to be literate in your discipline and make sense of the stuff you read. You want to be better informed and a more critical thinker. You don't imagine yourself doing research, but you want to understand better what others have done (or are doing).
2. You intend to do a research study as part of your training. This could include anything from a final project or master's thesis to a doctoral dissertation. In order to complete this task, you will need to know how to interpret and evaluate the research literature and how to formulate good questions, design studies, collect data, analyze results, and make sense of what you discovered.
3. Someone is making you do this. Never in your wildest dreams would you *choose* to take a research course. It is part of your program, a prerequisite for other courses, or a requirement for graduation.

All of these reasons are honorable and legitimate (if the third can be called a "motive"). Of one thing you can be certain: Whatever your current motives might be, they may change over time. Don't take our word for it—do your own research. Talk to professionals in the field for which you are preparing and find out how often they need to consult literature to solve a problem that plagues them. Learn how frequently they need to conduct their own systematic study in order to understand better what is going on in their work. You may not have selected this class as a high priority in your educational training, but you will be surprised how much of the content is going to make you better at what you do.

WHAT WILL BE COVERED

Content in the text is organized using a basic learning principle: Begin where the student is and move forward in small and directed steps. In this instance, the starting point is your ability to intelligently read and evaluate published studies. We believe that first you should be able to understand and critically review studies before you ever attempt to do one, and that is the primary objective of this text.

The text is organized with chapters that mirror a typical published research report. After an introductory chapter, we will focus on the skills needed to do the following:

- examine the research questions, hypotheses, and the literature review (Chapter 2)
- evaluate the appropriateness of the sample used in the study (Chapter 3)
- apply logical principles to evaluate the research design and measurement tools (Chapter 4)
- make sense of the results, including the statistics (Chapter 5)
- evaluate the researchers' summary of their findings in the discussion (Chapter 6)

Our last chapter is then a "do-it-yourself" exercise to practice evaluating studies with two different approaches.

When this class is over—when you have closed this book and given it an honored spot on your bookshelf—we hope that you will have changed in more ways than one. Certainly you will "know stuff" that you didn't know before, enough to at least impress your friends and family for a few months afterward. It is also reasonable to assume that you will indeed be able to read research with some modicum of proficiency. But far more than that, if you truly open yourself up to what this course can offer you, you will find yourself operating from a more informed, logical, analytic style in the ways you approach any problem or challenge you may face. That is indeed a goal worth working toward!

ACKNOWLEDGMENTS

We owe a debt of gratitude to a number of individuals who have offered guidance and assistance in the preparation of this text, only some of whom can be listed here. Our editors, Autumn Benson and Kevin Davis, have been consistently supportive throughout the process. We are grateful to a large number of our prior students over the years whose struggles with traditional research methods textbooks motivated the preparation of this book and helped in selection of its content and style. We appreciate the assistance of LeAnn Putney, University of Nevada, Las Vegas; and David Plummer, University of New England (Australia) for their guidance related to qualitative research design. We benefited immensely from the comments and insights of the reviewers of the manuscript: George F. Arthur, Marshall University; Mary Aspedon, Southwestern Oklahoma State University; Karen Banks, George Mason University; Gail Delicio, Clemson University; Andrew Furco, University of California, Berkeley; Stanley D. Ivie, Texas Woman's University; Antony Kunnan, California State University, Los Angeles; Barbara LaCost, University of Nebraska, Lincoln; Larry H. Ludlow, Boston College; Salvatore R. Paratore, George Washington University; and W. Paul Vogt, Illinois State University.

Finally, we thank our wives, Dorothy Jones and Ellen Kottler. Their patience while we postponed other tasks to work on this book was essential. Both are professionals working in the fields for which this book is intended, and we appreciate their continuing insight into what needed to be said and how best to communicate it.

Research Navigator:
Research Made Simple!

www.ResearchNavigator.com

Merrill Education is pleased to introduce Research Navigator—a one-stop research solution for students that simplifies and streamlines the entire research process. At www.researchnavigator.com, students will find extensive resources to enhance their understanding of the research process so they can effectively complete research assignments. In addition, Research Navigator has three exclusive databases of credible and reliable source content to help students focus their research efforts and begin the research process.

How Will Research Navigator Enhance Your Course?

- Extensive content helps students understand the research process, including writing, Internet research, and citing sources.
- Step-by-step tutorial guides students through the entire research process from selecting a topic to revising a rough draft.
- Research Writing in the Disciplines section details the differences in research across disciplines.
- Three exclusive databases—EBSCO's ContentSelect Academic Journal Database, *The New York Times* Search by Subject Archive, and "Best of the Web" Link Library—allow students to easily find journal articles and sources.

What's the Cost?

A subscription to Research Navigator is $7.50 but is **free** when ordered in conjunction with this textbook. To obtain free passcodes for your students, simply contact your local Merrill/Prentice Hall sales representative, and your representative will send you the Evaluating Online Resource Guide, which contains the code to access Research Navigator as well as tips on how to use Research Navigator and how to evaluate research. To preview the value of this website to your students, please go to www.educator learningcenter.com and use the Login Name "Research" and the password "Demo."

About the Authors

Paul Jones is a practicing clinician, active researcher, and university faculty member who regularly teaches the introduction to educational research course. He has published extensively in refereed professional journals and authored two books: *Deciphering the Diagnostic Codes: A Guide for School Counselors* and *Educational Psychology: The Teaching-Learning Process*. His Web-based instructional programs in basic measurement tools and single-case design are widely used. Previous collaborations with Dr. Kottler include a combined qualitative-quantitative journal publication and coediting a recent book on enhancing clinical skills, *Doing Better: Improving Clinical Skills and Professional Competence*.

Paul's forty-plus years of professional experience include teaching and counseling at the public school, community college, and university levels; full-time practice as a psychologist; and corporate assignment as a research psychologist. He joined the faculty at UNLV in 1987 and has three times received the college award for excellence in educational research. He serves as cochair of the university's Social/Behavioral Sciences Institutional Review Board

Paul is currently Professor of Educational Psychology at the University of Nevada, Las Vegas.

Jeffrey Kottler is one of the most prolific and successful authors in the fields of counseling, psychology, and education. He is the author of more than 55 books, including some of the most popular texts in his field and some of the best-regarded books for practitioners.

Examples of his recent work include *Making Changes Last, On Being a Therapist, Secrets for Secondary School Teachers, Students Who Drive You Crazy, Children with Limited English*, and *Bad Therapy*.

Jeffrey has been an educator for 25 years. He has worked as a teacher, counselor, and therapist in preschool, middle school, mental health center, crisis center, university, community college, and private practice settings. He has served as a Fulbright Scholar and has worked in dozens of countries as a consultant and trainer specializing in multicultural issues.

Jeffrey is currently Professor and Chair of the Counseling Department at California State University, Fullerton.

Brief Contents

Contents

Understanding Research

Becoming a Competent and Critical Consumer

1

What Is Research and Why Should You Care?

CHAPTER OUTLINE

BASIC CONCEPTS

Definitions of research
Discussion in a research report
Introduction in a research
  report

Method in a research report
Operational definitions
Qualitative research

Quantitative research
Results in a research report

Y ou have some physical symptoms that could be the flu and have decided to seek medical care. You have two choices. You can schedule an appointment with a physician who graduated from medical school last year, someone of ordinary talent from a respectable but not necessarily distinguished institution. Or, through some magical process, you could have your appointment with one of the most famous physicians from the distant past. Which appointment would you choose?

You have another decision to make. You've decided to purchase some artwork. Your choices are a painting completed by an artist who graduated last year with average reviews from a respectable but relatively obscure school of art. Or, for the same price, you can have a painting by one of the recognized masters from the distant past. Which painting will you choose?

In both of these instances the best choice, of course, is obvious. You'll want to own the painting by one of the recognized masters from the past, and unless you are into things like bloodletting and leeches, you'd better choose to get your flu symptoms treated by the physician who graduated last year.

Wondering where this is going and what these examples are doing in a book about research? The answer is coming, with just one more illustration. What if your choice involved choosing an instructor for a course or a therapist to help you with symptoms of depression? You could choose to take the class with a master teacher from the past, perhaps someone like Socrates, or you could choose an instructor who graduated last year with average grades from a typical graduate school. You could participate in a therapy session with Freud or with a therapist who was trained last year. Who would you choose? The best way to answer the question is with research.

The social sciences, like the practice of medicine, are a combination of science and art. But in medicine the scientific progress evident in published research obviously makes the newly trained physician a better choice than even the most renowned physician from the past. In contrast, a class with Socrates or a therapy session with Freud may seem more appealing at first, even though the practice of the contemporary educator or therapist has the benefit of knowledge from years of research studies.

We anticipate and encourage the notion that you will and should remain an artist in the practice of your profession. A goal in this book, though, is to provide information to strengthen the extent to which there is also a scientific base for the art, and you'll find that base in published research studies.

Critically reviewing a published research study requires only some basic skills, core attitudes, and a little experience. The task is essentially an exercise in problem solving in which you ask a series of well-constructed questions and then search for answers. This book is designed to help you learn what you need to know in order to examine most any journal article, scholarly book chapter, or monograph, and quickly evaluate its worth and relative value for your own needs.

RESEARCH IN THE SOCIAL SCIENCES

What Is It?

To define the word *research* we could simply start with its roots. If *search* means "to look," then *research* could be defined as "to look again" (re-search). We'll be more precise a bit later, but for now, this is a useful image. You need to do something in your work. You searched for the best answer, found it somewhere in your training, and now you are applying what you learned. The basic idea is that this should be an ongoing process in which you continuously evaluate what you are doing and frequently search again for the most current information to further inform your work.

Research can also be defined as studying in order to acquire information or applying one's mind to the acquisition of knowledge. In essence the idea is to find out things that you want to know, especially things that enrich your life and help you become more effective in what you do and how you do it.

To be even more precise, the Code of Federal Regulations for the Protection of Human Subjects (2001) that guides the design of research studies says: "Research is a systematic investigation, including research development, testing and evaluation, designed to develop or contribute to generalizable knowledge" (Paragraph 46.102.d).

The key elements in this definition are "systematic investigation" and "generalizable." To be systematic, research must be well planned, well organized, and conducted in a way that can be described precisely and repeated. To be generalizable, its intent must go beyond the specific setting in which the information was obtained. In other words, the discovery process must be designed to elicit information that can be applied to other situations and contexts.

Putting these various views of research together, we have a model that begins with a belief that you should never be completely satisfied with how you conduct your professional practice; you should always be re-searching, working toward improvement and increased performance. The task of re-searching involves a commitment for continuing study to acquire more knowledge. This can involve studies that you conduct yourself, but a vast amount of potentially useful information is available to you through careful review of research studies that have been done by others.

Why Is It Important?

We anticipate that most of you have embarked on this study of research as part of your training for some professional practice—perhaps as an educator, an administrator, a school psychologist or counselor, or any of a variety of other such careers. Let's assume, for illustration purposes, that you are now employed as a teacher, and you are enrolled in a degree program for which a research methods course is required. The following are three examples of circumstances in which there is a need for the skills to evaluate published research:

1. You have an idea for a new instructional strategy. Before you use it with students in your classes, you'd like to know whether others have tried the strategy, and, if so, how well it worked in other settings.
2. You have just attended a workshop in which a dynamic speaker spoke persuasively, recommending a significant change in the way you now manage your classroom. Dramatic results are promised, but implementing the change requires a great deal of your effort and time.
3. The syllabus for a course you are taking requires you to submit critical evaluations of three published research articles.

All of the examples are situations in which you will need to evaluate research literature effectively. In the first example, you have an idea: How many others have already experimented with this strategy? What were their results? What were the limitations of the method? Using the work of others to guide your own practice is equivalent to having a personal consultant available at your beck and call. When you are feeling lost or confused or uncertain, when you are hungry for new ideas, delving into research literature will provide you with material that not only is informative but also may provide validation for your instructional ideas.

In the second scenario, in which you consider instructional changes, it is quite likely that the speaker made statements along the lines of "Research has shown . . ." or "Research studies support . . ." or some such verbiage. Almost any idea can claim to be supported by a research study of some kind. Most anything can happen by chance; the reported outcome could have been no more than a fluke. Both here, and throughout this book, we encourage you to ask two questions over and over:

1. What is the evidence for the study's conclusions?
2. What *exactly* is the evidence for those conclusions?

Advice about what we should and should not eat, how much exercise we should get, and how we should conduct ourselves in our personal and professional lives is seldom in short supply. The first and obvious question you should ask is simply, "What is the evidence? Has anyone checked this out, or is this just someone's opinion?"

This first question is essential but often not sufficient. You need to know *exactly* what that evidence is. Let's say, for example, that one type of instructional modality produced dramatic results far superior to another. Should this study warrant further attention? Answers to the "What exactly is the evidence?" question would include (1) whether the two groups came into the study with equal ability and/or motivation, (2) how many students were in the study, and (3) where did the participants come from? In other words, it is not enough to simply read an abstract or a summary. It is essential that you look for and analyze the nitty-gritty details in the study.

Still thinking about the second scenario, the workshop presentation, one way to evaluate claims made in a presentation is to use the references often included as a handout. Selecting a few of those references and doing your own evaluation of the findings might reveal whether suggestions or claims are in fact clearly supported with research evidence.

As to the third scenario, your course assignment, okay . . . no further explanation is needed here.

Reflective Exercise 1.1
Let's Think About It

This would be a good time to reflect on how examination of prior research could have been helpful in your own practice. Either as an individual activity or in a small group, list a few instances from your own area of practice where you have thought about trying a new technique. This can be something you've thought of on your own, or perhaps something you heard presented by others. Be prepared to discuss the barriers, if any, that have limited your use of research data in your professional practice.

Where Do I Find It?

Suppose your instructor has included the evaluation of a published research study as a part of the requirements for your course. Where will you find something to evaluate? The obvious answer, a library, is in this case also the correct answer, especially if you include its electronic equivalent on the Internet.

Looking for a book might be your first choice but may not be your best option, depending on what's motivating your search. If you need to review and/or evaluate the report of a specific research study, a book is probably not the optimal source. Books often provide excellent summaries of research studies done by others but only sometimes provide detailed information about individual studies. More often, what you will find is the author's interpretation of the results of a study, and not the report of the study itself. On the positive side, those summaries can be invaluable for information to guide your professional practice. But you are trusting the author's ability to glean the relevant information from other studies, and, because of publication timelines, there will be often be a significant delay between completion of the study and its appearance in a book.

Another logical choice is the myriad of journals published by professional associations. Dissemination of research through professional journals is one of the time-honored missions of professional associations, and the cost of their publication is a significant part of the dues you send them each year. Remember, though, that the articles in most journals will be some combination of opinion pieces and research reports.

Some professional journals are almost completely focused on providing information on the science underlying your discipline. Others give nearly exclusive attention to providing help in your practitioner role, and some professional journals attempt to provide a balanced mixture of the two. There is a place and a need for all of these areas of focus, and many professional associations publish more than one journal in order to target specific needs.

A report of a single research study is more likely to be found in a professional journal than in a book, and the time delay from study to publication will often, though not always, be somewhat shorter. You will, though, want to be aware that the focus of the journal will have a relationship to the findings likely to be reported in it. For example, over the last few years several new journals have been created with focus on applications of technology in specific disciplines. Examples include the *International Journal of Educational Technology, Journal of Special Education Technology, Journal of Technology in Counseling, Journal of Technology and Teacher Education*, and so forth. While we have a deep commitment to technological applications, it would be folly to suggest that all studies would be equally welcomed for possible publication. Each of these journals publishes studies that pinpoint specific areas where technology does and does not appear to be useful. But a study with apparent intent to trash the whole concept of integrating technology and education would not likely survive the editorial process intact.

That brings us to the latest entry in the pool of resources for finding research reports, the increasingly ubiquitous Internet. At first glance, this would appear to be the optimal source. Information stored on the Internet is readily available, and the timeline from completion of a research study to online publication of its report can be a matter of hours, rather than months or even years. Some professional journals are exclusively online, and there is a growing trend for professional associations to make their printed journals also available in an online format.

Your authors are among the many who have enthusiastically embraced the use of Internet resources as a significant, if not primary, tool to stay current with research findings in our individual areas of interest. With that said, there is a need for caution. Before most books in our field are published, the information in them is scrutinized for accuracy by peers and by editors specialized in the field. Articles in professional journals typically go through a rigorous screening process before they are published, and in fact, the majority of submissions to these journals do not make it through the scrutiny. With the exception of online professional journals that differ from their hard-copy counterparts only in being available on the Internet, no such scrutiny is applied to most of the information on the Internet.

When the information is in the form of a stream-of-consciousness "blog," the lack of quality control is evident. Our caution is that something can easily be posted on the Internet that looks very much like a research report from a professional journal but may have been critiqued for accuracy by no one other than the person who prepared it. This isn't, by the way, necessarily a bad thing. It enables information to be available for your review that otherwise might have ended up in a desk drawer somewhere. It does, though, speak directly to the need for caution with the information, and also, we believe, to the need for the criteria for evaluating research reports that are the focus of this book.

TWO VIEWS OF THE WORLD: QUANTITATIVE AND QUALITATIVE

When evaluating any research report, regardless of the venue in which it appears—as a paper at a professional conference, a journal article, a grant proposal, a book, or an Internet posting—one of the first things you will notice is the particular methodology that was employed. Some approaches to research attempt to measure variables very carefully, resulting in numbers that are reported and analyzed; others attempt to investigate questions through more exploratory means that produce data in the form of narratives.

The historical tradition for research in the social sciences has been distinctly **quantitative** in nature. The emphasis has been on reducing characteristics to a form that could readily be described with numbers, and then using the numbers to identify relationships among the characteristics.

To illustrate, let's assume that a group of researchers wants to know whether there is a relationship between intelligence and socioeconomic status. Before you read further, take a few minutes with Reflective Exercise 1.2.

Reflective Exercise 1.2
Defining Intelligence and Socioeconomic Status

Either as an individual activity or in a small group, think about and perhaps discuss with other students how you might assign numbers to the characteristics of intelligence and socioeconomic status in order to conduct a quantitative study. Administering a test is the obvious approach to quantify intelligence, but think about how the test selected might affect the answer you would get about whether there is a relationship between the two characteristics. For example, would you be likely to come to a different conclusion about the relationship if you used a nonverbal test? What kinds of things would you consider in assigning a numerical value to socioeconomic status? Be prepared, if asked, to share the outcome of your analysis with the rest of your class.

Before the researchers can conduct a quantitative study to answer their question about whether there is a relationship between intelligence and socioeconomic status, both characteristics have to be transformed into numbers. Doing so is not an especially difficult task. As suggested in the Reflective Exercise, the most feasible approach for quantifying intelligence would be simply the score on an IQ test.

Several possibilities could be used to assign a number to socioeconomic status. For example, researchers often use a scale in which two measures are obtained: a prestige rating of the occupation of the primary breadwinner in the family and the educational level of that individual. Those two scores are then combined to provide a single numerical index of socioeconomic status.

In research studies, the outcomes of the tasks we just described are called **operational definitions,** in which a characteristic is defined by the activities used to measure it. Researchers have a great deal of freedom in how this is done. For example, it would be equally legitimate for researchers to define socioeconomic status by where one lives and ignore level of occupation and/or education. The choices are almost limitless. The researchers' obligation when reporting results is just to be completely clear in describing how the characteristics were defined in the study.

After the numerical scales have been identified and applied, a quantitative study to answer the research question would be relatively easy to conduct. Participants for the study would be located and measured with the two scales. One of several available statistical tools would be used to determine whether there did appear to be a relationship between these two characteristics. The research process itself is a set series of sequential steps, culminating with a statistical probability statement about whether what the researchers found would be likely to have occurred by chance alone. In actual use, the quantitative approach is usually more sophisticated than this example, but the underlying foundation of quantification remains the same.

While this approach is ideally suited to answer some research questions, it has inherent limitations, particularly related to depth of understanding. There is more to the experiential difference in living on the edge of poverty, as compared to living with large amounts of discretionary income, than can be conveyed by a single numerical label. The breadth and depth of human ability is more than can be easily expressed as an IQ test score.

Building on a foundation of tools used by anthropologists to study cultural patterns in natural settings and on the detailed, contextual case studies in the early history of psychotherapy, an approach different from the traditional quantitative model has emerged. The approach, typically identified as **qualitative** research, is increasingly evident in research projects in the social sciences. It is not just a different way of "doing" a study, it is a different way of thinking about the study itself, with identifying relationships often seen as much less important than in-depth exploration.

You probably will not be surprised to hear that when the qualitative approach began receiving increasing attention near the end of the 20th century, there was more than a small amount of rancor, at times even animosity, between researchers who identified with one approach or the other. Some of the quantitative-versus-qualitative discussion was akin to, and at times conducted with the same intensity of, the arguments we sometimes have about the best computer operating system, or even which is the preferred soft drink.

More recently, though, the quantitative-versus-qualitative dialogue has moved in a healthy direction, with recognition that both approaches are viable tools to use in answering questions. The question itself guides which approach is preferable. For example, if the question involves seeking tests to use as predictors of success in some activity, a quantitative approach is clearly the better choice. If your question is about gaining more understanding about the meaning of success to individuals who did or did not achieve it, one of the several available qualitative research strategies would be the clear choice.

On a practical level, in understanding and critically reviewing research reports, some criteria are common to both approaches and some criteria apply only to one or the other. In the chapters that follow, you'll find attention to understanding and applying criteria equally applicable in reports of quantitative and qualitative studies, and you'll find attention to tools for evaluation whose relevance is contingent on the research approach used in the study.

Even though the evaluation criteria have some differences, there is fortunately a relatively easy way to differentiate between research reports based on quantitative and qualitative research designs. In quantitative designs, the characteristic being studied will be defined, presented, and summarized using numbers. For example, when reading comprehension is defined in the study as a mean score of 31.4 with a standard deviation of 3.55, you probably have a quantitative study. Qualitative designs, in contrast, usually place emphasis on verbal descriptions of the characteristics being investigated. This is not to say that finding a number in the research report automatically excludes it from the qualitative category (and obviously you are going to find verbal descriptions in quantitative studies). But a qualitative study of reading would be expected to provide detailed narratives, rather than statistical data, about characteristics of the individual readers.

It may strike you as strange to think of "data" as something other than numbers or equations, but qualitative studies present words in the form of verbal or written narratives as the data in the report. The information can come from a variety of sources, including interview transcripts, observation field notes, diary entries, and even official institution records. Just as "raw data" in a quantitative study would be the information as it was directly measured and collected as a result of some intervention, the same can be true for qualitative studies. The raw data often takes the form of what was said by interviewees before it was organized and analyzed. What this means, then, is that to differentiate between quantitative and qualitative studies, all you have to do is look in the section of the report where the researchers present their results and see whether the information provided is mostly in the form of numbers or words. Special considerations that are contingent on the type of design are addressed in the chapters that follow, including what to do when the researchers have combined the two methods in a single study.

Reflective Exercise 1.3 is for a quick check of your understanding of two of the concepts we've presented thus far.

Reflective Exercise 1.3
Pick the Journal

The following article titles were selected from issues of two journals associated with the field of education. Review the titles and then try to answer the questions that follow.

Journal A	Journal B
Reading achievement: A longitudinal study of 187 children from first through sixth grades	Using centers to engage children during guided reading time: Intensifying learning experiences away from the teacher
Is native-language decoding skill related to second language learning?	What do reading specialists do? Results from a national survey
Predictors of exception word and nonword reading in dyslexic children: The severity hypothesis	Second-language reading: Insights from Nigerian primary schools
Individual differences in reading to summarize expository text: evidence from eye fixation patterns	Why don't you use your finger? Paired reading in first grade

Which of these journals appears to be targeted for the scientist and which for the practitioner? Or do both appear to have the same audience?

Bonus question: Which appear to be qualitative studies?

(Answers are at the end of the chapter.)

DECIPHERING A RESEARCH REPORT: PARTS OF THE WHOLE

As we prepare to begin our journey together in deciphering and making sense of published research studies, where we are going is illustrated in Figure 1.1.

Published research studies are usually composed of several easily identified sections, as shown in Figure 1.1. Following an **introduction,** which may or may not have a heading, you will typically find a section called **method** that describes the procedures that were employed to investigate the phenomenon. The method section will often have identified subheadings in which the researchers describe the sample of participants

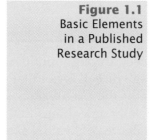

Figure 1.1
Basic Elements
in a Published
Research Study

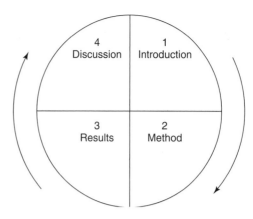

used in the study and the research design, including the specific procedures that were used. The description of the research design will also typically include a detailed description of the measurement tools used in the study.

Quite logically, a **results** section would follow in which—you guessed it—the results of the study are described, often in the form of a narrative description as well as a summary of the data (data can include both numbers and direct quotes). The paper ends with a section frequently identified as **discussion** in which the researchers have the opportunity to talk about the results in the previous section. In this section the main themes and key points are summarized, after which recommendations are usually made for further research in this area. (In some articles, the discussion section content is presented under separate headings; for example, summary, discussion, and/or conclusions.) While not all published studies follow this topical outline, most use comparable headings.

We use this same organizational structure in developing the chapters in this book. The next chapter is focused on how to evaluate the information in the Introduction of a research study. Chapters 3 and 4 address how to critique the method used in the study—first the participants and then the procedures and instrumentation. Chapter 5 describes the presentation of the outcome of the study in the results section, including a primer on how to translate the numerical symbols often found in this section. Chapter 6 addresses how to assess the validity of the conclusions reported in a study and the relevance of the findings included in the discussion.

In addition to the four basic elements, most published studies include an **abstract,** a brief summary typically at the beginning of a published study. The concept of the abstract is noble: to provide for the reader an accurate, well-written, concise, and specific overview of the study. In practice, however, this component often provides little information of value in critique and/or evaluation of the publication. Journals impose strict word limits for the abstract, and you'll learn a little about the content but often not enough to make an informed decision.

THE SKEPTICAL MINDSET

In the language that we've used throughout this chapter you will have noticed a fairly cautious writing voice. It is not that we are suspicious or critical by nature, but that one of the useful skills of research training is to look at the world, and especially new things that we encounter, with both wonder and awe, but also a degree of healthy skepticism.

The heading for this section of the chapter may be surprising with its implicit (and about to become explicit) suggestion that you are best served by an extremely skeptical mindset when reading a published research study. The proposition may seem particularly odd because having an open mind is a primary value associated with the research enterprise.

We do not believe that most research studies are conducted with a nefarious agenda. It is true that some studies have obviously been slanted to support either the researchers' prejudice or a specific product, but these studies are not the norm. It seems reasonable to assume that most published research is instead intended to extend the frontiers of knowledge and increase the information available to those working in the field so that they might operate more effectively.

So why the need for skepticism? In any published research study, quantitative or qualitative, the reader must take a remarkable number of things for granted. The researcher *claims* that people were randomly assigned to two treatment conditions. Were they? The researcher *reports* that people who got Treatment X had an average score of 25 while people who got Treatment Y had an average score of 45. Were those the actual scores? And if those were the true results, how do you know that one group wasn't given assistance that the other one was not?

A listing of questions like these could go on and on. You weren't there when the study was being conducted. You don't know, with absolute certainty, whether people were actually randomly assigned to experimental groups. You don't have the actual test data—just the summaries provided by the researcher. You don't really know whether a study was conducted at all. You don't know; the journal editor doesn't know; the people who provided the reviews of the manuscript and recommended its publication don't know.

A British psychologist, Cyril Burt, published a series of papers in the early 1940s showing that heredity had a much stronger influence than environment on IQ test scores. The studies involved identical twins reared together and reared apart. His work had significant influence on the schools in England, and he was knighted by King George VI. Thirty years later, within months of his death in 1971, questions about the authenticity of Burt's data began to emerge, leading in 1976 to a formal, public accusation of fraud (Joynson, 1989).

In another situation an American psychologist, Robert McConnell, became quite famous with an intriguing, though not especially palatable, study of planaria (McConnell, 1962). Using classical conditioning, a group of planaria (worms) learned a specific response. They were then ground up and fed (we warned you that this wasn't palatable) to another group of worms. Responses of the new group suggested that they had "learned" the same responses by simply ingesting the genetic material of the smart group.

Many were certain that this was evidence that a magic memory pill was just around the corner. But after this study had been widely quoted in the academic and popular press for decades, the research project collapsed when other scientists did not find comparable results in follow-up studies (Rilling, 1996).

Did Burt simply fabricate his data, as was charged at the time, or was his crime simply sloppy recordkeeping? Did McConnell rush to publish a finding in order to gain fame, or were others too quick in disseminating a really interesting finding? As investigations have evolved, the real answer to both of these questions remains uncertain. Later studies have shown a strong link between genetics and IQ scores, and each year brings more information about the biochemistry of memory. What is clear is that caution in interpreting and accepting research data is continually warranted. (Also clear is that learning something new can't be accomplished by just grinding up and eating someone who already knows it, a fact for which we are quite grateful.)

Our premise is simple: If the information that is verifiable is flawed, then it is reasonable and prudent to have serious doubts about the information that we are being asked to assume. The language in the introductory section of a research study, for example, might clearly indicate that the researcher had strong biases about the outcome. Did the researcher manipulate the data to support that bias? We can't know that for sure, but we propose that if there are mistakes in the known, the unknowns should not be taken at face value.

In suggesting such a strong filter, we recognize that this will result in many otherwise legitimate studies being eliminated from consideration. In the illustrations about IQ scores and worms, the researchers may well have been completely objective and accurate in conducting and reporting the results of the study. Completely honest researchers can make omissions and/or errors in writing the report. It is important to recognize that a poorly written study does not, in and of itself, demonstrate that the study was poorly conducted. But the point remains clear: A mistake in what can be known casts a cloud on the probable accuracy and veracity about the things that must be assumed.

Your personal life experiences support this premise. If a friend or classmate tells you something that you know is not true, then you are hardly likely to trust other things he or she tells you—at least not without healthy skepticism. If research data is to have much value to you, then you must be able to trust that what is offered is true as it was reported.

On a practical level, this strong filter might be more difficult to implement if there were few research studies available for consideration. The reality, however, is just the opposite. The number of studies published each year, magnified by the number available online, is overwhelming. A vast number of published studies do meet the criteria to be presented in this text.

SUMMARY AND CLOSING THOUGHTS

Implicit in this chapter is our belief that the quality of the services we deliver will be significantly improved with more attention to the knowledge available in the research literature, but also that not all published research studies warrant more than just a cursory glance. Thus there is an ongoing need to review and critique what others have already done. To be honest, some of that need comes only because of course assignments. But the importance of informed evaluation skills extends far beyond your training programs. Answers are available in the research literature for many of the questions you confront in the practice of your profession, as well as in your everyday lives. Unfortunately, though, there are contradictions in those answers, with some studies clearly suggesting one thing and others equally clearly suggesting just the opposite.

In this book we will explore tools that can be used to make sense of the conflicting recommendations. The objective is to be able to identify what *exactly* is the evidence to support recommendations made by the researchers. Specific factors used to comprehend and evaluate published studies will be examined one by one, beginning with how to find and evaluate the research question in a published study and how to determine whether the literature review provides a foundation for the research question.

Next, two chapters are devoted to evaluating the method used by the researchers to find the answer to their research question. First, we will examine factors to consider in deciding whether the researchers have selected a sample from which an answer to the question could even be anticipated. We will then identify features to consider in assessing whether the researchers have chosen a design with which the sample could provide an answer to the question, and whether the measurement tools used in the study were sufficient to generate appropriate information.

For many, a particularly off-putting element in published quantitative studies is a results section that appears to have been written in a foreign tongue—the language of inferential statistics. Our premise here is twofold. First, some understanding of the language is crucial. Simply skipping over the reported statistics is not a viable choice. They provide essential information in evaluating whether the conclusions are actually supported by those results.

On the other hand, coping in a setting with a different language does not require one to be absolutely fluent in the language being used. If you've traveled in a country where English is not the first language, you no doubt already know that certain key phrases (for example, *where is the bathroom*) suffice to meet basic needs.

This is not an argument against obtaining a strong foundation in educational statistics. In fact, the travel example could easily be used to support the value of being fluent in the language of the country being visited. But it is important to recognize that comprehension and evaluation of quantitative research do not mandate statistical fluency. You are likely to encounter only a few statistical key phrases; for example, $F(2, 200) = 2.48$, $p < .05$. Understanding those "phrases" will be our focus. You'll learn in Chapter 5, by the way, that this phrase tells you a great deal. The researcher used a technique called analysis of variance (F) and found at least one difference unlikely to be the result of chance alone ($p < .05$). From the numerals in the parentheses in the phrase, you're told that three groups were compared (add 1 to the first number) and that the study involved approximately 200 participants.

After considering the results section, we will address the features expected in the discussion section of a research report, in which we find the researchers' ideas about the actual usefulness of their findings and about future studies that may be needed.

This book will then conclude with our thoughts about where we hope the information in it will lead you. Both motivating and assisting you to become a more active and a more critical evaluator of the research studies done by others is clearly our primary goal. As you become more fluent in the language of research and the expectations in reporting the results of research studies, we think you may find yourself giving more thought to conducting your own research studies, inquiries to get answers specifically focused on enhancing your own professional practice.

ANSWER FOR REFLECTIVE EXERCISE

Reflective Exercise 1.3

Which of these journals appears to be targeted for the scientist and which for the practitioner? Or do both appear to have the same audience?

The audience for Journal A (Journal of Educational Psychology, March 2002) is primarily behavioral scientists. Journal B (The Reading Teacher, May 2002) is a practitioner-oriented journal.

Bonus question: Which appear to be qualitative studies?

Be careful! While some of the articles in Journal B appear to be qualitative, you can't be sure without reading the actual article.

2

What Is the Question and Why Is It Important?
Evaluating the Introduction of a Research Report

CHAPTER OUTLINE

BASIC CONCEPTS

Applied research
Basic research
Directional hypotheses
Holistic design

Linear design
Nondirectional hypotheses
Null hypotheses

Primary sources
Review of related literature
Secondary sources

A book, a movie, a story, and yes, even a research article always begins with an introduction to what will follow. This can be in the form of an opening scene, a narrator who sets the stage, or simply a presentation of coming attractions (as we are about to do). Introductions are constructed to provide an overview of contents, but they are also designed to capture interest. For example, consider the opening lines in a novel by Sebold (2002) about the aftermath of a crime:

> My name was Salmon, like the fish; first name, Susie. I was fourteen when I was murdered on December 6, 1973. In newspaper photos of missing girls from the seventies, most looked like me: white girls with mousy brown hair. This was before kids of all races and genders started appearing on milk cartons or in the daily mail. It was still back when people believed things like that didn't happen.[1]

While it might seem like a stretch to compare the introduction to a work of fiction to that of a research study, this example illustrates how an author, in a few sparse sentences, can both set the stage for what is to follow and grab a reader's attention. Only 71 words were required to introduce the main character and her unique voice and provide the context for the book.

INTRODUCING THE INTRODUCTION

In this chapter we explore the specific elements in the introduction of a published research study report. First, we will discuss the parts of the introduction, including general criteria for evaluating all research studies. Next, from information typically available in the introduction, we will examine how to identify whether the report you're evaluating is quantitative, qualitative, or a mixture of the two. Finally, we will examine special considerations needed for evaluation of the introductory sections for quantitative studies and then for those that are qualitative in design.

When you have completed reading this chapter, you will be able to do the following:

- analyze and critique the information provided in the introductory section of both quantitative and qualitative research studies
- use that analysis to screen out research articles that probably do not warrant any further attention from you

---

[1]Sebold, A. (2002). *The lovely bones* (p. 1). New York: Little, Brown and Company.

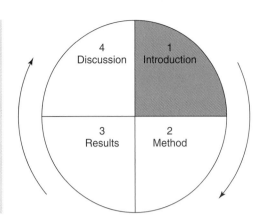

Figure 2.1
Evaluating the
Introduction

WHAT TO LOOK FOR IN THE INTRODUCTION

We begin the evaluation of the introduction (Figure 2.1) in published research studies with initial focus on the elements that are common in reports of both quantitative and qualitative research. Differences, and there are some important ones, are examined later in this chapter. There are usually three identifiable components in the introduction of a research report:

1. Description of a general problem area, including context and significance
2. Review of related literature
3. Statement of the objectives of the investigation

The excerpt in Example 2.1 illustrates the description of the problem area and the statement of the objectives in a typical research article.

Example 2.1
Excerpt Illustrating a Typical Introduction in a Research Article

Sources of Sexuality Information for University Students

Sexual learning occurs continuously throughout the lifespan in a variety of ways (Roberts, 1980). **The purpose of this study was** to examine different sources of sexuality information and to determine those sources that had the most influence on university students' sexual learning. . . .

. . . **it was hypothesized** that female students receive more information from parents than do male students, and that mothers play a more dominant role in sexual education in comparison to fathers. . . . It was also hypothesized that either trade books (e.g. romance novels, popular magazines, etc.) or sexuality textbooks are an important source of information for the university students in this study.

Ballard, S. M., & Morris, M. L. (1998). Sources of sexuality information for university students. *Journal of Sex Education & Therapy, 23,* 278–287.

The introduction of a research report (often without a heading) begins with information about the context and importance of the study and ends, as in Example 2.1, with the researchers' hypotheses, research questions, or statements of objectives for the study.

The first part in the introduction identifies the topic and the research problem being studied. The topic is the broad subject matter addressed in the study. The research problem is a more specific framing of the topic. For example, in the first sentence in the study in Example 2.1, the researchers note the topic: that sexual learning occurs across the life span. While the statement is perhaps obvious, it immediately provides the reader with some justification for conducting a study about sex education with a sample of university students: context and significance. This part may be, as in Example 2.1, quite brief, but in some studies the researchers provide several paragraphs to set the context and emphasize the importance. A study comparing different modalities for teaching reading, for example, might begin with a lengthy explanation of the importance of acquiring reading skills, perceived deficiencies in current instructional tools, societal impact of impaired reading, and so forth.

The second part of the introduction, the review of related literature, is easy to identify. The literature review is a summary of previously published research used by the researchers in designing their study. In it the researchers provide support both for the importance of the topic and for the research questions they intend to address. In the last part of the introduction, the researchers describe what their study was intended to accomplish. The last part of the introduction is typically quite short and, depending on the specific study, may describe some general goals or may instead list some very specific objectives.

The information at the beginning of the introduction has a singular purpose—to set the stage for what follows in the rest of the article. From the content in the introductory section, you will make preliminary decisions about the significance of the study and the questions addressed in it. You also will draw inferences about the competence and possible biases of the researchers who conducted it. (For the purpose of clarity in writing, we will consistently assume that the study you are evaluating has more than one author.)

In essence, the decisions you make while evaluating the introductory section should form the basis for a judgment about whether it is worthwhile to continue reading the article. From the very beginning, the authors should be able to convince you that what they have done is important and that they have the skills and the appropriate perspective to have accomplished what they claim. By the end of the introduction, the researchers' intent for the study should be quite clear. If, by that point, you are not convinced that there was some value in doing the study, or if the objectives remain unclear, then you might make a better use of your time to move on to another study.

EVALUATING THE INTRODUCTION

The next three sections explore general criteria you can use in evaluating the introduction of a published research study. These criteria are useful whether the strategy employed by the researchers was quantitative, qualitative, or a combination of the two methods.

Evaluating the Context and Significance

The introductory section begins with the investigators' explanation of why this research was needed. The researchers may include some citations at the beginning of the report to establish the context and significance of their study. This is the "hook" of any piece of writing, whether it is a novel, screenplay, essay, biography, or quantitative report. Unless the introduction (or opening scene) grabs your interest, convinces you that what you are about to read is useful, then you won't likely go any further.

Before the research study appears in print, several professionals have already judged that the topic warranted the investigation. This is the peer review process in which the editor of the journal found the study sufficiently important to send it, without identifying the authors, to professionals who have some expertise in the general area for critique and evaluation. When you are evaluating the context and significance of a published report, you are thus not only checking the work of the authors, but also of people associated with the journal.

Two primary factors are considered in this part of the review:

1. Is this topic important?
   a. Is it significant to society?
   b. Is it personally relevant?
2. Is the presentation clear and objective?

The first question, importance of the topic, is actually twofold. Do the authors in this introductory content make the case that there is a good reason for the investigation? And, is this topic something of interest to you?

Benefit to Society. While societal significance is an obvious factor, be cautious because some degree of individual perception often colors such an assessment. Research studies are sometimes categorized as either *basic* or *applied.* The purpose of basic research is knowledge itself, regardless of whether any practical application is apparent. Applied research is composed of studies obviously intended to solve problems. While studies specifically designed to solve problems may appear more relevant, it is important to remember that a topic you and I might classify as of little significance could turn out to have lasting and important implications. An example of this is illustrated in a story about a 19th-century scientist, Michael Faraday, who, while attempting to explain his findings in electro-magnetism to a prominent politician, was asked, "But what good is it?" Faraday's alleged replies were, "What good is a newborn baby?" and "Why, sir, there is the probability that you will soon be able to tax it." This story illustrates an important point. We should not be too quick to dismiss a research study's potential value to society. Some implications may not be immediately apparent.

Personal Relevance.   Whether the general topic of a research study is relevant to you depends on several factors. Are you looking for help with a particular problem in your practice? Are you interested in broadening your knowledge about other human service areas? Maybe you're just curious. Perhaps you are just interested in learning more about a particular facet of human behavior, human learning, or some unexplained phenomenon.

Whatever your reason, personal relevance is a key factor in the evaluation of research studies. Let's face it: There is a fair degree of concentration and commitment involved in reading carefully, scrutinizing, and making sense of a research article. Given a choice between two items on the nightstand by your bed—a professional journal or a riveting piece of fiction—which would you reach for first? Perhaps a few of you (and we're not among them) would indeed go for the journal, but for the rest of us, if we are going to devote an hour or more to perusing a journal, it had better offer us something that we can use in our lives and work.

Clear and Objective Presentation.   Your next task, after deciding whether a piece interests you, is to assess the clarity of presentation. Writing style is certainly a part of the consideration, but you should look for more than just smooth prose. As you begin reading the study, do the words clearly portray the general intent of the study? Is the general problem area quickly evident, or do the researchers appear to be rambling around a variety of topics?

Second, you will want to look for evidence of bias in the language chosen by the researchers. This will be a value judgment and is a bit tricky. Researchers are human. They bring to every study their own beliefs, values, and even biased attitudes.

The rules of science do not prohibit a researcher from prior beliefs or even hoped-for outcomes. What you are looking for is any evidence to suggest that the researchers in this study may have such strong beliefs that, either purposefully or inadvertently, the design of the study, or the results obtained, may have been slanted toward the desired outcome.

The hypothetical article in Example 2.2 illustrates how language in an introductory section may identify an unacceptable bias.

Example 2.2
A Biased Introduction

Efficacy of Selected Instructional Modalities for Teaching Reading
I. Am Sure, Ph.D.

Although many arguments have been offered to explain the unacceptable failure rate in the public schools, most (Doe, 2004) concur that competence in reading is the critical factor. Thousands of school-age children have become victims of instructional approaches that give insufficient attention to basic phonics.

Jones (2001) compared whole-language and direct instruction approaches with sixth graders and found significantly higher achievement test scores for students in the direct instruction group. Brown and Sure (1998) compared outcomes of phonics and other approaches with middle-school students and found higher word recognition scores in students in the phonics treatment group. A comprehensive study of fifth-grade students (Sure, Brown, Jones, & Doe, 2000) suggested that students in the whole-language group were at risk for failure in any classes requiring minimal reading skills.

The objective of the present study is to compare the outcomes of strategies for teaching reading.

Notice in Example 2.2 that both of the first two sentences include strong opinions of this researcher. The first sentence expresses a belief that reading is the most important factor in school success. This sentence does not, in and of itself, suggest a bias risk. The researcher provided a citation for the belief, but that is not the key factor. This study (from the title) is not about comparing different content areas to determine which is most important in reference to school failure. The first sentence appropriately provides a context for the significance of the study: why it is important to compare different strategies for teaching reading.

The second sentence is a different story. The problem word in the second sentence is *victims*. We can assume that this researcher conducted a study that included some contrasting of phonics and non-phonics-based approaches to teaching reading. Given the author's word choice, the question you would now ask yourself is how much trust to place in the objectivity of the researcher.

By itself, the use of a value-laden term in the introduction does not prove guilt. But, it certainly warrants suspicion. In Example 2.2, Dr. Sure may have conducted a completely appropriate and objective study, but the word choice gives you reason to be extremely cautious when examining the results.

Evaluating the Literature Review

We are now ready to for the second category of information provided in the introduction, the review of related literature. This is the background section of a research report that accomplishes several tasks, including establishing the author's credibility and mastery of the material and informing the reader about what has already been done on this subject. As you will see later in this chapter, in some types of studies the literature review is the basis in providing the foundation for the questions to be asked in the study.

Four primary factors are used when evaluating the review of literature:

1. Is a balanced viewpoint evident? (Not all cited sources should have the same outcome.)
2. Do the dates indicate attention to both historical precedent (older publications) and more recent work?
3. Is a coherent theme evident, including a brief summary of findings?
4. Did the authors appear to emphasize primary, rather than only secondary, sources?

Balanced Viewpoint.   The literature review is used to make the case that a study is important and the direction is supported by previous research. Thus, it is neither surprising nor problematic to find most of the citations supporting the beliefs of the authors. Objectivity, however, is a critical element in research, and it would be hard to think of any important topic in which all previous studies pointed in the same direction. You can reasonably expect that the review of literature should include some disparity in the previous findings. For example, the second paragraph of the hypothetical study in Example 2.2 might have begun with "Although some (Smith, 1991; Green, 1993) have suggested no loss in word recognition performance when a whole-language approach is used, more recent studies have challenged that assumption."

Appropriate Time Frame.   The time required from initiation of a research study to its publication in a professional journal is usually a period of several years. So it is not necessarily a weakness for the most recent citation in a study to be dated four or even five years earlier than the year the study was actually published. But when the most recent citation is more than about five years old, you should expect the authors to provide some explanation for why more recent studies are not included.

There is another side to this coin. A time-honored tradition in research, particularly in quantitative studies, is that efforts are always built on the basis of accumulated knowledge. It is expected that researchers will construct the case for their own efforts by showing a sequential, logical flow of work, in which each subsequent step advances what has been accomplished previously. Credit is meticulously cited to the appropriate contributors.

When all studies cited in the literature review are relatively recent, you would have reason to question whether the authors really did their homework. Did they consider historical precedents for their investigation? Did they give credit where credit was due?

In addition to the earliest and latest citation dates, you should also be concerned about any lengthy unexplained gaps in the dates. If, for example, the literature review cites studies published in the 1970s and studies published in 2000 with nothing in between, it is legitimate for you to wonder why. There may be a reasonable explanation; sometimes a topic receives a great deal of attention for a while and then interest in it seems to disappear. But it is the authors' responsibility to acknowledge the gap and provide some possible explanation for it. Otherwise, you are left to wonder whether they actually even looked.

Coherent Theme.   The literature review in a research study is probably reminiscent of the term papers you've prepared over the years to meet requirements in your courses. That is not necessarily a bad model (depending, of course, on how well you write term papers). In this section of the introduction, the researchers' selection of previous studies should be directly related to the purpose of their study, and that relationship should be clearly evident.

When reading this section, you should be able to identify how each cited study relates to the purpose of the study and how it relates to the other studies included in the literature review. It is especially helpful if the researchers provide an overall summary of the previous research.

Primary and Secondary Sources.   Okay, let's admit it. We've probably all done it. It was a term paper required in an undergraduate course. The professor was known for counting citations when assigning grades. You found one of those "gold mine" articles, relatively recent, and with a very long list of references. There was no time to actually read them yourself (you had much more interesting things to do). So your paper was replete with references you hadn't actually consulted, relying instead on what was reported by another writer. A *primary source* is a firsthand account, an original document, a report of a study written by those who actually did the study. A *secondary source* is a description provided by someone other than the original observer, results of a study reported by someone other than the actual researchers. The references you didn't actually consult are defined as secondary sources.

Using secondary sources is permitted and may have been the authors' only choice. Some journals are difficult to find, and a new concern, aptly labeled "web rot," exacerbates the problem with references published on the Internet. The latter occurs when an electronic file is intentionally or inadvertently deleted or when a web site has been reorganized without sufficient attention to maintaining links to the files. Relying on secondary sources is dangerous because you can only assume that the one that was actually read provided an accurate description of the one that was not.

One example of the danger of secondary sources is evident earlier in this chapter in the presentation about basic and applied research, where we described a conversation between a politician and a 19th-century scientist. Although this alleged interchange is often quoted in defense of basic research, Faraday never mentioned the incident in his own writings. So it is unlikely that the conversation ever actually occurred.

When secondary sources are used, they should be identified as such. For example, assume that the authors want to cite a study conducted by Jones in 1997. They haven't actually read the Jones study, just a summary of it in an article by Kottler published in 2003. It is not appropriate for the authors to assume that Kottler's summary was accurate, so the Jones study should not be included in their reference list. The appropriate format in the narrative would be as follows: "A study by Jones (as cited in Kottler, 2003) found . . .," and only the Kottler article would be included in the references. (Of course, a preferable option would be to locate and read the original source.)

When evaluating a published research study, it will not usually be easy for you to identify the extent to which the authors may have used but not identified secondary sources in their review of the literature. You could, of course, actually read each cited resource yourself (we're not suggesting that this would be a good use of your time). One clue, though, may become evident if you check the titles of cited articles in the reference list. If the word *review* appears with some frequency, it may be reasonable to be suspicious about the extent to which the authors relied on secondary sources. If this is of some concern, you might want to actually locate one of the more recent citations, particularly if it appears to be a lengthy publication, and see if its references appear to match those in the article you are evaluating.

The hypothetical study in Example 2.2 illustrates warning signs that can be evident in the related literature review even if you are not especially familiar with the topic. Notice in the citations of related literature (the second paragraph of the hypothetical study) that there appears to be a working relationship among all of the authors cited. Finding citations of prior work by the author of a study is not at all unusual, but in this example, there does not seem to be any recognition of studies by people who have no relationship to the author. Notice also that all of the cited results are in the same direction—an outcome that certainly seems unusual for a topic such as reading methods. A date of publication was not given for the article, but since the context section included a 2001 citation, one could question why none of the related research citations were dated earlier than 1996. Apart from the specifics that we are mentioning, you can already get a sense for the critical mindset in place when evaluating an article you are reading—it is not that you are being unduly negative, mistrustful, and doubtful toward everything you read, just healthily skeptical. And this is indeed the appropriate attitude for a practitioner or scholar.

Evaluating the Objectives of the Study

The last part of the introduction takes different forms, depending on whether a qualitative or quantitative approach was used in the study. Criteria specific to the two approaches are presented later in this chapter. But for both approaches, the most important factor in evaluating this part of the introduction is clarity. Can you tell what the researchers were attempting to accomplish with this study? By the time you finish the content in the paragraph or two that concludes the introduction, the reason for doing the study should be quite evident.

IDENTIFYING THE RESEARCH STRATEGY: QUANTITATIVE, QUALITATIVE, OR MIXED METHODS

The general information we have provided about what to expect in the introduction of a research report can be applied to most studies. Some differences in specific criteria for evaluation of the introduction are needed, however, depending on which of the two primary categories of educational research was used in the study: quantitative or qualitative. Differences between these two approaches in the introduction to a research study are evident particularly in the expectations for the literature review and in the specificity expected in the description of objectives for the study near the end of the introduction. The differences are examined in the next two sections of this chapter.

It is important to be able to identify whether the study you are evaluating used a qualitative or a quantitative approach, and some hints for quickly doing so were discussed in Chapter 1. In the introduction itself, the difference may be evident in a more open-ended statement of the objectives of the study. For example, "We will examine perceptions of feeling safe in a classroom setting" would probably signal a qualitative study, while "We will compare the effects of teacher experience, neighborhood socioeconomic level, and age of students on ratings of feeling safe" would be more likely to be used to describe a quantitative study.

In some research reports, the authors make this task easy by telling you in the introductory material whether their design was qualitative or quantitative. If you find it difficult to differentiate between the two study types when the design is not explicitly identified, you may want to review the material in Chapter 1.

The situation is a little more complex when the authors have chosen a **mixed-method** research design. Just as you might expect from the label, this method combines elements of both qualitative and quantitative methods in the same research study. The researchers will typically emphasize in the report that both types of methodology were used and clearly indicate where and how each method was used. In this case, you will need to decide whether the study is balanced more in one direction or the other so that you can determine which criteria to apply when evaluating the quality of the introduction.

SPECIAL CONSIDERATIONS IN QUANTITATIVE STUDIES

You may find it helpful to picture the introduction of a quantitative research report as a series of concentric rings, each defining increasingly specific boundaries for the study, as illustrated in Figure 2.2. The researchers

Figure 2.2
Concentric Rings
in the Introduction
of Quantitative
Research Studies

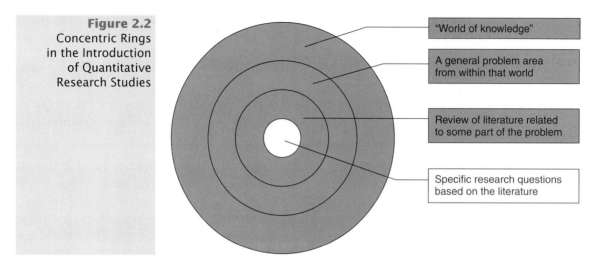

begin with a circle representing the "world of knowledge." At the beginning of the introduction, the researchers "draw" the first inner circle, carving out a general problem for their investigation from within that world. The next inner circle identifies the review of previous studies related to that problem, and then another circle names the specific objectives of the study. These circles correspond to the elements previously identified as the components in the introductory section of a research report.

The basic idea in the quantitative research strategy is that of an ongoing process in which each new study adds to, clarifies, or disputes the findings of earlier research, incrementally adding to the knowledge base about a topic. Each scientist, in effect, is expected to stand on the shoulders of the scientists who came before.

Linear Approach

In this traditional research strategy, the introduction is linear by design. It is assumed that

1. general knowledge about a topic led the researchers to
2. more specific knowledge from prior studies related to some part of that topic, with which the researchers developed
3. specific hypotheses/research questions, which were then
4. tested by gathering data.

In quantitative studies each element is completed in a set chronological order. Quantitative researchers are not supposed to gather the data and then go back and create the research questions.

The hypothetical study in Example 2.2 illustrates problems in both clarity and the link between literature review and study objectives. The purpose of that study is no more clear after reading the third paragraph than it was from the title alone. The hypothetical author provides little information about what exactly was being investigated, nor any explanation of why prior research showed any need for this study.

Evaluating the Context and Significance

In all studies, it is expected that the introduction will begin with the researchers' setting the stage with some context for the problem they investigated. This often includes a historical perspective (what has been done previously in this area?), as well as a more contemporary framing of the study (why is this being examined now?).

The general criteria for evaluating this part of the introduction apply to both quantitative and qualitative studies—importance and presentation. The language in this section of a quantitative report is, however, expected to be consistent with the perspective of an "outsider looking in" with few, if any, personal references. The objective tone in Example 2.1 is typical for the introductory section of a quantitative study.

Evaluating the Literature Review

While there is little difference between quantitative and qualitative studies in terms of the presentation of context and significance, the requirements for the literature review section are quite different. The literature review in a quantitative study has one primary purpose: to provide credibility for the research questions addressed in the study. It is *not* intended to serve as a comprehensive review of all prior research on the topic.

The review of literature in quantitative research studies may bring back memories of writing term papers, but the objective is quite different. The obligation of the researchers is to provide the foundation in prior research on which their specific hypotheses/research questions rest. They are narrowing the scope of the investigation; in effect, drawing a circle inside the first one with more limited boundaries.

Consider two scenarios. In the first, the objectives of the study were chosen by the authors after careful and extensive review of previously published work. These are both related to their research question and appear to be extensions of the previous work. In the second scenario, the authors went searching for some previously published research to fit a study that they had already completed.

Scenario 1 gets a grade of A; Scenario 2 gets a grade of F. Surveying the literature after a study is already completed is not an accepted method in quantitative research. Think of these two scenarios when you are reading the literature review in a published study. From what you are reading, which of the two seems more likely?

Clarity in writing style is important, and excellent writers might well have the skill to make Scenario 2 look as if it had been done the correct way. Most often, though, we believe that an "after the fact" or incomplete literature review will be evident in the way the material is presented. Some of us have been accused of using commas in our writing the way we use salt with our dinners—just sprinkle one in every once in a while. In like manner, if it appears that citations have just been "sprinkled in" where they are supposed to be, you have evidence of a poorly conducted review of the literature.

Identifying an "after the fact" literature review is not necessarily an easy task. Differences are subtle, and a lack of cohesiveness could be the result of poor writing skills rather than an inappropriate review of the literature. But for example, suppose that the researchers were investigating the impact of providing visual cues with videoconferencing for delivery of online mental health services. If their literature review began with a general reference on videoconferencing software, jumped immediately to a study using text chat for counseling, then cited the history of video telephones, and turned then to a citation describing key elements in mental health counseling, you probably should be suspicious about citation sprinkling. All of those sources could be relevant for their study, but there would appear to be no developing theme in the order they were presented.

Evaluating the Objectives of the Study

The other part of the introduction in which there is a large difference in expectations between quantitative and qualitative studies is how the objectives for the research are presented at the end of the introductory section. Remember the linear approach expected in quantitative studies; the shading in Figure 2.3 illustrates the completion of the circle, which is specific research questions supported by the literature review.

The Role of the Hypotheses. Scientists are expected to begin a research study with a prior belief about its outcome (called a hypothesis). They must be willing to subject this opinion to some form of experiment or test and then modify the belief based on the outcome of the study. Essentially, the *hypothesis* is just an educated guess about the outcome of a study, even before it is undertaken. Now why, you might ask, would anyone want to predict the results of a study before it has even been done?

There are at least two ways to address that question, one practical and one more philosophical. The practical answer is that this step is the tradition-bound expectation in a quantitative research study: first the

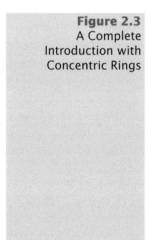

Figure 2.3
A Complete Introduction with Concentric Rings

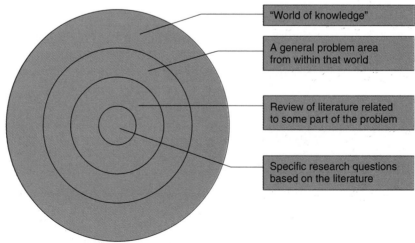

"World of knowledge"

A general problem area from within that world

Review of literature related to some part of the problem

Specific research questions based on the literature

context, then the related literature review, then the hypotheses warranted by prior research. It has always been done this way. (We realize, by the way, that "because you are supposed to" doesn't really answer the question.)

A practical reason for stating a hypothesis is that making such a prediction has the impact of informing the reader that the researchers do, in fact, know enough about this topic to be able to generate plausible predictions. One could argue that a researcher who doesn't know enough about a topic to form a hypothesis probably doesn't know enough about the topic to be doing the study in the first place.

Let's try to answer the question once more, this time with a more philosophical base. Is there anything in the world about which absolutely nothing is known? The perspective of the quantitative researcher is that the answer to that question is a resounding *no*. Obviously, how much is known about different topics varies dramatically. But the premise that drives quantitative research is that, regardless of the topic, there is some information out there, some prior research, some previous experience, maybe even someone's insightful idea. The tradition of quantitative research is that all new studies are to be informed by the results of prior information. And with access to and comprehension of that information, it is possible to form a plausible prediction about the outcome of a new study. This is the essence of quantitative research: making a prediction based on prior knowledge and then testing the accuracy of the prediction.

When stated as specific hypotheses, prior beliefs about the outcome of a research study can be divided into three types:

1. directional
2. nondirectional
3. null

Need a break? The brief time-out in Figure 2.4 may help.

Figure 2.4
A Brief Time-Out

We interrupt our regularly scheduled program with a brief announcement. . . .

Before we talk about these terms further, we wish to alert you that we were not kidding earlier when we mentioned that there were some challenges in developing "fluency" in the language of research. You are literally learning a whole new vocabulary, and even "syntax" and "grammar." So we ask you to be patient with yourself (and with us) as you augment your skills with new concepts, and especially new terms with which you might be only marginally familiar. This "null hypothesis" business is one such example. You may have heard it before—you may even have learned it in a previous class even if the meaning now escapes you. Treat the acquisition of this new learning just as you would if you were learning any new language—say Sanskrit, Czech, or Fortran. You must commit certain words to memory, learn their meaning, and practice their application in various verb forms. Most of all, you must be realistic about the amount of time and effort that is needed in order to master this new language.

Okay, back to our regularly scheduled program. . . .

Hypotheses deal with predicted relationships between or among variables. A variable is simply something that varies, or doesn't always have the same value. Time is a variable. Age is a variable. Test scores are variables. In a *directional* hypothesis, the researchers believe that there will be differences between the groups being compared on some variable (or that there will be a significant relationship between two or more variables) and that the direction of difference or relationship is predictable. Both of the following hypotheses are directional:

- Male students are more likely than female students to prefer distance education using self-directed e-mail.
- There is a significant positive relationship between amount of study time and scores on midterm examinations.

A *nondirectional* hypothesis is quite similar. The researchers who stated the following hypotheses believe that there will be a difference between groups (or a relationship between variables), but the expected direction is not stated.

- There is a gender difference in preference for distance education using self-directed e-mail.
- There is a significant relationship between amount of study time and scores on midterm examinations.

Notice that the difference between the directional and nondirectional hypotheses associated with study time and midterm examinations is only one word. The word *positive* in the directional hypothesis says that the researchers believe that more study time results in higher scores. In the nondirectional hypothesis, the researchers suggest only that there is some relationship between the two variables. The nondirectional hypothesis would thus be supported either if more study time is associated with higher grades or if more study time is a predictor of lower grades.

The *null* hypothesis, as you would expect, represents a prior belief that there will be no difference between the groups, or that there is no relationship between the variables. The null forms of the preceding examples would be as follows:

- There is no gender difference in preference for distance education using self-directed e-mail.
- There is no relationship between amount of study time and scores on midterm examinations.

Objectives, Research Questions, or Hypotheses.   In the preparation of a quantitative master's thesis, research proposal, or doctoral dissertation, a student will usually be required to state explicitly the hypotheses investigated in the study. It is easy to identify the form: directional, nondirectional, or null. In articles published in professional journals, however, the hypotheses are more likely to be implicit rather than explicit. The word *hypothesis* may not even appear in the publication. The use of research questions and statements of purpose is so prevalent, in fact, that if the introductory section ends with explicitly stated hypotheses, identified as such, it is a reasonable guess that this article is probably an outgrowth of a thesis or dissertation by one of its authors.

More and more often, researchers are choosing to close the introduction with stated objectives of the study or research questions rather than listing specific hypotheses. The alternate form (stated objectives or research questions) is primarily a matter of style, not substance. It is reasonable to infer that those stated objectives and/or questions have roots in the hypotheses of the researchers.

Examples of research objectives identified as statements of purpose or in the form of research questions include the following:

- The purpose of the present study was to investigate the relationship between gender and preference for distance education using self-directed e-mail.
- The purpose of this study was to address the question of whether gender differences are evident in the preference for distance education using self-directed e-mail.

When the research question or objective statement format is used, it will be difficult to identify whether the researchers' prior beliefs were directional, nondirectional, or null. In effect, the objective statement or research question typically just assumes the characteristics of a null hypothesis.

SPECIAL CONSIDERATIONS IN QUALITATIVE STUDIES

A good qualitative research report is, in some ways, like a good novel. Most students find qualitative reports much easier to read than the reports that describe quantitative studies. One reason for this is that they more closely resemble the kinds of things that you already read and use a narrative style that is familiar.

Holistic versus Linear

In contrast to the linear requirement in quantitative research, qualitative research studies are holistic by design. Qualitative research does not typically consist of a series of discrete steps that must be completed in a specific order; the researchers have more flexibility to adapt the investigation to fit specific needs in much the same way that an educator may make adjustments in relating to a particular student or classroom, depending on responses elicited and ongoing information as it is gathered.

The holistic focus does not, however, suggest that qualitative researchers can be haphazard or less rigorous in conducting or reporting the study. In evaluating the introductory section of a qualitative study, you will consider general criteria and some specific features associated with this design.

In the introductory section the researchers are expected to provide some general information about the problem area, but specific questions will often not emerge until after data are gathered. In some qualitative studies, the researcher may even discuss his or her personal motives for doing the study. For example, in a study of aggressive teenagers and how they respond to school-based interventions, the author may mention that she was motivated to pursue this study not only because of her work with this population, but also because of very personal experiences that took place in her family of origin. While objectivity is a primary value in quantitative research and subjectivity is the enemy, in qualitative studies one's personal motives, perceptions, and subjective experience are acknowledged and can even be embraced.

The image of a ring with increasingly specific boundaries in Figure 2.3 does not work particularly well with qualitative research studies. A general boundary from the world of knowledge—the first inner circle—is drawn, but the concept of concentric rings with increasing specificity does not often apply. In the introduction the interior boundaries might not be sharply drawn at all. While remaining within the same general area of investigation, qualitative research is characterized by a continuing interaction among data gathering, literature review, and research questioning. An initial circle identifies the general parameters, but what happens inside the boundary remains open to change throughout the investigation.

Evaluating the Context and Significance

The introductory section of a qualitative study begins, as in the other approach, with identification of a general area of study. In effect the researchers will be attempting to persuade the reader that it was important to conduct the investigation. Your evaluation of the initial part of the report will again rely on two criteria: (1) its importance, and (2) its overall clarity.

Blatant bias in the language would, as before, raise doubts about the researchers' willingness to be guided by the data. This is unacceptable in all forms of research inquiry. But when evaluating a qualitative research study, you need to use some caution in how you apply this criterion. Qualitative research, by design, is research in which the investigators are typically involved with, rather than attempting to stand apart from, the topic being studied. A style of writing with a more personal approach does not necessarily signal a biased researcher. What you are looking for is any evidence that the authors were so involved with their prior beliefs that they would be likely to identify and report only the findings consistent with them. Value-laden terminology will often be more evident and is not unacceptable, particularly when a reference is cited.

A warmer, less distant tone is usually evident in qualitative research reports, communicating the involvement of the researchers with the participants. Consider, for example, the beginning of the qualitative study in Example 2.3.

Example 2.3
An Introduction in a Qualitative Study

Examining Transformative Process and Practices: A Cross-Case Analysis of Life in Two Bilingual Classrooms

"Our Tower Community is very unique and different from most other classes. This is why. . . . The teacher of the Tower is usually Ms. Yeager, but everyone gets to play different roles, like teaching. Lots of time we have to work in groups and we have different roles in that too. . . . When you're in the Tower you have to look at different points of view. . . . Most of all, in our community you need to know respect for everyone and everything and be responsible for what you do."

—Chris, Grade 5

In the opening lines of this essay describing his classroom community, Chris claimed that his classroom community was not like others in which he had participated during his years of schooling. He described four ways in which this classroom community differs from others. . . .

Putney, L. G., & Floriani, A. (1999). Examining transformative process and practices: A cross-case analysis of life in two bilingual classrooms. *Journal of Classroom Interaction, 34,* 17–29. Used with permission.

The excerpt in Example 2.3 illustrates the more personal writing style typical in qualitative research reports. At the beginning, the reader is encouraged to recognize that the study involves real people like Chris, with real feelings. To assist in this communication, quotations from participants are extensively used in the reports and often help to quickly engage the reader.

Evaluating the Literature Review

Differences between qualitative and quantitative approaches are especially evident in expectations for the literature review. The literature review is ongoing throughout the study; as the researchers learn something in the collection of the data, the literature review is extended and the new information may change the way additional data are collected. Qualitative researchers typically provide a preliminary literature review in the introductory section, but that initial review (with relevant citations) is expanded as the study evolves and can continue throughout other sections of the research report.

You will be looking for clues indicating that the review was balanced and sufficiently comprehensive, that it included more recent work as well as historical context, and that the researchers tied outcomes together with some form of summary. Also, there should be an emphasis on primary sources.

Evaluating the Research Questions

Significant differences between the qualitative and quantitative approaches are also evident in expectations for the final part of the introductory section. In qualitative studies it is typical to begin with only a preliminary identification of the question to be addressed in the study, often identified as the "foreshadowing" problem or question. The content serves as a general framework, not a specific statement, for the qualitative study. Revision of the question is anticipated as data are gathered.

The outcome is that the criteria appropriate in evaluating the research questions in quantitative studies are essentially reversed when evaluating this part of a qualitative research report. Research questions in quantitative studies should be limited and specific. In contrast, questions within a qualitative study should be sufficiently open-ended to facilitate exploration of themes that emerge during the study.

Consider the following two research questions:

- Do students in technology-rich classrooms have higher scores on standardized achievement tests than those in classrooms without such technology?
- How do technology-rich classrooms affect the educational process?

The first question suggests a quantitative study. The second one would be more appropriate for a qualitative study. It identifies a general framework that can be reformulated as data are gathered during the study. For example, the qualitative research strategy might begin with the researchers conducting interviews with students about their experiences in the technology-rich classroom. From those interviews, the researchers may believe they have detected a theme of a more isolated, less interactive environment when a personal computer is available for each student. This could lead to a reformulated question, going from "How do technology-rich classrooms affect the educational process?" to "Is there an increase in feelings of isolation in technology-rich classrooms?"

Are you comfortable with distinguishing between qualitative and quantitative studies? Reflective Exercise 2.1 will help.

Reflective Exercise 2.1
Distinguishing Between
Qualitative and
Quantitative Studies

This is a good time to take a break from the text and see if the qualitative-quantitative categorization is as easy as we have claimed. Team up with a partner. Using a recent journal from your area of specialization, quickly go through the articles, identifying the studies with quantitative emphasis and those with qualitative emphasis. (Remember that many articles in professional journals are opinion pieces that fit neither category.)

SUMMARY AND CLOSING THOUGHTS

Implicit in this chapter is our belief that not all published research studies warrant more than just a cursory glance. Our objective was to provide specific guidance for critical evaluation of the introductory section of research reports.

In quantitative and many qualitative studies, the boundary of the introduction will almost always be followed by a section with a heading of "Method." This tells you that you are about to move into the realm of what was actually done, rather than just how this study was conceived conceptually. The introduction is usually presented without subheadings, but you can expect to identify content in the introduction that addresses

1. the general context and importance of the investigation,
2. a review of related literature, and
3. the research questions to be investigated.

Because the specific criteria to be used in critique of the introduction are not identical in quantitative and qualitative studies, your first step in evaluation is to identify which approach was used in the investigation. The questions to be asked in evaluation are quite similar, but some of the desired answers will depend on the approach being used. If the researchers do not label their approach (and many do not), look through the article and decide whether the things being studied are usually defined with numbers or with extended verbal descriptions.

For both types of studies, the first question is this: Have the authors made their case that this study was an important study? Does this study seem likely to provide information that I would find useful?

If the answer to the first question is *yes*, then the next concern is about the language: Is the language used consistent with the selected methodology (quantitative or qualitative)? Does the language suggest that the researchers have sufficient objectivity for their conclusions to be guided by their data, rather than vice versa?

After the general context has been presented, you should find a review of previous research studies related to the question being investigated. You will be looking for the following:

- balance (most important topics have studies that appear to support more than one viewpoint)
- timeliness (studies with only dated citations should have some explanation for why no current references are available)
- relevance (coherent themes, rather than isolated citations, should be evident)
- emphasis on primary sources

The introduction of a research report ends with the presentation of the objectives of the study. Sometimes these are provided in the form of hypotheses. More often they will be in the form of research questions or purpose statements.

If the focus of the study is quantitative, your questions are as follows:

- Are the objectives of this study clearly stated?
- Are these objectives supported by the review of related literature that was presented just before them?

If the study is qualitative, you will look for clarity, but not for the specificity essential in the introduction of a quantitative report. In qualitative studies, there is expectation that the initial research question will evolve and be reformulated during the course of the study. Thus, your question for this part of the introduction of a qualitative study is the following:

- Is the initial research question defined to accommodate continuing refinement as data emerge during the study (for example, "What are themes of discomfort associated with combining career, family, and graduate study?" rather than "Do assigned term papers interfere with family demands when students combine graduate school and work?")?

In the introduction of a research report, from the vast scope of what could be studied, both quantitative and qualitative researchers first identify a boundary, in effect drawing a circle surrounding the general problem area. In a qualitative study, the area within that circle remains pliable throughout the investigation. In a quantitative study, concentric rings are drawn inside the initial circle. Inside the first ring are the results of prior research related to a segment of the broad problem area. Then, based on the prior research, a second ring further limits the area to a specific focus of investigation for the study being reported.

Finally, we suggest that you take a rather harsh approach in your critique. If a report fails to meet the criteria for evaluation at any point along the line, our advice is to move on to another study.

AN EXERCISE FOR REVIEW

Try using the evaluative criteria from this chapter with the introductory sections of two published articles, one quantitative and one qualitative. Use the following template to evaluate the material in the introduction. Our evaluation using that same template immediately follows the excerpts.

Template for Evaluating the Introduction

Beginning of the Article
☐ Significance—context, importance of the study
☐ Language—style consistent with approach, objectivity

Review of Related Literature
☐ Is a balanced viewpoint evident? (not all reported studies had the same outcome)
☐ Do the dates indicate attention to both historical precedent and more recent work?
☐ Is a coherent theme evident in this section of the introduction?
☐ Does there appear to be emphasis on primary sources?

Research Objectives
☐ Clearly identified
☐ Supported by literature review and/or emerging data (qualitative)
☐ Open-ended to facilitate theme exploration (qualitative)
☐ Limited to questions with direct foundation in literature review (quantitative)

Selected Content for Evaluation

Quantitative Study

This is an excerpt from: Sapp, M. (1995). Teaching ethics to mental health practica students at the master's level: A comparative study. *College Student Journal, 29,* 333–339. The complete text appears in Appendix A.

Teaching Ethics to Mental Health Practica Students at the Master's Level: A Comparative Study

Marty Sapp

Dewayne, Gordon, Joyce, and Maureen (1991) defined ethics as the process of making moral decisions that are designed to protect the rights and welfare of clients. In terms of practice guidelines, both the American Psychological Association (1981; 1992) and the American Counseling Association (1988) have established a set of principles to guide the ethical behavior of counseling professionals. Welfel and Lipsitz (1984) pointed out that research is needed to determine the impact of formal coursework in ethics upon actual practice. Also, Corey, Corey, and

Callanan (1993) noted that the literature is sparse in supporting the premise that ethics courses have a positive impact on students in actual practice. Similarly, it is not known from empirical research the impact that ethics courses have upon the actual behaviors of mental health counselors with clients. Moreover, there are no data to determine whether ethics is better taught in a separate course or integrated within existing courses. In addition, Welfel and Lipsitz (1984) also questioned if ethical training translates into actual practice.

Many articles on ethics in counseling and psychology have appeared in academic journals (Adair, Linsay, & Carlopio, 1983; Britton, Richardson, Smith, & Hamilton, 1983; Dalton, 1984; Handelsman, Rosen, & Arguello, 1987; Korn, 1984; McGovern, 1988). This article differs in that its purpose is to describe and evaluate three methods of presenting ethics to mental health practica students at the master's level.

Various models have been proposed for teaching ethics, three of which seem quite distinct. First, Kitchener (1986) recommends the integration of psychological processes and educational goals. In fact, Kitchener believes that counseling programs can equip counselors with the critical thinking skills needed to evaluate and interpret ethical codes. Moreover, according to Kitchener, mental health counseling programs can also provide counselors with the ability to evaluate their own behavior during ethical dilemmas. In summary, the foregoing author suggested that ethical training should involve four components: 1) sensitizing students to ethical issues, 2) stimulating the ability of students to reason about ethical issues, 3) encouraging in students a sense of moral responsibility to act ethically, and 4) instructing students how to tolerate the ambiguity involved in ethical decision making.

Second, Pelsma and Borgers (1986) proposed an experience-based developmental model of teaching ethics. Their model integrates the learning process formulated by Kolb (1976) and a developmental scheme of ethical reasoning proposed by Van Hoose (1980). Essentially, this model has four components: 1) concrete experience with feelings that involve ethical concerns, 2) reflective observations about ethical dilemmas, 3) abstract conceptualization—the ability to generalize from concrete ethical principles to abstract ethical dilemmas, and 4) active experimentation—the use of complex strategies to reason out ethical concerns. In summary, this is an integrated model of teaching ethics. As students experience new ethical dilemmas, their new reflections and observational skills result in novel perceptions and a solid basis for the formulation of ethical behavior.

Finally, Strom and Tennyson (1989) developed a problem-posing model for teaching ethics, stressing critical reflective thinking. They emphasize that students develop the capacity and inclination to make rational, defensible, practical, and moral judgments through a problem-posing model. This can be done by presenting students in Fieldwork or Practicum with potential ethical dilemmas that can occur in actual practice. Then, students are allowed to reflect critically upon how they would respond to various ethical issues.

The purpose of the project covered herein was to assess the ethical knowledge of mental health practica students at the master's level who had previous exposure to the ethical principles of ACA and APA and to determine if students' reactions to three different methods of presenting ethics differed from those of students in an attentional control group.

Qualitative Study

This is an excerpt from: Henze, R. C. (2001). Segregated classrooms, integrated intent: How one school responded to the challenge of developing positive interethnic relations. *Journal of Education for Students Placed at Risk, 6,* 133–155. The complete text appears in Appendix B.

Segregated Classrooms, Integrated Intent: How One School Responded to the Challenge of Developing Positive Interethnic Relations

Rosemary C. Henze

During the past 3 years, several colleagues and I have carried out a research project called Leading for Diversity to document proactive approaches that school leaders are using to reduce racial and ethnic conflict and to promote positive interethnic relations (Henze, Katz, Norte, Sather, & Walker, 1999). One of the assumptions underlying this work is that schools can indeed make a positive difference in race relations, and therefore the activities they engage in to do so are worth documenting so that others can learn from them.

In the process of visiting many of the 21 schools participating in the study, I was from time to time challenged to look critically at this assumption. Can schools really be vehicles for improving race relations? On what basis can we answer this positively? What evidence is there to suggest that schools, as currently configured, cannot serve this function, or can only serve it partially? This article explores these questions in the context of one particular elementary school, Cornell, which served a diverse population of vibrant, hopeful children from low-income homes.

Kozol (1991) wrote that "Most of the urban schools I visited were 95 to 99 percent nonwhite" (p. 3) and "reminded me of garrisons or outposts in a foreign nation" (p. 5). He questioned why, in a country that calls itself a democracy, "we would agree to let our children go to school in places where no politician, school board president, or business CEO would dream of working" (p. 5). What emerges from his analysis, and from that of others such as McDermott and Varenne (1995), is the flip side of the traditional risk equation. These scholars, rather than focusing on factors in families and children that may predict school failure, asked instead how schools fail students and families, and indeed how our school system is structured so tightly around the label of "at riskness" that there is a necessary corollary: In addition to children acquiring at-risk factors, the at-risk label has to acquire children. We have, according to McDermott and Varenne, developed a culture that requires some of its members to be disabled, poor, illiterate, and low achieving.

Although many schools work hard, often against great odds, to address risk factors such as poverty, limited English proficiency, racial minority group membership, and others, a few take the brave step of beginning to look at how the school system itself structures inequality and how school staff, school policies, school curriculum, and so on, are part of the problem. An example is Hollinger Elementary school in Arizona, where teachers worked with a group of applied anthropologists to implement an approach called "funds of knowledge." Key domains of change in this approach are as follows: "(1) the development of teachers as qualitative researchers; (2) the formation of new relationships with families; and (3) the redefinition of local households as sites containing important social and intellectual resources for teaching" (González et al., 1995, p. 445). By recasting low-income, Latino households from sites that are culturally deprived to sites where valued knowledge and skills are transmitted from one generation to the next, González and her colleagues fundamentally shifted the way we think about schools and communities. Another example of schools seeking to examine their own part in creating student failure are those that try to eliminate or reduce tracking. Recognizing that the practice of grouping students by presumed ability has resulted in low-ability and high-ability tracks that too often become permanent pathways with no exit, "detracking" schools are moving toward less rigid and hierarchical grouping practices, high academic standards for all students, and the provision of supports that enable all students to reach their highest potential (Oakes, Wells, & Associates, 1996).

In the process of reaching this understanding that the structures, policies, and practices of school systems often create or reinforce existing societal inequalities, schools may question specifically how they help or hinder the development of positive intergroup relations. Given that the society in which U.S. schools are nested has a historical legacy of racism that still affects us today (Banks, 1997; Sleeter, 1991), schools are in a position to reinforce racial and ethnic inequality and stereotyping, which are primary causes of racial and ethnic conflict (Kreisberg, 1998). Schools can also ignore racial inequality and stereotyping or take actions to counter them. The nature of schools as partially bounded cultures within the larger national culture gives them this potential to shape a particular, local culture that may deviate somewhat from the norms and practices of the larger society. In a volume appropriately titled *Shaping School Culture: The Heart of Leadership*, Deal and Peterson (1999) pointed out that school cultures are "shaped by the ways principals, teachers, and key people reinforce, nurture, or transform underlying norms, beliefs, and assumptions" (p. 4).

If we want all children to grow and learn to their fullest potential, then certain basic elements have to be in place in schools. Children who feel physically unsafe because of threats of violence, or who constantly fear verbal abuse such as racial slurs or mockery of their language, are not going to be ready to learn (Bolman & Deal, 1991; Maslow, 1954; Norte, in press). Schools that do not safeguard these basic human needs place children at great risk of school failure. For this reason, it is vital that we consider what schools can do to constructively alter the societal conditions of racial inequality and stereotyping, to nurture a positive racial and ethnic identity among students as well as adults, and to create a strong sense of shared community in which differences are respected and valued.

Several models have been proposed in the literature for the enhancement of interethnic relations. The first of these is Allport's (1954) equal status contact theory, which asserts that positive intergroup relations will develop when the following conditions are present: (a) Groups have equal status within the context; (b) there is one-to-one personal interaction among individuals of different groups; (c) cooperative activities encourage people to work together on superordinate tasks, and (d) there is explicit support for and modeling of intergroup relations by relevant authority figures.

Building on and extending Allport's (1954) theory, Fine, Weis, and Powell (1998) wrote about three high schools that ranged along a "continuum from desegregated but racially separate to integrated communities of difference" (p. 248). However, Fine et al. found equal status contact theory to be inadequate by itself to explain what they saw in the one "integrated community of difference." They suggested that in addition to Allport's four conditions, schools need to "(1) build a sense of community among students; (2) demonstrate a commitment to creative analysis of difference, power, and privilege; and (3) invest in democratic practice with youth" (p. 249).

The reasoning behind these suggestions is that, even though many schools are technically desegregated, there is also tremendous resistance to inclusion. Fine et al. (1998) cited research by Braddock, Dawkins, and Wilson (1995), which showed that over time, sites that purportedly have equal status contact devolve into sites where inclusion and interaction barriers such as differential expectations, or subtle forms of social exclusion, counter the move toward positive intergroup relations. It is worth noting that the three conditions Fine et al. suggested are predicated on work with high school students, and that a "creative analysis of difference, power, and privilege" might look and sound quite different at the elementary level, as would an investment in "democratic practice with youth" (p. 249).

Similar conditions are part of what Tatum (in press) called the ABCs of intergroup relations: (a) affirming identity, (b) building community, and (c) cultivating student leadership. What is different in Tatum's set of conditions is the notion of affirming identity. This grows out of her understanding of the stages of racial identity development that individuals of different racial groups experience (Cross, 1978; Helms, 1990). For somewhat different reasons and at different stages, both Black and White students (and, one would assume, students of other racial and ethnic backgrounds) need to feel secure in a sense of their own racial and ethnic identity to move outward into meaningful relationships with others. A focus on affirming identity in elementary schools might, for example, include such activities as family heritage projects in which children are asked to share with the class information they have gathered from interviews with their families. A focus on building community might include class projects in which children of different ethnic backgrounds work together to solve a shared problem such as cleaning up a park near the school that has become unsafe due to drug trafficking. Cultivating student leadership at the elementary level could involve, for example, teaching students democratic leadership skills so that they can form their own student council or serve as conflict managers on the playground. Such leadership opportunities are important for all students even at the elementary level because they foster a sense of social responsibility and empowerment.

These models for the improvement of interethnic relations provide a framework that is useful in analyzing the efforts of particular schools, like Cornell Elementary.*

---

*The schools and individuals mentioned in this article have been assigned pseudonyms to protect the confidentiality of information shared.

Examples of Evaluation

Quantitative Study

Beginning of the Article

☒ Significance—context, importance of the study
The importance of the study is noted in the author's statement that despite many publications associated with ethics, there are no data about the impact of different instructional styles.

☒ Language—style consistent with approach, objectivity
Although the style at times appears somewhat stilted, the objectivity expected in a quantitative study is evident, and there were no indicators to suggest bias toward one or the other of the instructional approaches.

Review of Related Literature

☒ Is a balanced viewpoint evident? (not all reported studies had the same outcome)
The author noted questions in the literature about whether content in ethics courses is reflected in actual behavior. Absent from the review were citations related to the different instructional modalities with other content.

☒ Do the dates indicate attention to both historical precedent and more recent work?
The range of dates appears reasonable, with some more distant (1979) and others close to the date of the publication.

☒ Is a coherent theme evident in this section of the introduction?
A theme of studies directly associated with ethics instruction is evident. The style of writing could be clearer.

☒ Does there appear to be emphasis on primary sources?
From the excerpt alone this cannot be determined.

Research Objectives

☒ Clearly identified
The purpose of the study is clearly identified in the last paragraph. The writing style, as previously noted, is awkward.

☒ Limited to questions with direct foundation in literature review (quantitative)
The identified purpose appears to be grounded in the literature review.

Qualitative Study

Beginning of the Article

☒ Significance—context, importance of the study
In the first paragraph, the author provides a context for this study, explains why it is important, and identifies her involvement.

☒ Language—style consistent with approach, objectivity
The writing style appears appropriate for the qualitative approach. While she is not particularly "objective" in regard to whether there are race

relations problems in the schools, she provides foundation for her beliefs and appears open to what can be learned from study of this particular school.

Review of Related Literature

☒ Is a balanced viewpoint evident? (not all reported studies had the same outcome)
While it would have been helpful to see some citations acknowledging questions about whether improving race relations should be the responsibility of the schools, a range of sources was included in the review. It is also important to remember that in qualitative methodology, the literature review may extend beyond the introduction as new questions emerge.

☒ Do the dates indicate attention to both historical precedent and more recent work?
The review noted that current perspective may have roots back to 1954 and included studies close to the date of this publication, even including a study that was "in press" at the time of this publication.

☒ Is a coherent theme evident in this section of the introduction?
A coherent theme was clearly evident.

☒ Does there appear to be emphasis on primary sources?
From the excerpt alone this cannot be determined.

Research Objectives

☒ Clearly identified
Remember that a gradual narrowing of focus from the beginning of the introduction to the research objectives is not a required feature of qualitative methodology. The objective of the study is clearly stated in the last sentence of the second paragraph and acknowledged again as the last paragraph.

☒ Supported by literature review and/or emerging data (qualitative)
There is an evident link between the objective of the study and the literature review.

☒ Open-ended to facilitate theme exploration (qualitative)
The objective is open-ended. The author suggests that a specific school with a diverse population can provide important information regarding race relations but does not limit the possibilities about what specific information will be sought.

3

Who Answered the Question?
Evaluating the Participant Sample

CHAPTER OUTLINE

BASIC CONCEPTS

Accessible population
Cluster sampling
Convenience selection
Higher-risk sampling
    techniques

Lower-risk sampling
    techniques
Purposive selection
Quota selection
Replicate
Research sample

Simple randomization
Strata
Stratified randomization
Systematic sampling
Target population

We'll now move from learning how to make some preliminary assessment about a research study by reviewing the introductory section to scrutinizing the section that follows—a description of the methods employed in the study. Imagine that you're engaging the researchers in a conversation that goes something like this:

Okay," you begin cautiously, "I am intrigued enough with your overview to read further."

"Good." The author nods her head. "And I'm sure you'll agree . . ."

"Wait one second," you interrupt, putting the brakes on. "Before I agree to anything, I want to know a whole lot more about *how* you did this study. You already told me what you *intended* to do, now I want to know *what* you did, and *why* you did it that way."

"Well sure," the author agrees. "But before we go there, I want to tell you why I had to proceed the way I did. Most people don't understand . . ."

"Look," you tell her, becoming impatient. "I don't have a lot of time. This journal is sitting by my nightstand, but so are some really interesting things waiting to be read. Let's get to the point here. Besides, you already told me in the introduction what you had in mind. I don't want to hear the whole thing again. Just tell me what you did—*exactly* what you did."

In one sense, any good piece of writing, whether a journal article, a research text, or a novel, is a conversation between the author and the reader. And at this point in your dialogue with the researchers you are indeed asking them what they were up to. Presumably, you have already been persuaded by their general rationale and have now moved on to their plan. This set of procedures is described in the method section of the article.

PRIMARY TOPICS IN THE METHOD SECTION

As illustrated in Figure 3.1, the three primary topics usually included in the method section are participants, instruments and procedures. Each of these will sometimes (though not always) be identified with a subheading in the actual journal article.

The first subsection of the method section is about the individuals who were the **participants** in the study. Participants are the individuals

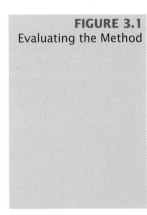

FIGURE 3.1
Evaluating the Method

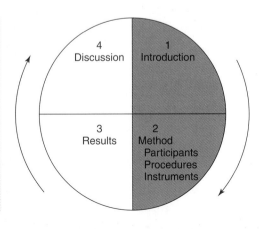

who were studied by the authors. These folks can be called "subjects," which sounds kind of impersonal, or sometimes they are referred to as the "co-researchers" in qualitative studies to communicate that they were collaborators in the inquiry process.

The next subsection of the method section usually details the **instruments,** the techniques and tools used to measure, observe, or document the information gathered about the variables or phenomenon investigated in the study. This means that the participants engaged in some sort of activity and some aspect of their behavior was observed, examined, described, and/or measured.

This could include some specific variable such as the frequency of eye blinks as a measure of anxiety, or it could involve a more general, internal process such as the kind of thoughts that accompany preparation for an exam. In some cases the researcher instigates the activity. In others, the researcher uses information such as test scores, memoranda, or cumulative records that are already available. This subsection also includes a description of any apparatus used to gather information for the study—for example, stopwatches or videotaping equipment.

The last subsection of the method section, the **procedures,** describes the research design. The procedures tell you exactly what the researchers did and why they did it that way. Not only does this provide you with information that allows you to assess whether the study was well designed, but if you decide to **replicate** the study, to do a comparable study with a different group of participants, you would know exactly how to proceed.

In this chapter our focus is on the first of these topics: evaluating the researchers' choice of participants for their study. Instruments and procedures are considered in the chapter that follows.

DEFINITIONS

In this section you will be introduced to the terminology often used by researchers to describe the process used to select the participants in a research study. The specific terminology may be new, but you'll find that the terms are usually self-descriptive.

Target Population

The **target population** is the group about which results are supposed to provide information or generalizations. Generalizability is the extent to which the information obtained from a selected group reflects the ultimate target, the people whom the researchers would ideally want to study. In some studies the ultimate target is composed only of the actual participants in the study. More often, especially in quantitative studies, the participants instead are serving a surrogate role, representing an ultimate target group. In some research reports the ultimate target population is explicitly identified. In others, you have to infer the target population from information provided in the research questions.

For example, consider a research study involving vocabulary acquisition and reading comprehension in which the researchers compared the effectiveness of elementary school basal readers alone to the use of basal readers plus computer drill. It is highly unlikely that the researchers would be interested only in the results of the students used in that study. Instead, the ultimate goal would be to use those results to predict (or generalize to) a much larger group, perhaps all elementary school students in North America.

The researchers investigating sources of sexuality information in the study described in Chapter 2 had a much larger group in mind than just sophomore students at one university in the Southeast. Their objective was to use the information from those sophomores to draw conclusions about university students in general.

Research Sample

In both of the preceding examples and in the vast majority of quantitative research studies, the actual data come from a sample selected to represent the target group. The **research sample,** also referred to as the **participant sample,** is a subgroup of the target population. Researchers proceed in this way because often it is impossible to work with everyone in the target population. They instead use a representative sample of the population and then attempt to generalize results. When sampling is used, you as the consumer of its findings will have to be the one to decide the extent to which you believe the sample accurately reflects the target population.

Accessible Population

When actually conducting a research study, there is often an intermediate group between the target and the sample, identified as the **accessible population.** This is defined as the members of the target population who are available for the research study. For evaluation of most published research studies, this intermediate tier is not a primary concern. You will typically only need to look for information to support whether the target population is consistent with the research questions, and, if so, whether the research sample would be likely to adequately represent the target.

The relationship among these elements is illustrated in Figure 3.2. We start with the **general population,** simply defined as everyone. From the general population, the researchers select a target population based on their research objectives. From the target population, they may have to select an accessible population group. Finally, from either the target or accessible group, they often draw a sample of research participants for their study. The critical question in sampling is whether the research or participant sample is a mirror of the ultimate target.

Inanimate Research Sample

One more consideration and we will be ready to proceed. In most research studies in the social science field, the research or participant sample is composed of people. For simplicity and clarity, the examples in this

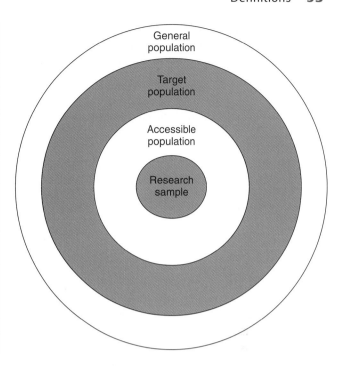

FIGURE 3.2
Relationship of General Population, Target Population, Accessible Population, and Research Sample

General population

Target population

Accessible population

Research sample

chapter will usually assume a human sample of research participants. Don't forget, though, that there are instances in which the researchers' target is inanimate—for example, a study designed to summarize the findings of several other studies in a field. For instance, if the objectives of a study are to provide a review of literature in some specific topic area, the sample described by the researchers would be the specific articles used in the review and the criteria used to select them. To illustrate, the researchers in a study titled "Research on Telehealth and Chronic Medical Conditions: Critical Review, Key Issues, and Future Directions" (Liss, Glueckauf, & Ecklund-Johnson, 2002) identified how they searched for relevant research articles and the specific criteria used to select those articles.

Try Reflective Exercise 3.1 to understand how the individuals or documents sampled affect the usefulness of the research findings.

Reflective Exercise 3.1
Why Does the Type of Sample Matter?

Imagine that the instructor of your class has come up with a new and apparently really good idea about how to motivate students who are taking their first course in research methods. The new approach will be tried out in your course this term, with a plan to share the results with other instructors.

In small-group format, discuss how the concepts of *target population, accessible population,* and *research sample* would influence the usefulness of the results in other settings. For example, to whom do you think the instructor will want to generalize the results? Are there characteristics of your group that would make you a good or a poor sample? Be prepared to share your thoughts with the class. (Our thoughts about some implications are at the end of the chapter.)

THE FIRST QUESTION

Before we consider specific criteria for evaluating the adequacy of the participants in a research study, consider the following scenario: A professor in a prestigious law school begins each first-year class by writing the following on the board:

$$\text{equals} \quad \frac{\begin{array}{r} 2 \\ 2 \end{array}}{?}$$

The professor then turns to the new students and demands, "What's the answer?" Eager to please, one or more of the new students quickly respond, "The answer is four."

The outcome for these students is a lengthy and not especially positive prognosis for their future in law school, punctuated by the words, "And how, may I ask, can you possibly know the answer, when you don't even know what the question is?"

That scenario illustrates a simple and key point in evaluation of the participants. You have to know what the question is in order to answer whether the criteria used to select the participants used were adequate and appropriate.

Therefore, when evaluating the selection of the participants, your first step will be to review what the researchers stated as the research questions for their study. That information, as described in Chapter 2, should be provided in the introduction to the article, just before the method section begins. The questions might have been presented in the form of hypotheses or statements of purpose. Regardless of format, they are the primary templates you will use in a critical evaluation of the participant selection.

For example, in the study on sources of sexuality information described in Chapter 2 (Example 2.1), the research questions were stated in the form of hypotheses about gender differences and the extent to which books were an important source of such information for *university students.* That objective is critical in evaluating whether their use of undergraduate students as a participant sample was appropriate.

In essence, remember that evaluating participants in a research study begins with, and is focused on this single question:

Do the participants identified in the research report appear appropriate and sufficient to address the questions identified by the researchers as the objectives of the study?

FIGURE 3.3 Evaluating the Participants	What is the target population? Who participated in the study? Where were the participants? When were the data gathered? How was the sample selected? Why was this sample selected?

WHAT DO YOU NEED TO KNOW?

Journalism students are taught that a news story should include *who*, *when*, *why*, *what*, *how*, and *where*, preferably in the first sentence of the story. To evaluate the adequacy and appropriateness of the participant sample, we'll use those same tools but with a slight variation (see Figure 3.3).[1]

The questions in Figure 3.3 will be the tools to provide the information you will need to answer the critical question: whether these participants can answer the research questions.

EVALUATION TOOL ONE: WHAT IS THE TARGET POPULATION?

Evaluating the adequacy of a sample begins with identification of the target population. In many qualitative studies, and some quantitative studies, the target population is the only relevant group. For example, if the objective of a survey research study is to describe characteristics of teachers in a certain school district in a specific school year, the researchers might choose to gather data from all teachers in the district. In that case, there would be no separate research "sample." The sample is the population.

Note, though, that the "gathering from all" is not what defines this as the target population, but rather that the research objective is to describe only this particular group of teachers. If the researchers plan to use these data to make inferences about characteristics of teachers in similar school districts, or even in that district in other years, the group now becomes a research sample for a different target. That new target population could be all teachers in certain kinds of school districts, or teachers over a period of years in that district.

---

[1]The "six honest serving-men" were first identified in a 1902 poem by Rudyard Kipling that begins: I keep six honest serving-men/(They taught me all I knew);/Their names are What and Why and When/And How and Where and Who.

In Reflective Exercise 3.2, the objectives are provided for three studies. See if you can identify who the researchers had in mind for the target populations in those studies.

The following excerpts from three published research articles describe the objectives for each study. Read each excerpt and identify the likely target population for the study.

Our purposes in the present study were (a) to examine differences in reported teacher efficacy in early-childhood and elementary preservice teachers in Taiwan and the United States and (b) to see if reported teacher efficacy changes as a function of the learning experiences in the teacher education programs. . . . We hypothesized that differences between Taiwanese and U.S. preservice teachers at the beginning of the program would be attributable to prior experience with different educational and sociocultural perceptions. Also, . . . we hypothesized that differences between Taiwanese and U.S. preservice teachers at the end of the program would be attributable, at least in part, to the nature of the respective programs, to the content of the teachers' studies, and to their increasing experience.

Lin, H., Gorrell, J., & Taylor, J. (2002). Influence of culture and education on U.S. and Taiwan preservice teachers' efficacy beliefs. *Journal of Educational Research, 96*, 37–46. Reprinted with permission of the Helen Dwight Reid Educational Foundation. Published by Heldref Publications, 1319 Eighteenth St., NW., Washington, DC 20036-1802. Copyright © (2002).

Our purpose . . . is to review the rites of passage concept, to describe reentry women in both university and home environments; and finally, to discuss the possible purposes and the degree of necessity for such rites.

Redding, N. P., & Dowling, W. D. (1992). Rites of passage among women reentering higher education. *Adult Education Quarterly, 42*, 221–226.

The purpose of this study was to determine whether training students in a specific self-supervision technique can have a positive effect on their ability to evaluate their own professional work.

Donnelly, C., & Glaser, A. (1992). Training in self-supervision skills. *The Clinical Supervisor, 10*, 2–10.

Bonus question: From the objectives included in the excerpts of these three articles, which appears to identify a qualitative research study?

(Answers are at the end of the chapter.)

EVALUATION TOOL TWO: WHO PARTICIPATED IN THE STUDY?

If the target population seems an appropriate potential resource (which is usually, but not always, the case), your next question for evaluation of the participants is, who actually provided data for the study? In other words, who participated in the study? Your ability to answer this question depends on the amount of information provided in the article by the researchers. Obviously, you can't know everything about the participants, but the general rule is that the more information you are given, the better you will be able to judge the extent to which the results can be generalized. What you are particularly looking for is any information about the participants' characteristics that might have some impact on responses to the research questions.

For example, a research question might involve the effect of different instructional techniques on achievement test scores. If there is some reason to suspect gender differences in those scores, the researchers should certainly tell you how many males and how many females were in the study. Age, race/ethnicity, socioeconomic status, and disability status are among the other demographic factors that are often helpful to know.

In evaluating a published study with this tool, you may find that the problem is simply insufficient information. For example, if the researchers tell you only that the participants were elementary school students and nothing else about them, it will be essentially impossible for you to evaluate the significance of their findings. Remember the "skeptical mindset" from Chapter 1. If you are not given enough information about the participants to judge whether they could provide answers for the research questions, don't spend any more time with that research study.

You will want to be alert to unusual characteristics, especially if the researchers provide little or insufficient explanation. For example, the researchers might tell you that participants were elementary school students selected from Grades 3, 4, and 6. What happened to the fifth-grade students? Why were they not included in the study?

You will also want to be cautious about the language used to describe the specific characteristics of the participants. Researchers, for instance, might report that the majority of participants in the study were children whose parents were in the lower socioeconomic strata. The troublesome word in that sentence is *majority.* The researchers would be technically correct in using that word if the actual percentage of those children was anywhere from 51 percent to 99 percent of the participants. That's too wide a range to understand the characteristics of the group. A better way to describe the participants in this particular study would be: "The majority of participants in the study (67%) were children whose parents were in the lower socioeconomic strata."

When you are using this tool, your role is very similar to that of a detective. You are carefully examining each piece of information about the sample that is available to you. What seems to be missing in the description? If essential information does not appear to be there, was it just poor writing on the part of the researchers, or could the omission warrant suspicion that the researchers were attempting to mask some problems in the study?

We continue to suggest a "guilty until proven innocent" mindset during the evaluation. It is the researchers' responsibility to provide sufficient evidence for you to evaluate the extent to which the participants are in a position to provide answers to the research questions. If the evidence is not there, stop reading.

EVALUATION TOOL THREE: WHERE WERE THE PARTICIPANTS?

The information from the *where* question extends the description of the participants. If the participants were school-age children, were the data gathered as a part of a regular school day or as an after-school activity? Where was the school located? Were any special characteristics of the school itself (for example, private or public, traditional or experimental, large or small) likely to have had an impact relevant for the research questions? Participants, for example, from small public schools located in rural settings may or may not have provided the same answer to a research question as participants in an inner-city school district.

Information from university subject pools can be gathered in a variety of settings from a large lecture hall to a small lab. Again, the question is whether the setting would appear likely to have influenced the pattern of responses. Clearly, for example, an instructional technique that works well in a small university lab might be a total failure in a regular classroom. Also, participants from a small exclusive private college might have vastly different characteristics from those drawn from a large public university.

Any one of these settings could provide an appropriate setting in which to investigate specific research questions. In evaluating the sample, you should use your judgment as to whether the setting was conducive to the objectives of the study. The researchers obviously believed it was. Did they provide sufficient information to convince you as well?

EVALUATION TOOL FOUR: WHEN WERE THE DATA GATHERED?

This question needs to be asked because the answer will occasionally influence your evaluation of the adequacy of the participants. The two pieces of information needed are the date when the data were gathered and the date when the article was actually published. Expect some time lag between these two dates. A period of at least two years is typical, and the gap could be much longer in some journals or if the manuscript had to be revised and resubmitted several times before it was accepted for publication.

The *when* question is included as a tool for evaluation because events can occur between the conducting of a research study and its publication that could dramatically influence the relevance of the findings. The most obvious example might be a study in the United States on perceptions of safety in the school setting conducted prior to September 11, 2001, and published after that date. At the time such a study was conducted, the researchers could have done an exemplary job in all phases of the research study, including a completely appropriate participant group. But the subsequent event could severely limit the extent to which the findings could be generalized to the present.

EVALUATION TOOL FIVE: HOW WAS THE SAMPLE SELECTED?

In almost all quantitative and some qualitative studies, the researchers use a sample, a group of participants selected to represent the target population. When sampling is used, we also have to consider whether the sample seems likely to provide adequate representation of the target population.

The logic in this is hopefully quite clear. The application, however, quickly becomes a bit complex for a couple of reasons. First, the researchers may not have clearly identified the ultimate target population, leaving it to you to infer this from their description of the sample. Identifying the authors' target population should be possible, though, even if the authors were not explicit. Try to carefully read the information in the introductory section of the article and the description of the participants in the method section.

Second, unless you have a crystal ball in front of you, it will be difficult (actually close to impossible) for you to know for sure whether this sample did in fact adequately represent the target. Judging whether a participant sample seems to be representative of the target population is aided by the information about them obtained in the *who, where,* and *when* questions. And, when sampling is used to select the participants, two more questions should be asked:

1. How was the sample selected?
2. Why was this particular sample selected?

Keep in mind that the manner in which a sample is selected (the *how* question) can only increase or decease the odds that the sample represents the target population. The answer to the question "What could happen by chance?" is always the same: "Anything." Using the most statistically sound sampling procedure does not guarantee that the selected sample is actually representative of the target population. By chance alone, even the best sampling techniques will sometimes produce a group that just isn't like the target group in some important characteristics. As just one example, the sample used for exit polls during the 2000 U.S. presidential election was chosen with tools that would seem to guarantee their accuracy in predicting the target population of all who voted. But a lot of red-faced network newscasters found themselves backpedaling after making an initial call of the election results that turned out to be inaccurate.

The reverse is equally true. A sample that is representative of the target population can sometimes emerge by chance alone, regardless of the techniques employed by the researchers to select it. (This is not, by the way, a recommendation for how to select samples when you do research. Simply hoping that a representative sample will emerge by chance alone is a really bad idea!)

Researchers might be able to use sampling procedures that increase the odds that the sample will actually be representative of the target population. In the material that follows, these are categorized as the *lower-risk* sampling procedures. The researchers may instead, for a variety of reasons, choose procedures in which the odds are only neutral at best that a representative sample will be selected, identified here as the *higher-risk* techniques. Remember, though, that using the former does not necessarily result in a representative sample, and using the latter does not always result in peculiar samples. The choice of a sampling technique just affects the odds that the sample will be representative of the intended target. Using a higher-risk technique in hopes of obtaining a representative sample is somewhat akin to betting on your favorite sports team, now at the bottom of the standings, to emerge as the eventual champion. It could happen, but it probably won't.

What all this means is that researchers often have some difficult decisions in how they do things, in this case deciding how participants are selected. Choices, each with some benefit and some cost, must be made. Researchers try to make the best decisions they can with the resources they have available. They have to consider factors such as the time available, the cost of some procedures over others, and the accessibility of various groups. Research studies that involve human participants require approval from university institutional review boards. These boards, composed of professors and representatives of the general community, review proposed research studies to be sure that participants are not placed at risk through participation in a study and have been given enough information about the study to be able to provide an informed consent to participate. Thus, the researchers have to consider the possible difficulty in getting approval when they decide how a sample will be selected. Also crucial in decisions about sample selection is how ambitious the researchers are in terms of the scope and potential significance of their study.

In the next sections, we provide you with some of the common sampling procedures, discussing their relative advantages and risks. Some need for memorization is inevitable, but try to keep a focus on the bigger picture as you read about each sampling technique. Keep in mind that your ultimate concern is the extent to which the selection procedure is likely to produce participants who will help answer the identified research questions.

Lower-Risk Sampling Procedures

One or more of the following might be evident in the researchers' description of how they selected the research sample.

- Simple randomization
- Stratified randomization
- Cluster sampling
- Systematic sampling

Simple Randomization.   Selecting a sample through **simple randomization** is the easiest method to describe but may be the most difficult to implement in actual research studies because it assumes the availability of a master list of the population. To use the simple randomization technique, researchers begin with a master population list and select participants using a random-number procedure. The concept is straightforward—a condition is created in which every member of the target population has an equal chance of being selected for the research sample.

For example, if researchers were planning to conduct a study of characteristics of the graduate students in the college or university in which you are now enrolled, they might begin with a list of all graduate students currently enrolled, their target population. Then a sample of predetermined size would be randomly selected to participate in the study. To make the random selection, the researchers might use a book with a table of random numbers that provides instructions on how to select a random group. More likely they would instead use one of the widely available computer software programs in which they indicate the predetermined total and are provided with a list of random numbers.

Simple randomization is not a bad procedure (in fact a quite honorable technique), but notice that researchers using this technique would have to begin with a listing of all possible participants in a target population. Such a listing could be available to the researchers, but in real-life studies that doesn't happen very often. It is just too time consuming, too expensive, and too impractical.

Simple randomization is sometimes practical and appropriate as a second selection step in qualitative studies that begin with the *purposive selection* technique, described later in this chapter. If the purposive sample has more members than are needed or would be practical to use, the qualitative researchers could randomly select participants from the master list of the purposive selection.

Stratified Randomization.   A **stratified randomization** procedure is a derivative of simple randomization in which the researchers take steps before selecting the sample to ensure that characteristics that are relevant for their study are adequately represented in the sample selected. The name is from a term, *stratum,* that you may have encountered in reference to geology. A stratum is an internal layer. In our context, the term is used to indicate that relevant layers, defined as subgroups or subpopulations within the total population, are represented in the sample in the same proportion as they are found in the population.

To illustrate, let's assume that you are in a college with 1,000 graduate students, and 65% are female. Could a sample selected with simple randomization have 70% males? The answer, of course (anything can happen by chance), is *yes,* and the odds of an inappropriate gender distribution go up as the size of the sample goes down. If different responses to the researchers' questions could be contingent on gender, this could be a significant problem.

To avoid the problem, researchers ensure representation through the process of stratification. Randomly selecting participants from within the strata rather than randomly selecting from the total group ensures that the sample has proportional representation from relevant subgroups. In the preceding example, if the researchers wanted a total sample of 100, they would randomly select 65 from the list of females in the target population and randomly select 35 from the list of males in the target population.

Cluster Sampling.   Another derivative of simple randomization is **cluster sampling.** Usually in simple and stratified randomization, the basic unit is the individual person. In cluster sampling the basic unit instead is a naturally occurring group of people—for example, a classroom, a school, or a club. We can extend the example of the study of graduate students to illustrate how it works. Assume that the researchers want to administer a questionnaire to gather data about the graduate students. It would be much easier to do this with a group than to find each individual graduate student. Where do graduate students cluster together? Graduate students cluster together in classes. Thus, instead of using simple randomization or stratified randomization to select from a list of names of all graduate students, the researchers could instead use a list of all graduate classes.

Before we go further, the cooperative learning exercise in Reflective Exercise 3.3 will help ensure that the basic concepts are clear (and it's probably time for a break!).

Reflective Exercise 3.3
Selecting a Sample

In a small-group setting (or on your own), consider the following questions:

1. How could researchers use cluster sampling to create strata in a study investigating characteristics of graduate students on your campus?
2. What would be a primary stumbling block for use of cluster techniques in such a study, and how could it be resolved?

(Answers are at the end of the chapter.)

Systematic Sampling.   The final derivative in the lower-risk category to be considered here is the use of **systematic sampling** procedures. In systematic sampling, the researchers again begin with a master list of all potential participants. The list could be composed of individuals or, if cluster procedures are being used, a list of potential groups. After deciding how many are desired for the sample, the researchers systematically go down the list, selecting participants according to some predetermined system (such as every tenth name or every seventh classroom).

In essence, the systematic procedure approximates randomization and is much simpler to do (if it's being done by hand). The primary risk, assuming that the list is alphabetical, occurs when the beginning letter used for alphabetizing is not a random occurrence. For example, the researchers might be conducting a study in which ethnicity is an important variable and the likelihood of having a last name beginning with a specific letter is influenced by one's ethnic background. (Consider asking for extra credit if you noticed that a systematic sampling procedure would result in a randomized sample if the original list is in random order.)

Table 3.1 illustrates how different participants would be selected using systematic and simple randomization procedures.

Table 3.1
Examples of Systematic and Simple Randomization Procedures for Selection of Participants

Systematic Sampling	*Simple Randomization*
From the 20 names in the master list, the researchers want a sample of 5 participants. Starting at the top of the list, they select every 4th name.	From the 20 names in the master list, the researchers want a sample of 5 participants. From a table of random numbers, the numbers selected are 15, 9, 7, 8, and 1.
Adams, John	**Adams, John**
Arthur, Chester	Arthur, Chester
Buchanan, James	Buchanan, James
Fillmore, Millard	Fillmore, Millard
Garfield, James	Garfield, James
Grant, Ulysses	Grant, Ulysses
Harrison, William	**Harrison, William**
Hayes, Rutherford	**Hayes, Rutherford**
Jackson, Andrew	**Jackson, Andrew**
Jefferson, Thomas	Jefferson, Thomas
Johnson, Andrew	Johnson, Andrew
Lincoln, Abraham	Lincoln, Abraham
Madison, James	Madison, James
Monroe, James	Monroe, James
Pierce, Franklin	**Pierce, Franklin**
Polk, James	Polk, James
Taylor, Zachary	Taylor, Zachary
Tyler, John	Tyler, John
Van Buren, Martin	Van Buren, Martin
Washington, George	Washington, George

Table 3.1 can also be used to illustrate a feature of stratified randomization. You may have noticed that a remarkably high proportion (20%) of the first 20 presidents of the United States were named James. But when we used a simple randomization procedure for selection, not one of these was selected. If for some reason this mattered (okay, we know it's really not important), the researchers could have ensured a proportional representation of the James's with the following steps:

1. Presidents with the first name of James constituted 20% of the list.
2. Presidents with the first name of James should constitute 20% of the sample.
3. Researchers want a total sample of 5 participants, so 1 of the 5 should be a James.
4. Researchers construct two lists: a James list (five potential participants) and a non-James list (15 potential participants).
5. Researchers randomly select 1 from the James list and 4 from the non-James list.

We admit that this example is a bit far-fetched. Strata are used in real life only if there is some likely relevance. This example, however, does illustrate the process.

Higher-Risk Sampling Procedures

Common sense might suggest that studies using higher-risk sampling procedures would be automatically suspect. But for many important areas of inquiry in the social sciences, the lower-risk techniques simply cannot be applied. Using any one of those techniques with human participants assumes that the researcher has or can acquire a master list of all members in some usually very large group. Going from target population to accessible population would make it a little easier, but the latter, when done honestly, will still be a quite large group.

For example, a researcher might want to use children in his or her classroom as participants in a research study. There are several designs for which this would be a completely legitimate action. But to define that group as the accessible population, randomly sample from it, and then claim to be able to generalize from that sample group to all students in North America at that grade level would be rather suspect at the very least.

A question you might be asking is that if researchers cannot use a pure form of randomization to select a participant sample, what can they do instead? How did these people come to be a part of the participant sample in this research study?

Because the comprehensive master list of the target population may not be available to the researchers (or may not even exist anywhere), there has to be another option. The research articles you read will very seldom include samples selected by truly random procedures. Instead, the samples in those research studies will have been chosen using one or some combination of the following techniques:

- Convenience selection
- Quota selection
- Purposive selection

Convenience Selection.   The use of **convenience selection** techniques is so pervasive that it is tempting here to define it simply as "what most researchers actually do." Essentially convenience selection is, as would be expected from its name, a procedure in which the researchers choose the participant sample because they provide a convenient, easily accessible group. Many universities include participation in a research study as a requirement in some lower-division classes. Researchers who use these subject pools—in this case, undergraduate students—to get their samples are using convenience selection.

Convenience selection is a higher-risk procedure because the risk of obtaining a sample that doesn't represent the target population is higher than would be evident with true randomization. But it isn't necessarily a bad procedure. The key in evaluating the adequacy of a convenience sample is whether the subjects seem likely to be representative of the actual target. We should be able to assume that the researchers who use the convenience technique have made some effort for these participants to bear some resemblance to the target population. In evaluating that effort, it is especially important for the researchers to provide extensive information about the people who were used, a topic considered earlier in the section on who the participants were. Reflective Exercise 3.4 is designed to demonstrate the frequency with which the convenience selection procedure is used.

Reflective Exercise 3.4
Convenience Sampling

> We've claimed that convenience sampling is used more often than the other techniques to select participant samples. Let's check this out (actually, we want *you* to check this out). Either by yourself or with a partner who has similar interests, get a copy of a recent journal from your area of specialization or interest. Go to the method section in each research article in the journal and count the number of articles in which convenience seems to have been the criterion for selecting the participants. Be prepared to give a report to the rest of the class about what you find.

Quota Selection.   The **quota selection** procedure is an interesting derivative of the stratified random technique. A primary difference is that a master list of potential participants is not required. In quota sampling, the researchers instead begin with quotas to fill in a variety of predetermined categories—for example, 11 females who are between ages 35 and 44, 15 females who are between the ages 45 and 54, and so forth. Using the quota selection procedure provides a sample that is stratified but not really random. You may not find it often in research articles you are reviewing, but there's a good chance that while walking across your campus you've been asked to participate in a study using this technique. To use quota sampling, the researchers will typically begin with some desired total number of participants and a goal related to some specific demographic characteristics of the sample—for example, an equal gender representation. The demographic criteria are selected to include characteristics judged to be possibly relevant in the specific study.

For example, suppose that you have a series of questions you'd like to have answered about whether your school should change its parking regulations. You're going to obtain the information through interviews, so you've decided to limit the size of the sample to 100 participants. On your campus, approximately 40% of the students are classified as lower division (freshmen and sophomores), 36% are upper division (juniors and seniors), and 24% are graduate students. Armed with your clipboard, you then set out across campus to find people willing to answer your questions. You keep at it (perhaps making some new friends along the way) until you've gotten answers from 40 lower-division students, 36 upper-division students, and 24 graduate students.

The simple quota in the example could easily be elaborated. If 75% of the graduate students on your campus are female, your quota would be to get answers from 18 female and 6 male graduate students. The big question remains the same: Does this sample produce results comparable to those that would have been obtained from the target population, in this case all students on your campus?

Obviously this is a higher-risk sampling technique, in part because you are meeting the strata criteria but with a limited group from whom to choose. For example, in the hypothetical parking study, if you chose 100 people who were driving around looking for a parking place around midday, you might get a far different response pattern than if you did the 100 interviews at 7:30 in the morning.

Quota sampling is especially evident during election season with those annoying automated phone calls. The actual sample may match the target population in many demographic characteristics, but the answers will come only from people who are able (and willing) to interrupt their lives to answer and respond to the phone call.

Purposive Selection.   The last of the higher-risk techniques is **purposive selection.** In quantitative studies, purposive samples may be chosen because the researchers know (or at least think they know) things about the characteristics of people in the sample that would probably make them reflective of the target population. The adequacy of this kind of sampling for quantitative studies rests on the judgment of the researchers and is sometimes even called *judgment sampling.*

For example, a student was studying personality characteristics and needed a sample that would include people with a broad spectrum of career interests. The education department's subject pool wasn't a viable alternative because those students had already chosen a college major and thus typically included people with personality characteristics primarily consistent with careers associated with that major. The solution was to use instead a sample of people enrolled in introductory courses at a local community college.

This example also illustrates that the higher-risk techniques are often combined when selecting the participant sample. In this case, the sample was *purposive,* chosen because a variety of vocational interests would be likely, and it was *convenient,* easily accessible by the researcher.

Purposive sampling is sometimes used in quantitative studies, but it is the most frequent technique employed in qualitative studies. As described earlier, in some qualitative studies the idea of sampling doesn't really even apply, at least in the traditional sense. Generalization does not apply since the study is more often focused only on the group or site being studied. The sample *is* the target population.

When not all of the possible participants are to be included in a qualitative study, the sample selected will most often be purposive. For example, the researchers will choose participants who seem most likely to

Table 3.2
Key Characteristics of Sampling Procedures

Category	Type	Process	Strengths	Concerns
Lower-risk	Simple randomization	Randomly select participants from a master list	Ensures equal chance to become participant	Must have a master list; important subpopulations may be missed
	Stratified randomization	Identify subgroups; randomly select participants within subgroups	Participation by relevant subgroups is ensured	Subgroup information must be included in the master list
	Cluster sampling	Sample intact groups (such as classrooms) instead of individuals	Reduces time required to gather data	Important individual differences may be lost when using many participants from a single location
	Systematic sampling	Systematically select participants from a master list (such as every 25th name)	Simpler process (if a computer program for random selection is not available)	Inadvertent bias in selection is possible (such as ethnic influence on last names in an alphabetical list)
Higher-risk	Convenience selection	Choose readily available participants (such as university subject pools)	Easiest selection procedure	May not be representative of intended target population because of researchers' location
	Quota selection	Predetermine subgroups and select until the desired number of participants is reached	No master list is required	May not be representative of intended target population because of participants' location
	Purposive selection	Select participants because of known similarities to the target population	Easy selection procedure	Prior knowledge of characteristics of selected group is required; risk of researcher bias in selection

provide the in-depth interview and observational data needed for the study design. Further, participants may be chosen to represent the broadest range of possible responses in order to reach a point of data *saturation*—the point at which the same themes come up several times. A great deal of time is often spent with the participants in qualitative studies, so combining purposive and convenience selection can be a critical factor.

A summary of key characteristics of the lower- and higher-risk sampling options is provided in Table 3.2.

EVALUATION TOOL SIX: WHY WAS THIS SAMPLE SELECTED?

We've come to the last tool in evaluating the sample. You are looking for any evidence that might suggest that the researchers either purposefully or inadvertently selected a sampling procedure that could cause a bias in the answers to the research questions. There are no hard and fast rules to apply. This part of the evaluation is based on your own judgment (which will develop with experience) after reviewing the research questions and reading the material about the sample in the method section.

For example, consider a research question about whether teaching effectiveness in public schools would be improved through greater use of instructional technology. A sample drawn from the members of the International Society for Technology in Education could provide information about whether people with special interests in this field would think that more emphasis on technology in education would be a good thing (although the study would be a bit redundant). But even if a total list of membership in the society was used with random stratification to produce a sample that matched the population of educators on characteristics such as gender, age, and years of service, results would most likely be biased in favor of technology. Because of the sample selected, you would probably not give much credence to the results, nor read beyond the method section even if the introduction section had seemed interesting.

A researcher cannot draw a sample from a group made up only of one segment of a population and then make that segment representative of the whole population by applying randomization, stratified randomization, or any other sophisticated sampling procedure. Valid inferences from such a sample to a general population are just not likely.

Over the years, this procedural error has created problems. Early norm-referenced standardized tests, for example, used data obtained from middle- to upper-middle-class, mostly suburban schools to create norms that were then portrayed as representative of the entire population. Participant groups made up largely of upper-middle-class, Caucasian college students have been used to create diagnostic codes and other entities and then sometimes applied without consideration of their relevance to marginalized, minority, or culturally diverse groups.

Convenience sampling, defended earlier, is certainly a form of sampling from a narrow segment, and it would be unfair to automatically define such samples as biased. In this part of your evaluation task, the burden of proof is on the researchers in preparing the report. If the selected sample even suggests a possible bias in the answers to the research questions, it is the researchers' responsibility to acknowledge the possibility and explain how it was dealt with in the study. We would like to emphasize again that in learning to be an informed and critical consumer of research, it is extremely important that you retain your doubts as well as your curiosity. If you are not satisfied with a question about the adequacy of the participants to answer the research questions, at best you should look skeptically and critically at the results and you may be better served by simply ignoring the study.

 ## SUMMARY AND CLOSING THOUGHTS

It seems prudent here to emphasize that having a suspicious mind does not automatically preclude being willing to "cut a little slack" when evaluating the adequacy of the participants in a research study. Researchers are obligated to provide sufficient information for you to make an informed judgment about whether the data were gathered from a group likely to have provided unbiased answers for the research question. When sampling is used, you are unlikely to be able to judge for sure whether the sample was actually a good representation of that target because you don't know all characteristics of that target. You instead are left only with your own best judgment about the target and the research questions and with a set of tools to use in applying that judgment about whether the sample effectively represents the target group.

The "slack" recommended earlier is in recognition of the fact that real-life samples used in research studies probably don't provide a miniature mirror of the target population. Without funding from large research grants, researchers often have little choice other than the use of convenience samples for their studies. A remarkably large number of studies in professional journals in the social sciences come with samples drawn from subject pools (one could probably make a good argument, in fact, that most of our current knowledge about human behavior is based on studies with laboratory animals and college sophomores).

As emphasized earlier in the chapter, the sampling procedure selected by the researchers at best only increases or decreases the odds that the sample truly represents the target population. Whether the sample actually reflects the population is ultimately the key question, not how it was selected. We encourage you to save your harshest criticism for two situations: those in which the researchers fail to provide you with enough information to make an informed judgment, and those in which the researchers' conclusions go far beyond what is reasonable from the participants in their study.

The tools proposed here for you to use in evaluating the adequacy of the participants began with identification of the target population, the group to whom the results of the study were ultimately to be generalized. You look then for detailed information about the participants themselves, including where and when the data were gathered. If a sampling procedure was used, you look for information about whether samples were selected using lower-risk (simple randomization, stratified randomization, cluster) or higher-risk (convenience, quota, purposive) techniques. Finally, you look carefully for any indications that participants may have been selected who were unlikely to be capable of providing unbiased answers to the research questions.

Before you complete an exercise at the end of the chapter, some caution is warranted about the word *random.* It's probably safe to say that researchers, whenever possible, will try to have that word appear in their research reports. The very word seems to have an aura of science around it.

The words *random, randomized,* and so forth may appear in the method section of a research article in two quite different contexts, only one of which has anything to do with the selection of participants. In reference to the participants, we believe that true random selection will very seldom be evident, and we have cautioned that randomly choosing from a non-random list is not likely to produce a sample that reflects the larger group.

After the participants have been selected, in some study designs the researchers create a condition to make two groups within those participants different from each other by doing something to one group and something else to the other. That may (and usually should) be done on a random basis and will be identified as such in another part of the method section of the report. We'll address that in the next chapter.

AN EXERCISE FOR REVIEW

We believe that the best way to review your grasp of the content in this chapter is to actually practice applying it. The stimulus is an excerpt from a published study regarding factors associated with procrastination among college students. It begins with the paragraph in the article that immediately precedes the methods subheading and continues through the description of the participants. Remember that there is one critical question:

Do the participants identified in the research report appear appropriate and sufficient to address the questions identified by the researchers as the objectives of the study?

Now use the following template to evaluate the adequacy of the participants in this study. Our evaluation using that same template immediately follows the excerpt.

Template for Evaluating the Participants

- ☐ What is the target population? Can you easily identify the ultimate target?
- ☐ Who participated in the study? Were sufficient details provided? Do the participants appear to reflect the target population?
- ☐ Where were the participants? In what setting were the data gathered? Does this appear to be an appropriate setting to represent the ultimate target?
- ☐ When were the data gathered? Can you identify the time period? Is the time at which data were gathered likely to influence generalization of the findings?
- ☐ How was the sample selected? If a sample was used, can you identify the procedure for selecting the sample? Which sampling techniques were evident?
- ☐ Why was this sample selected? Is there reason to suspect accidental or purposeful bias by the researchers in use of this sample?

Selected Content for Evaluation

Excerpt from: Haycock, L. A., McCarthy, P., & Skay, C. L. (1998). Procrastination in college students: The role of self-efficacy and anxiety. *Journal of Counseling & Development, 76*, 317–324. The complete text appears in Appendix C.

Procrastination in College Students: The Role of Self-Efficacy and Anxiety

Laurel A. Haycock, Patricia McCarthy, and Carol L. Skay

. . . The focus of this study concerned the extent to which procrastination can be predicted by variables that are theoretically or empirically tied to the construct. We hypothesized that efficacy expectations would be the strongest predictors of procrastination and that they would be inversely related to procrastination. It was further hypothesized that anxiety would be the next strongest predictor and that it would be positively related to procrastination. No hypotheses were generated concerning either gender or age, given the equivocal nature of the gender findings and the lack of research on age and procrastination.

METHOD

Participants and Procedure

One hundred and forty-one college student volunteers (87 women, 54 men), enrolled at a major midwestern university, participated in this study. Seventy-nine percent ($n = 111$) were enrolled in a learning and study skills course, and 21% ($n = 30$) were in a counseling procedures course for students who were not counseling majors. They ranged in age from 18 to 54 years ($M = 24.50$, $SD = 7.40$). The majority, 86%, identified themselves as White, and 14% identified as persons of color, primarily Black (4%) and Hispanic (4%). The sample included both undergraduates (82%) and adult extension and graduate students (18%). A variety of academic majors were represented.

Participation was solicited by one of the researchers during class time. The study was described as an investigation of factors that might be related to procrastination. The participants completed the questionnaires anonymously during the class. Of the 143 possible participants, 141 completed usable questionnaires. . . .

Example of Evaluation

⊠ What is the target population? Can you easily identify the ultimate target?
The target population, although not specifically identified, would appear to be university students throughout the United States, a target group that seems a reasonable resource to address the research questions.

⊠ Who participated in the study? Were sufficient details provided? Do the participants appear to reflect the target population?
The researchers provide sufficient detail in their descriptions for readers to make informed judgments about the extent to which their findings might apply to the target population.

⊠ Where were the participants? In what setting were the data gathered? Does this appear to be an appropriate setting to represent the ultimate target?
Data were gathered during class time in two courses at a "major midwestern university," which would appear to be an appropriate setting. (The researchers followed standard procedure in not specifically naming the

university. From the author identification in the actual article, however, it would not be hard to make a good prediction about which university was involved.)

☒ When were the data gathered? Can you identify the time period? Is the time at which data were gathered likely to influence generalization of the findings?

The date when the data were gathered is not reported in the study, but the research questions in this study do not appear likely to have been significantly influenced by when the research was conducted.

☒ How was the sample selected? If a sample was used, can you identify the procedure for selecting the sample? Which sampling techniques were evident?

There was no indication of use of the procedures required in the lower-risk techniques and no evidence indicating that the characteristics would meet criteria to be defined as a purposive or quota sample. This is a convenience sample, apparently classes taught by the researchers.

☒ Why was this sample selected? Is there reason to suspect accidental or purposeful bias by the researchers in use of this sample?

There were no apparent indicators of intentional bias in the selection. It is not known, however, whether the topics of self-efficacy and procrastination had been covered in a lecture immediately prior to the administration of the questionnaires.

ANSWERS FOR REFLECTIVE EXERCISES

Reflective Exercise 3.1

Why does the type of sample matter?

You obviously are accessible. The question is whether you are also the target population or instead an accessible group or research sample intended to represent a larger target. With a plan to share the results with other instructors, it would appear that representing others is what the instructor might have in mind. If that is correct, are you like the target population in ways that might affect the results (such as ability, age, and previous experience with this content)? The issue is generalizability—that is, to what extent your results would be comparable to results with your instructor in future terms and/or with other instructors.

Reflective Exercise 3.2

What is the target population?

For the first study, the target populations appear clear from both the researchers' stated objectives and the title of the article. The efficacy beliefs found in the study are to represent those of preservice teachers in the United States and preservice teachers in Taiwan.

The target population for the second study is also clear from both the objectives and the title. The findings are to be generalized to women who have left higher education and are now resuming university studies.

The third study illustrates the fact that there are times when identifying the target population for a study requires you to look further than the stated objectives. From the objectives, you know that the population is students. From the title of the journal, it is reasonable to infer that the students are in some kind of clinical training program. That's about as far as you can go from the information provided. (If you had the entire article, however, you would have been able to quickly identify from the introduction that the clinical field for the target population was speech-language pathology.)

Bonus question: From the objectives included in the excerpts of these three articles, which appears to identify a qualitative research study?

Only the study on women reentering higher education suggests a qualitative focus. Both of the other articles appear to involve comparing the effects of different conditions. Description and discussion were identified as purposes of the reentry study.

Reflective Exercise 3.3: Selecting a Sample

How could researchers use cluster sampling to create strata in a study investigating characteristics of graduate students on your campus?

To keep the example reasonably simple, let's assume that just one stratum will be considered: the department in which classes are taken. A first step, using information available from a registrar's office, would be to find out how many graduate classes were being taught in a given semester by each department in the university and obtain a list of all of those classes, including the number enrolled in each class.

Your next task then would be to select the number of classes to use for participants in the study based on the total number of responses you want to obtain. If, for example, 10% of the total number of graduate classes are taught in the special education department, you would need to choose 10% of the classes in your sample from that department, and so forth. You then would need only to randomly select classes to participate in the study (easy) and obtain permission of the instructor to use the class (not necessarily so easy).

What would be a primary stumbling block for use of cluster techniques in such a study, and how could it be resolved?

There are actually several stumbling blocks. Sampling from intact class groups, for example, leaves open the possibility that one student may be given several opportunities to respond to the same study. You could resolve that one simply by including an instruction to participants to complete the questionnaire only once. A problem not so easy to resolve could come, though, if some departments offer a lot of small-enrollment graduate courses each semester. The department strata could result in an oversupply of participants from that department. Fixing this is also possible by adding another stratification (size of courses), but doing so dramatically complicates your task in selecting the sample. (Evaluating research studies is much easier than doing them.)

4

Could They Answer
the Question?
Evaluating the Procedures
and Instrumentation

CHAPTER OUTLINE

BASIC CONCEPTS

Criterion variable
Dependent variable
Experimental variable
Extraneous variable
Independent variable

Internal consistency
Outcome variable
Reliability
Replicate

Research design
Treatment variable
Triangulation
Validity

When you want to do something, what do you do first? To start, you need to figure out exactly how you are going to do it. You need a plan. Whether you want to cook something or investigate why your students are falling asleep in class, you need to design a set of procedures to complete your task. Before anyone else can decide whether the results you obtained are useful, they need to evaluate whether the route you chose was appropriate. Of course, your creation might taste delicious, or the data you collected on your students might be quite interesting, but it would still be important to know just how you arrived at your conclusions. Maybe it was sheer luck. Or perhaps the result is impressive but it cannot be duplicated by anyone else.

For example, let's suppose you want to make a batch of gazpacho, a delicious chilled soup. You know the basic ingredients, and you know the general directions for preparation (see Figure 4.1). Is that enough?

For the novice cook, the answer is clearly *no*. Figure 4.2 illustrates some of the questions left unanswered in the basic recipe.

In case you may be wondering, the publisher did not accidentally get this chapter mixed up with a book about research in the food services. We simply want to emphasize that investigation requires a plan and that assessment of the outcome requires that complete information is included in that plan. (And even if you haven't yet become excited about research, you'll have to admit that you got something useful from this book. Enjoy the gazpacho!)

In this chapter we continue the exploration of tools to evaluate the method section of published research studies. Our focus moves now to the appropriateness of the procedures and instruments, often referred to as the **research design.** First we will look at how to evaluate the specific procedures; then we will look at the instruments, or how the researchers went about gathering the information. It is important to remember that

FIGURE 4.1
Gazpacho Recipe

Ingredients:

4 cups tomato juice	2 cups diced tomato
1 cup chopped green pepper	1 diced cucumber
1 small chopped onion	2 chopped scallions
juice of 1 lime	2 tbsp. wine vinegar
1 can corn	1 tbsp. basil
1 tbsp. crushed garlic	2 tbsp. olive oil
1 tsp. cumin	1 tsp. honey
¼ cup chopped parsley	pinch of garlic salt
pepper to taste	dash of Tabasco sauce

Directions:

Combine all ingredients.
Chill in refrigerator.

FIGURE 4.2
The Missing
Information in the
Gazpacho Recipe

What kind of tomato juice is used, and does that matter? (It doesn't matter. You can even use V-8 vegetable juice if you want.)

Is it okay to use canned chopped tomato, or does the tomato need to be fresh? (Canned is fine.)

How finely should you chop the green pepper, onion, and cucumber? (Small.)

Should you remove the seeds of the cucumber? (Yes. First, peel the cucumber and slice it in half lengthwise; then scrape the seeds out of each half with the tip of a spoon.)

How much is "a pinch," "a dash," and "to taste"? (Now *that's* a very good question.)

Does it matter in what order you combine the ingredients? (No.)

How long should you chill the soup? (At least two to three hours.)

How long does it take to make this recipe? (About half an hour.)

procedures and instruments work together in your evaluation of whether the research questions could actually be answered in the study. The procedures could be elegant but without adequate techniques to describe the variables, the outcome would be akin to owning a new Mercedes automobile that never left your garage. (It may look good, but it won't get you anywhere.)

Our decision to focus on procedures before instruments in this section is purely arbitrary. In fact, when the report includes a separate subheading for the instruments, the recommended order is in the other direction: instruments first, then procedures. We chose this order recognizing that many studies do not separate the data-gathering tools into a subsection, but instead incorporate them under the overall procedures heading.

Notice that the title of this chapter is not "*Did* they answer the question?" That issue is addressed in the results and discussion chapters that follow. The concern here is whether the researchers used a set of procedures that at least *could* have provided the desired information.

RESEARCH DESIGNS

Many procedures or research designs could legitimately be used to address the research questions identified by the researchers. But there are also boundaries. Some designs simply cannot provide the information needed to answer the questions.

For example, if researchers, want to know whether a certain math skill is typically mastered in schools by third grade, a qualitative study would be a very poor choice. The in-depth nature of qualitative research just doesn't lend itself to questions that have in essence a *yes* or *no* answer. If, on the other hand, the researchers want to provide an in-depth analysis of the influences that create an excellent instructional environment for development of that math skill, a qualitative approach would be the clear method of choice.

The number of different research designs available in both qualitative and quantitative approaches is staggering. That's good news because it means that researchers have a wide range of options for selecting procedures that best fit the questions they have identified. It would create a rather large obstacle, though, if your task in evaluating a research study required you to identify the specific name of the design that was employed and to evaluate whether the researchers exactly followed all steps in that particular research design.

Fortunately, your evaluation of the procedures used by the researchers does not require you to identify by name the specific design used, and in fact that information would not even be particularly helpful in the present task. In the introductory material of the research report, the investigators have identified what they were trying to learn. In this section we only have to inspect how they went about the task and decide whether the procedures and instrumentation they chose were likely to provide information relevant for their objective(s).

ANSWERING THE KEY QUESTION

In the previous chapter, we emphasized that when determining whether the participants used in the study were appropriate, you must take into consideration exactly what kind of research questions were being considered. *Appropriate* is a conditional term that must be defined with a reference—appropriate for what? The *what* is always defined by the purpose of the study, identified as the research questions, objectives, or hypotheses.

This same idea continues with a new key question:

Do the procedures, including tools used to gather information, appear appropriate and sufficient to address the research questions?

Answering this question involves four steps, each using information in the method section of the research report:

1. Are the procedures described in sufficient detail to allow you to make an informed judgment about their appropriateness?
2. Are the procedures relevant for the research questions identified by the researchers?
3. Are the instruments used in the study clearly identified?
4. Do the identified instruments appear appropriate and sufficient to define and describe the variables investigated in the study?

EVALUATING THE PROCEDURES: SUFFICIENT INFORMATION?

Evaluating the procedures in a research report begins with a simple question: Was sufficient detail provided in the report to do the evaluation? If the description does not include sufficient detail, the game is over.

How do you know whether enough information was provided? A useful rule of thumb is simply whether the researchers provided sufficient information for a reader to **replicate** the study. There are technically several types of replication (by now, you are no doubt convinced that there are usually several types of everything involved with research), but the simplest definition will suffice here: Did the researchers provide enough detail so that you could, if you chose to do so, conduct an essentially identical study? If not, you probably shouldn't waste your time reading the study.

Consider, for example, a study in which the research question was about the effect of three leadership styles on staff morale in an elementary school. Participants in the study were identified as all teachers and support staff in all elementary schools in a school district. At the end of the school year, each participant completed a questionnaire purported to tap important factors in morale.

In the procedures section the authors say that they identified administrators who consistently demonstrated "authoritarian," "democratic," or "laissez faire" styles of communication, and provide much detail about differences associated with those styles. But they neglected to include specifically how they determined the style being used by each administrator.

Could you replicate the study without that information? The answer, we think, is clearly *no*. A myriad of possible ways to identify one's leadership style are available, and without knowing which was used it is essentially impossible to make a reasonable interpretation of any comparative results.

How much information is enough information, though? At some point in the evaluation, a value judgment on your part will be required. A research report obviously cannot include every single detail about what was done during the study. The task is to be sure that all information essential for you to conduct an essentially identical study is provided.

We admit that the preceding example is a bit extreme. A report that didn't specify how a critical variable was defined would be very unlikely to be published. A concern more likely to be evident in articles you evaluate will be the omission of some possibly significant element of information with either no explanation, or an insufficient explanation. The preceding hypothetical study, for example, might include a sufficiently detailed explanation about how the leadership styles were determined, but go on to say that results from one school were not included because of incomplete data. While there could be a legitimate reason, more explanation would be helpful about what was incomplete. Otherwise you are left to wonder whether perhaps the information was excluded because it didn't come out the way the researchers had hoped.

EVALUATING THE PROCEDURES: APPROPRIATE FOR THE QUESTION?

In your assessment of whether appropriate procedures were used, the logical first step is to identify whether the approach was primarily qualitative or quantitative. This will not be difficult, of course, because you already will have made this assessment when evaluating the introductory section of the study (Chapter 2).

However, if you're having difficulty making the distinction in an article you are evaluating, the information that follows about procedures in qualitative and quantitative designs may help in clarifying which method was prominent. The keys that we present in the following sections are only tools to quickly differentiate between the two types of studies. The true differences between the qualitative and quantitative research techniques go far beyond which data type is preferred. Remember that you will occasionally encounter an article in which the procedures identify a mixed-methods design that could have a roughly equal balance of quantitative and qualitative procedures.

QUALITATIVE PROCEDURES

Overview of the Approach

We've pointed out the following key determinants:

- Qualitative studies place more emphasis on narrative than numerical data.
- The research questions in qualitative studies are more open-ended than those in quantitative studies.
- Participants in qualitative studies are more likely to be selected using purposive than random techniques.

Qualitative research methodology has been described as a phenomenon with a short history but a long past. It has only been within the last decade or two, for example, that this methodology has moved into the mainstream in educational research, and a variety of procedures could be subsumed under a qualitative heading.

Bogden and Biklen (2003) identified five elements that are especially characteristic of qualitative research procedures:

- Usually conducted in natural settings
- Extensive use of descriptive data
- Emphasis on process more than product
- Often based on inductive logic
- Search for meaning is often evident

We discuss each of these elements in the following paragraphs.

The Setting.   It would be very unusual to find a qualitative study in education conducted in a university lab. Natural settings (such as classrooms and schools) are the overwhelming preference for such studies, based on the belief that separating the phenomena being investigated from the site in which they occur diminishes the quality of the information provided. In effect, there is no substitute for "being there."

The Data.   Although qualitative researchers are more likely to describe a phenomenon with words than numbers, it would be a mistake to assume that they are concerned only with the big picture. In fact, in the spirit of a great detective, every type of data even remotely associated with the phenomenon, whether it can be reduced to a number or not, might be included in the study. A qualitative study, for example, might very well include a table with scores from standardized achievement tests, but would be extremely unlikely to provide such data without additional descriptive information about the context in which those data were gathered.

The Process.   The emphasis in qualitative research is as much on process as it is on outcome. For example, a qualitative researcher might have very little interest in whether a student arrived at the correct answer and a great deal of interest in the steps along the way. This emphasis in qualitative research is not unlike what is often the goal in preparing professional educators—observing not only the content of what takes place on a surface level of communication, but also on the level of the deeper process taking place.

   Consider a study in which qualitative researchers are investigating classroom interactions between teacher and students. A student raises her hand and says, "Teacher, is this going to be on the test?" A content analysis could focus on a surface-level response: "Yes, it is," or "No, it's not." Qualitative researchers, however, are much more likely to be interested in the meaning underlying the questions. Was this student asking a question, or was she perhaps making a statement or expressing a feeling? Instead of a simple *yes* or *no,* a process-oriented response might sound something like this: "You're really worried about the upcoming test and how you're going to do on it." This sort of mentality of looking beneath the surface; decoding underlying meanings of behavior; and examining the deeper, underlying, metaphorical meaning rather than just the literal, concrete behavior is what a process orientation is all about. It works well not only for operating more effectively in our work but in any interactive setting in which we are puzzled by what is going on. Whenever we are stuck in a situation we don't understand, we might apply a process orientation to ask ourselves: What is really going on here? What is this person saying with his behavior? How do the words I'm hearing fit with what I am observing and sensing?

The Specific to the General.   Most, though not all, qualitative research emphasizes inductive reasoning and analysis, going from the specific to the general. The qualitative researcher often uses extensive and detailed analysis in a specific setting to construct a theory explaining what was found. For instance, a theoretical explanation of test anxiety might begin with a series of in-depth interviews with students experiencing this distress.

The Search for Meaning.   The "search for meaning" focus in qualitative research is the deliberate attempt to learn how people try to make sense of their lives. *How it is* may not be nearly as important in a qualitative study as *how the participants think it is*. In simplest terms, qualitative researchers are probably much more likely than their quantitative counterparts to believe that there is no sound if a tree falls in a forest with no one around. More important than the sound itself would be the meaning that would be ascribed to it if it were heard.

Evaluating Procedures in a Qualitative Study

Qualitative studies typically share the preceding elements, but it would be a mistake to assume that all qualitative studies are alike. There are more than a dozen identified subtypes of qualitative design, each of which might or might not be relevant for a particular research question. But to evaluate the appropriateness of the procedures in a research report, assigning the correct label to the research design is not essential, and we purposefully are suggesting a different direction.

Let's start with whether the researchers appear to have made the correct decision in choosing a qualitative approach. Consider the research questions in Reflective Exercise 4.1.

Reflective Exercise 4.1
Research Questions

> 1. Does gender affect the likelihood of a student being recognized when hands are raised in classroom discussion?
> 2. What is the social structure of a classroom that includes mainstreamed students with physical disabilities?
> 3. What categories of discussion emerge from messages in an electronic mailing list?
> 4. Does completion of a symptom inventory prior to each counseling session influence the rating of that session by the client?

Two of these four questions suggest that the researchers should have selected a qualitative approach. Can you identify which two?

The correct answers are Question 2 and Question 3. The nature of Question 2 suggests a need for narrative, rather than numerical, descriptions. Answering the question would appear to require extensive observational detail of a specific setting.

Question 3 also would be best answered with qualitative procedures. To answer the question, the researchers will be seeking broader explanatory categories for the content in specific e-mail messages. Simply counting the number of messages would be insufficient. The researchers would instead be seeking to identify common themes in those messages to propose broad categories for explanation and understanding of the electronic messaging phenomenon.

Evaluating the appropriateness of procedures in a qualitative study does, of course, involve more than just deciding whether a more open-ended research question was evident. But the remainder of the task is just a matter of applying critical-thinking skills.

For example, imagine that you are talking to a friend, and the conversation turns to whether the two of you should buy tickets for a certain movie. That's the research question. How would you go about answering it? Your friend suggests that you simply poll some peers and ask them if you should go. Is that a good idea? It's certainly a place to start, but simply getting *yes* or *no* answers from others wouldn't be sufficient. You probably would want to limit your poll to those who had seen the movie, and limit it further to those whose preferences are similar to yours. You would also be unlikely to be satisfied with a *yes* or *no* answer and would want more specific information about why the preference was expressed. And most likely you would want to check out some reviews of the movie to confirm or dispute the opinions you gathered.

The movie scenario is obviously not rocket science, but neither is the process of assessing the procedures in a qualitative research report. The researchers begin with questions. Your task, always keeping the questions as a focus, is to decide whether the researchers stayed on track while seeking their answers.

As an illustration, at the end of Chapter 2, you evaluated the introductory material for a qualitative study (Henze, 2001) about interethnic relations in a school setting (see Appendix B). At the end of the introductory material, the researcher identified the general research question as the analysis of relationships among ethnic groups at one specific school.

In the method section of this article, the researcher then listed the procedures used for the analysis. Four types of data were gathered. Interviews were conducted with school personnel, students, and parents. Observations were conducted in classes, meetings, assemblies, and other events. A questionnaire was administered to faculty and representatives of the community. Documents and relevant school records were examined. The researcher went on to report the total number of interviews conducted, the number of classes and events observed, and the return rate of questionnaires.

Your task in evaluating the procedures is simply to make your own best judgment about whether you believe these procedures were sufficient to provide the analysis identified as the objective for the study. In this instance, they do appear both appropriate and sufficient.

Remember that in the qualitative approach, research questions and objectives continue to be developed throughout the study. The initial statement at the end of the introduction is often the foreshadowed objective that may become more specific as the study progresses. For this reason, when evaluating the procedures in a qualitative study, you must read the entire article. Additional procedures and/or more specific explanations of how data were gathered can continue throughout the report.

QUANTITATIVE PROCEDURES

Overview of the Approach

The key determinants for quantitative studies are essentially the mirror opposites of those used to identify a qualitative study. As we've discussed:

- Quantitative studies place more emphasis on numerical than on narrative data.
- The research questions in quantitative studies are intentionally narrow and specific.
- Participants in quantitative studies are usually selected with the expectation that their results will be generalized to a larger target population.

Quantitative researchers most often begin with an established theory, predict specific outcomes based on that theory, and then test the accuracy of the predictions. For example, in a counseling session, reinforcement theory would predict a significant increase in the client's positive statements about self if the "rewards" provided by the counselor (such as praise or a smile) are contingent on such statements. A quantitative researcher might begin with the theory and then design a study to determine whether the predicted outcome actually happened.

The various quantitative designs typically involve gathering information for one or more of the following reasons:

- Describing current status
- Identifying relationships
- Comparing outcomes

Current Status.   If the first element, describing current status, seems reminiscent of a qualitative research design, you are not off the mark. The difference is that a quantitative study would have a primary focus on presenting numerical data and a much more limited extent of providing context for those data. For example, the student course evaluation forms you may be asked to complete at the end of a course often are interpreted almost exclusively in reference to the average numerical ratings, not on comments written by students about the course.

Identifying Relationships.   In its simplest form, a study to identify relationships among variables is an extension of the current status procedure. Researchers are interested in knowing whether two or more variables tend to "go together." For example, are higher scores on aptitude tests associated with higher scores on achievement tests? As age increases, does motivation for high grades increase as well? The answers to the relationship questions are usually presented in the form of numerical correlation coefficients (Chapter 5).

Studies to identify relationships can also be conceptualized with a metaphor of prediction. Researchers may want to know whether a relationship exists between variable X (aptitude test scores) and variable Y (achievement test scores), in order to know how well Y can be predicted from X.

Comparing Outcomes.   The prediction metaphor also works when the researchers' question involves some form of outcome comparison. For example, one group of students received instruction with emphasis on classroom lectures. Another group of students covered the same content in a distance-learning environment. All took the same test at the end of the unit, and the average scores of the two groups were compared. In effect, the researchers want to know whether the overall level of performance on the test can be predicted by knowing the type of instruction that was provided.

The specific labels used when comparing outcomes in quantitative research studies are illustrated in the following example. A friend predicts that it will rain sometime during the afternoon. Another friend predicts that your least favorite candidate will win an election. A third friend predicts that your favorite professional sports team will lose a game by more than five points. Other than the fact that you appear to have some rather discouraging friends, what do these examples have in common?

First, each prediction anticipates a particular outcome (weather, election result, game score). The term used to identify the outcome in quantitative research is usually the **dependent variable.** The outcome is assumed to *depend on* some other factors. It's called a *variable* because the outcome varies (more than one outcome is possible).

Next, your friends made their predictions about outcomes using some available information. Perhaps, for example, a newspaper story just reported some particularly scandalous behavior about your candidate that led your friend to make the prediction. That information would be the **independent variable:** a variable (assuming that equal scandal wasn't reported for all candidates) presumed to influence the outcome.

An example of an independent variable in the weather prediction could be your friend's knowledge about a current cloud condition. Likewise, the football game prediction could have been made based on an independent variable associated with an injury to a star player. In each case the outcome, the dependent variable, is assumed to be predictable because of something going on with the independent variable.

Finally, for each of those predictions, factors other than the independent variable could influence the outcome. Because they are not directly considered as a part of the prediction, those factors would be identified as **extraneous variables.** Obviously, this would be the larger group. For example, voter turnout, voter indifference to scandal, and other news reports prior to the election are variables that could have a major influence on the election outcome.

In a study to determine the effect of computer drill on third graders' math achievement, the independent variable would be whether computer drill was provided. The dependent variable would be the math achievement; the researchers are attempting to learn whether math achievement is dependent on the presence or absence of computer drill. Possible extraneous variables, other factors that could affect the level of math achievement, would include the number of students in the class, the skill of the teacher, and familiarity with use of the computer.

Other, more descriptive, terms are now frequently used for dependent and independent variables. These terms, illustrated next, are increasingly evident in published research.

Historical Term	Also Known As
Dependent variable	Criterion variable, outcome variable
Independent variable	Experimental variable, treatment variable

Let's go back to the research questions in Reflective Exercise 4.1. The two questions that suggest that the researchers should have used a quantitative design are the following:

- Does gender affect the likelihood of a student being recognized when hands are raised in classroom discussion?
- Does completion of a symptom inventory prior to each counseling session influence the rating of that session by the client?

With both of these questions, the characteristic being investigated can easily be translated into a numerical value. Whether the design involved identifying relationships or comparing outcomes, prediction is implicit: Can the likelihood of being called on be predicted by whether the student is male or female? Can the magnitude of a postsession rating of counseling effectiveness be predicted by whether a symptom inventory was administered before the session began? The activity in Reflective Exercise 4.2 provides an opportunity to be sure you are clear about the differences among dependent, independent, and extraneous variables.

Reflective Exercise 4.2
Identifying Variables

Either by yourself or as a small-group activity, identify the independent and dependent variables for the gender and rating studies (this shouldn't take very long). Then think about possible extraneous variables that might influence the dependent-variable scores. Be prepared to share your thoughts with the rest of the class.

Evaluating Procedures in a Quantitative Study

Implicit in our description of how to evaluate the appropriateness of procedures in qualitative studies was a message that your task is mostly just applying common sense. That message applies equally when the report you are evaluating is a quantitative study.

The researchers have identified what they wanted to find out. In this section of the report, they tell you how they went about doing it. Your task is just to evaluate whether what they did would be likely to provide the information they were seeking. Don't allow yourself to be overwhelmed by numbers and formulas (we'll be providing assistance with those in the chapter that follows).

Look for how the researchers went about gathering their data. Look especially carefully for the possibility that the researchers did not give sufficient attention to the extraneous variables identified earlier. In their results, the researchers will be telling you what they found. In the procedures, did they appear to recognize and attend to other factors that might have influenced the outcomes they observed?

This concern is relevant even in the simplest form of quantitative study: the description of some current status. As an example, suppose the researchers were investigating teacher morale in a school district. Whom did they ask? (That was in the previous chapter.) How did they ask? (That's coming up in this one.) It's not difficult to identify a number of extraneous variables that could influence how a person responded in a current status study to questions about morale. An obvious one, of course, is who is asking the question.

Extraneous variables are of obvious concern when the quantitative study involves identifying relationships and/or making comparisons. For example, researchers might be interested in the effect of class size on student achievement. The question would be whether the level of student achievement could be predicted from the size of the class. Student achievement is the *dependent variable;* class size is the *independent variable.*

In this example, even if student achievement does appear to be related to class size, obviously many extraneous variables (such as student ability and teacher effectiveness) can also influence the level of achievement. The extraneous variables often require researchers to utilize some form of **control group** for comparison. Control groups are made up of people assumed to be comparable to the group being investigated in regard to everything except the independent variable.

EVALUATING THE INSTRUMENTS

We're now ready to evaluate the content in the method section that deals with how the information was gathered for the study. *Instruments* (also referred to as apparatus, materials, or instrumentation) refers to all of the various types of data collection activities (such as test scores, diaries, and observation) the researchers used in their study. The quality of these techniques sets a limit on the value of the study, and it is not unusual in published research studies to find elegant research procedures and sophisticated data analysis techniques accompanied by highly questionable data-gathering techniques. Unless appropriate techniques were used to gather the data, all of the time invested by the researchers in planning the study, selecting the sample, conducting the study, and analyzing the results is essentially wasted. If the data gathering is flawed, the study is flawed.

Let's begin with a perspective. From the quantitative tradition, "If anything exists, it exists in some amount. If it exists in some amount, it can be measured" (Thorndike, 1914). This often-quoted idea may be more applicable to quantitative procedures, because a precise definition of the term **measurement** is the assigning of numbers to a result. To ensure applicability in both quantitative and qualitative approaches, let's substitute "If anything varies, it varies to some extent. If it varies to some extent, the extent can be described." It's the same idea, and the idea enables investigation of a vast array of topics of interest to both quantitative and qualitative researchers. The focus in quantitative studies is typically on measurement, while in qualitative studies the focus is on description.

Whether the focus is on measuring or on describing, it is assumed that what is being measured or described is not identical in all research study participants. What you will be evaluating is how the measurements or descriptions were obtained. It should come as no surprise that quantitative and qualitative researchers tend to use different types of instruments to identify the differences. When the procedures indicate the use of one of the quantitative designs, the instruments will be those in which the outcome is easily described with numbers—for example, tests and questionnaires. Qualitative design procedures are instead much more likely to identify differences using instruments where the outcome is better described with words than with numbers—for example, classroom observations and documents.

In both quantitative and qualitative studies, it is the obligation of the researchers to provide sufficient information for a reader to evaluate the appropriateness of the tools used to gather the data. As we've said before, if the information is not complete or the techniques used do not seem appropriate, stop reading the study (or at least be suspicious of the results).

Reliability and Validity

Once you have identified the techniques used to collect the data in the study you are reading, you will need to determine whether those techniques appear capable of providing data that are reliable and valid.

The simplest definition of **reliability** involves consistency. If a researcher's observation of classroom interactions finds evidence of hostility between teacher and students, would another researcher observing at the same time have come to the same conclusion? If the dependent variable in a research study is scores on Form X of a reading comprehension test, would the results have been comparable if Form Y of that test had been used instead?

In either of these examples, the question is not whether the results would have been identical. Most likely, they would not. The question with those examples is how much difference might be evident with a different observer, or a different form of the test, or perhaps if the observational or test data had been gathered at a different time.

The concept of **validity,** sometimes interpreted as truthfulness, is better defined as relevance. An observation or a test, for example, could very well be valid for one purpose while not providing relevant information for another. Norm-referenced achievement tests are one example. Such tests can provide valuable information about how well a student is performing in comparison to a peer group, while providing essentially no useful information about exactly what a student has or has not mastered. Observations of a teacher's performance in a classroom during a planned visit by a supervisor may provide quite relevant information about that teacher's maximum level of performance, while providing little or no usable information about the teacher's typical performance.

In the strictest sense, evaluating reliability and validity involves some very complex issues. Most notably, to a degree each is situation-specific. The data used to estimate reliability come from a particular group of participants and may or may not apply when used elsewhere. Information about validity always requires a qualifier—valid for what use? These nuances and the various ways in which they are estimated are important, especially when developing instruments, but are not so crucial in the current task. You will only need to review the information provided by the researchers about the instruments they used and make your best informed judgment about whether the techniques used in the study appear to be up to the task for which they were employed.

Qualitative Instruments

Reliability and validity of the tools is easier to quantify in quantitative studies, but the quality of the instruments is equally important in qualitative studies (wordplay is intentional). A major influence on reliability in all types of data is the amount of information gathered. Conducting one 30-minute interview with a participant in a study is likely to result in less reliable data than would be available if there were three 60-minute interviews.

In like manner, increasing the number of participants can also provide more reliability in the data. Would you give more credence to a study in which the researcher interviewed 11 children in one school about their experiences being bullied, or double that number from a wider variety of schools, ages, and settings?

Much of qualitative research rests on observational data. Of particular interest in regard to validity are factors associated with the impact of **observer bias** and an **observer effect.** The former reflects our tendency to see what we expect to see; the latter is the extent to which being observed changes the nature of what is observed.

Qualitative researchers have often been leaders in recognizing the need to corroborate their findings with other data sources and/or through having colleagues independently consider the same data. This process is called **triangulation** (even when there are only two data sources).

What you look for when evaluating the quality of the data in a qualitative study is twofold: Did the researchers recognize that there could be some limitations in the data being used for their conclusions? What, if any, steps, did the researchers take to minimize the impact of the limitations? Reflective Exercise 4.3 is suggested to further explore issues of reliability and validity of the data in qualitative research studies.

Reflective Exercise 4.3 Reliability and Validity of Qualitative Instrumentation	A qualitative study of interactions between school administrators and teachers includes an analysis to identify themes in memos written by the principal to the teachers during one school year. Either by yourself or in a small-group setting, think about how the researchers might provide information about the reliability and validity of the information obtained from analysis of the memos. Be prepared to share your thoughts with the class. *(Our answers are at the end of the chapter.)*

Quantitative Instruments

When new measurement instruments—for example, a new test—have been developed for use in a quantitative study, researchers are expected to provide not only information about the reliability and validity of the instruments, but also some detail about how those data were gathered. If instead they used existing instruments, you are more likely to find citations to support their reliability and validity.

In either case, you can anticipate finding (1) an identification of which of the several types of reliability and validity is being reported, (2) some numerical data, and (3) a verbal appraisal of reliability and validity of the instruments as they were used in the study. For your use in evaluating, it may be helpful to remember that reliability estimates come in just two basic categories. Reliability associated with consistency over time is provided in the form of test-retest information. Reliability related to what might have happened with a different form of the test is provided with labels such as *split-half, Kuder–Richardson,* and *alpha coefficients* and is often identified as **internal consistency.** Reliability associated with both time and different questions is provided in the form of *alternate-* or *equivalent-forms* information. Validity information that comes from asking a group of experts to assess the test is identified as **content validity.** Validity information that comes from data-based studies is typically identified as **criterion, construct,** or **empirical validity.**

Your task does not require particular attention to the numerical values or to the subtle differences among the various types of reliability and validity. Instead you will want to be sure that the researchers provided information about the instruments used. It is especially helpful if the information provided appears to have been gathered in a situation comparable to how the instruments are being used in the study you are evaluating.

For example, reliability and validity data that were obtained in a study of undergraduate college students may or may not be applicable in a study involving participants from the general adult population. If researchers are using Test X with an assumption that it is effective as a predictor of academic performance, providing content validity evidence alone would not be sufficient. They should provide examples of previous studies in which this test was effective in predicting future performance. If, in their use of Test X, the researchers presume that it provides consistent measurement over time, the reliability information provided should be in the form of test-retest or equivalent-form data and not just in the form of split-half, Kuder–Richardson, or alpha reliability techniques.

Notice that the researchers' planned use of the instrument is the critical factor. All of the quantitative tools for assessing reliability and validity are legitimate, but not all provide appropriate information for use in a given study.

To illustrate, at the end of Chapter 2 you evaluated the introductory material for a study (Sapp, 2001) comparing different approaches for teaching ethics in a graduate school program (see Appendix A). Measurement of the dependent variable—scores on an ethics test—was provided by a questionnaire constructed by the author of the study.

In the article, the researcher provides specific details about the questionnaire: It used vignettes and 34 multiple-choice items based on ethical principles of the American Psychological Association and the American Counseling Association. Each item had a correct answer and four distracters. The report included the following:

> Since this was a criterion-referenced questionnaire, a validity coefficient was not calculated; however, a split-halves reliability coefficient comparing even-numbered and odd-numbered item responses produced a reliability coefficient of .88. The high split-halves reliability coefficient shows that the criterion-referenced questionnaire consistently measured the characteristic it was constructed to measure.

Because a new instrument was created for use in the study, the researcher had an obligation to provide sufficient information about the instrument for readers to judge its appropriateness. The information about how items were prepared would be in the category of content validity. Information about reliability was provided by first identifying the type of information (split-half), then the numerical description, and then the researcher's appraisal of the adequacy of the instrument for the task.

In the article itself, the researcher also reports some data-based information about characteristics of the individual items. We might quarrel with the author's statement that validity coefficients could not be obtained with criterion-referenced instruments. Also missing in the description was from whom the data were obtained to calculate the reliability coefficient, and the appraisal of reliability may be a bit strong since no data were provided regarding consistency over time. But overall, this author has provided a great deal of information for readers to use in evaluating the adequacy of the instrument, and, going back to the author's objective provided at the end of the introduction to the study, the instrument does appear adequate to address the research question.

 ## SUMMARY AND CLOSING THOUGHTS

Sometimes stated directly, and always intended to be implicit in this chapter, is our belief that the best way for you to approach evaluation of the procedures and instrumentation is through simple logic and common sense. The authors have identified the objective(s) for their study. Have they made clear how they went about conducting it? Do the procedures and tools for gathering data appear to be sufficient and appropriate for what they wanted to accomplish?

This is really not a difficult process, and we think that the greatest risk you face in making this evaluation is the possibility of getting sidetracked by the jargon. All you need to do here is make your best judgment about whether the researchers used procedures and instruments for gathering information that would appear to have a reasonable chance of providing relevant information related to what they were trying to find out by doing the study.

In making your decision, you have already determined whether the people they studied are likely to be able to provide the desired information. Now the question is, what did they do with those people? If the questions simply involved learning about some setting, what questions were asked and how were they asked? If the researchers were attempting to draw some causative inference through comparing what happens when different things are done to the participants, did the researchers consider what else might have caused the outcome other than the factors being manipulated?

Our goal with this chapter has been to encourage you to make more use of information from research studies in your own professional practices by helping you learn to make informed judgments about which of those studies warrant your attention.

Specific features about the variety of available research designs will be needed when you learn to design your own studies. But for now, focus as we did on the simple questions. Did the researchers tell you what they did? Does it appear to be enough?

AN EXERCISE FOR REVIEW

In the last chapter you evaluated the participant sample in a study about procrastination and college students. To review the content in this chapter, let's continue with the same study, this time with focus on the procedures and the instruments. The critical question now is as follows:

Does the research design, including the instrumentation, appear appropriate and sufficient to address the questions identified by the researchers as the objectives of the study?

Use the following template to evaluate the procedures and the instrumentation. Our evaluation using that same template immediately follows the excerpt.

Template for Evaluating Procedures and Instrumentation

- ☐ Did the researchers provide sufficient information about the procedures so that this study could be replicated with a different participant sample?
- ☐ Are the procedures relevant for the research questions identified by the researchers?
- ☐ Are the instruments used in the study clearly identified?
- ☐ Do the identified instruments appear appropriate and sufficient to define and describe the variables investigated in the study?

Selected Content for Evaluation

Excerpt from: Haycock, L. A., McCarthy, P., & Skay, C. L. (1998). Procrastination in college students: The role of self-efficacy and anxiety. *Journal of Counseling & Development, 76,* 317–324. The complete text appears in Appendix C.

Procrastination in College Students: The Role of Self-Efficacy and Anxiety

Laurel A. Haycock, Patricia McCarthy, and Carol L. Skay

. . . The focus of this study concerned the extent to which procrastination can be predicted by variables that are theoretically or empirically tied to the construct. We hypothesized that efficacy expectations would be the strongest predictors of procrastination and that they would be inversely related to procrastination. It was further hypothesized that anxiety would be the next strongest predictor and that it would be positively related to procrastination. No hypotheses were generated concerning either gender or age, given the equivocal nature of the gender findings and the lack of research on age and procrastination.

METHOD

Participants and Procedure

One hundred and forty-one college student volunteers (87 women, 54 men), enrolled at a major midwestern university, participated in this study. Seventy-nine percent (*n* = 111) were enrolled in a learning and study skills course, and 21% (*n* = 30) were in a counseling procedures course for students who were not counseling majors. . . .

Participation was solicited by one of the researchers during class time. The study was described as an investigation of factors that might be related to procrastination. The participants completed the questionnaires anonymously during the class. Of the 143 possible participants, 141 completed usable questionnaires.

Variables

Self-Efficacy.   The Self-Efficacy Inventory (SEI) was created as part of this study to assess behaviors related to the task of "doing an important and difficult project by a specific deadline." Participants were asked to imagine themselves doing a project such as finding a job, writing a paper, or making a big decision, and to respond to the SEI within the context of their imagined project. This approach was used to increase the likelihood that each participant would select a task that was personally meaningful, salient, and challenging. Participants also were asked to list their project.

The SEI items were developed to assess efficacy *level* and *strength* for distinct behaviors generally related to accomplishing tasks. Level is measured by asking respondents to indicate by answering "yes" or "no" whether they think they can do a series of behaviors that vary in difficulty. Strength is measured by asking respondents to indicate their degree of confidence that they can do each behavior (0 = *great uncertainty* to 100 = *complete certainty*). Although Bandura (1986) recommended arranging items in a hierarchy of difficulty, we used a random format as suggested for complex behavior domains such as career self-efficacy (Lent & Hackett, 1987).

A panel of four psychologists with knowledge and expertise in the areas of procrastination and self-efficacy independently rated 45 items, first for their importance to the behavioral domain and next for their difficulty level for a "typical" person. Forty-three items were rated by all four judges as important to the domain; 31 of these had unanimous agreement for difficulty level. These 31 items constituted the final form of the SEI, with 10 items of high difficulty (e.g., "Can you identify target dates for the realistic completion of your work?"), 17 of medium difficulty (e.g., "Can you establish specific goals for your work?"), and four of low difficulty (e.g., "Can you take time-outs as a break from your work?"). The final form was piloted on 12 mental health professionals, and no substantive changes were made as a result of this pilot testing.

Responses to the SEI were scored in three ways. In accordance with Bandura's (1977) guidelines, efficacy level was determined by summing the number of "yes" responses across the 31 items for each participant. Scores can range from 0 to 31, with higher scores indicating higher efficacy expectations. Efficacy strength was scored in two ways. First, based on Bandura et al.'s (1977) procedures, an average score was obtained for each participant by dividing the total strength score by the number of "yes" responses, with a possible range of 0 to 100. In addition, a cumulative strength score was obtained for each participant by summing the confidence ratings for all items with a "yes" response. Cumulative strength scores can range from 0 to 3100, with higher scores indicating stronger efficacy. This latter method was used because we questioned how average strength scores are affected by different efficacy levels. For example, an individual responding "yes" to a small number of items with high confidence would have an artificially high indicator of efficacy if average strength was calculated. A cumulative strength score takes into consideration both the number of "yes" responses and the confidence ratings and may contain more information regarding efficacy beliefs. Cronbach's alpha coefficients, calculated for efficacy level, average efficacy strength, and cumulative efficacy strength, were .81, .60, and .91, respectively, indicating adequate-to-high internal consistency reliability.

Procrastination.   A modified version of Form G of the Procrastination Inventory (PI; Lay, 1986) was used to measure procrastination. The original form of this self-report inventory contains 20 forced-choice items concerning general, everyday behaviors (e.g., paying bills, returning phone calls promptly, putting things off "until tomorrow"). It was modified to include three items from Form A of the PI pertaining to academic tasks, for a total of 23 items. Items were added to increase the breadth of behaviors measured. Responses reflecting procrastination were scored as 2, and those not reflecting procrastination were scored as 1. Scores are summed across items and can range from 23 to 46, with higher scores indicating greater procrastination. In contrast to Lay's (1988) use of a median split procedure to categorize participants into groups of high and low procrastinators, participant scores were treated as continuous variables.

Internal consistency reliability coefficients ranging from .81 to .89 have been reported in three studies (Lay, 1988; Lay & Burns, 1991; Lay, Edwards, Parker, & Endler, 1989). Test–retest reliability for a 9-month interval was .80 (Ferrari, 1989). There is adequate evidence of construct validity for the PI; for example, it has been positively correlated with the Procrastination Assessment Scale, a measure of academic procrastination (Solomon & Rothblum, 1984), and has low correlations with a social desirability scale (Lay, 1986). Cronbach's alpha coefficient for the modified form of the Procrastination Inventory was .84 for the current sample, indicating good internal consistency reliability.

Anxiety.   The Spielberger State-Trait Anxiety Inventory (STAI) (Spielberger, Gorsuch, & Lushene, 1968) was used to measure participant anxiety. The STAI is an anxiety inventory commonly used in procrastination research. It consists of two 20-item scales, the Trait scale and the State scale. The Trait scale is a measure of relatively stable individual differences in anxiety-proneness or a tendency to perceive situations as threatening or dangerous. The State scale measures more transitory anxiety in response to specific stimuli. For this study, participants were instructed to complete the State scale by imagining themselves doing the same important project identified for completion of the SEI. For each STAI item, respondents rate themselves on a 4-point Likert scale (1 = *not at all*, 4 = *very much*).

Scores for each scale can range from 20 to 80, with higher scores suggesting greater anxiety. The STAI is a widely researched inventory with substantial evidence of its reliability and validity (Spielberger et al., 1968). For example, test–retest reliability for the Trait scale ranges from .73 to .86 (Rothblum et al., 1986), but it is low, as expected, for the State scale, which measures transient anxiety (range = .16 to .54) (Spielberger et al., 1968).

Demographics.   A demographic questionnaire was developed to obtain descriptive information about participants. It consisted of nine questions concerning age, sex, ethnicity, relationship status, student status, educational level, income, and employment status.

Example of Evaluation

⊠ Did the researchers provide sufficient information about the procedures so that this study could be replicated with a different participant sample?
The answer is yes. All you would need to conduct this study yourself would be the instruments used in it and a convenient sample.

⊠ Are the procedures relevant for the research questions identified by the researchers?
This answer is clearly yes. The research questions identify an objective to investigate variables that could predict procrastination. The procedures appear completely consistent with this objective. Identifying that this study was quantitative was easy. The research questions emphasized prediction, so more than just quantitative description was involved, and no mention was made in the procedures of dividing the participants into subgroups during the study, so a focus on comparing could also be eliminated. This leaves, of the quantitative categories presented in this chapter, a study to identify relationships among variables, consistent with the reported procedures.

⊠ Are the instruments used in the study clearly identified?
This answer is also yes. An instrument was created to measure self-efficacy. Existing instruments were used to measure anxiety and procrastination. The authors were particularly diligent in providing detailed information about reliability and validity for the instruments. For the existing instruments, the authors not only cited available references but also summarized the findings. Providing reliability and validity data for a demographic questionnaire as used in this study is not necessary.

⊠ Do the identified instruments appear appropriate and sufficient to define and describe the variables investigated in the study?
This answer is another yes. You may or may not agree with the way self-efficacy was defined for the instrument in this study, but the authors clearly identified the rationale for the operational definition they used and data supporting the new and existing instruments.

ANSWER FOR REFLECTIVE EXERCISE

Reflective Exercise 4.3

How can researchers provide information about the Reliability and Validity of Qualitative Instrumentation?

Themes identified through analysis of memos sent by the principal to the teachers are being used as data in this hypothetical study. Probably the best way for the researchers to report the reliability of those data is by having the memos independently analyzed, using the same criteria, by more than one person. This, logically enough, is called inter-rater reliability and can also be used with other forms of qualitative data—for example, reports of observations either in person or on videotape. Remember that in this context, validity is defined as relevance, *not as* truthfulness. *So the issue is not whether the information in the memos is true. Validity information could be evident in the researchers' connection of the themes to the objectives of the study. Validity information (such as triangulation) could be in the form of reported consistency between themes from the memos and themes identified by analysis of interactions in faculty meetings. Although reliability and validity are not identical concepts, there is an underlying common focus: the extent to which these data can be generalized as descriptive of anything else.*

5

What Was the (Simple) Answer, Please?
Evaluating the Results Section

CHAPTER OUTLINE

BASIC CONCEPTS

Alpha level
Analysis of covariance
Analysis of variance
Chi-square
Confidence interval
Descriptive statistics
Effect size
Inferential statistics
Mean
Measures of central tendency

Measures of relationship
Measures of variability
Median
Mode
Nonparametric
Parametric
Probability value
Product-moment correlation
    coefficient

Quartile deviation
Range
Spearman rank correlation
    coefficient
Regression analysis
Standard deviation
Standard error of estimate
Statistical significance
t test

In the preceding sections of the report, the researchers told you what they chose to study, why they felt the study should be done, and how they went about doing it. As indicated in Figure 5.1, we're ready now to evaluate the results, the actual data in the study. This section of the research report has a single purpose—to tell you what was found.

The results section includes a summary of what was discovered, measured, manipulated, or treated. In the best possible circumstances, the results of this study may persuade you to change the ways you think about professional practice, leading you to modify the ways in which you operate in the future. The results of the study are what made it worth doing and worth reading.

For qualitative research studies the process of deciphering the results will be somewhat familiar, since the data are mostly presented as verbal narratives. You may not agree with the conclusions drawn by the qualitative researchers, but you most often will be able to understand the results as they are presented.

The situation with quantitative studies is quite different. In fact, many readers find themselves lost and confused in the results section of quantitative studies and either skip over it and move on to the conclusions or just give up on the article altogether. As you are probably already well aware, there are "math phobic" individuals who shut down their brains whenever they are called on to make sense of quantitative data beyond their checkbooks.

Because of the special challenges in deciphering the results of quantitative studies, most of this chapter is focused on interpreting the results of these kinds of research reports. We're confident that you will often be able to evaluate qualitative study results without as much assistance from us. Example 5.1 illustrates a typical difference in the presentation of qualitative and quantitative results. As you can see, the information provided in a qualitative study is typically much longer than in a quantitative study.

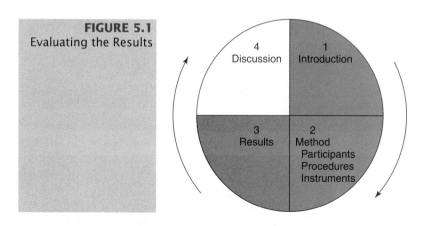

FIGURE 5.1
Evaluating the Results

Example 5.1
Contrast between Qualitative and Quantitative Results

Hypothetical Qualitative Results from a Study on Teacher Burnout

In an interview, Ms. J. clearly voices the feelings associated with being burned out from classroom teaching when she says: "I'm just tired of the kids, tired of the parents blaming me for their mistakes and failings. I'm sick of the administration and their crazy expectations without giving us the resources we need to do our jobs. I guess I've had just about enough. But after 16 years in the classroom, maybe what I'm really saying is that I need some sort of change. I just can't keep doing the same things the same way."

[She pauses and stares out window for one minute, then resumes.]

"I'm just not ready to give up. I don't want to blame the kids or their parents or the school board, or I'm acting just like they are. Kids always have an excuse for why they don't have their homework done. And I'm doing the same thing. I guess what I'm saying is that I've got to find that passion again that I once had when I started out in the field. Somewhere along the path I've lost my way."

Hypothetical Quantitative Results from a Study on Teacher Burnout

Mean scores on the *Teacher Burnout Questionnaire* for the first year teacher group, 10 year teacher group, and 10+ year group were 26.3, 27.4, and 38.5, respectively. Differences among the scores were statistically significant, $F(2,167) = 8.55$, $p < .01$. The difference between the first year and 10 year groups was not statistically significant ($p > .05$). A statistically significant difference, however, was evident in the burnout symptoms reported by the teachers who had been employed more than 10 years in comparison to both the first year group ($p < .01$) and the 10 year group ($p > .05$).

WHAT TO LOOK FOR IN THE RESULTS SECTION

To evaluate the content in this section of the research report, we begin with what by now is a familiar theme: The presentation of results should address the research questions identified for the study. Remember, though, that in qualitative studies, these include not only the questions identified at the beginning of the report, but also the questions that emerged as the study progressed.

The content in the results section should be focused directly on the evidence related to the research question(s), and you should consider two primary factors in evaluating this content in both qualitative and quantitative research reports:

1. Are the findings presented clearly?
2. Is sufficient detail evident in the findings?

Qualitative Features

Consistent with the philosophy of qualitative research, the reports are not necessarily organized in a neat and tidy fashion. Because of this, analysis and interpretation of the data often occur together and are not necessarily labeled as a "Results" section in the report. However, you won't have difficulty identifying when the researchers are presenting their findings.

The findings in a qualitative study should be focused on the research questions and typically provide rich detail about what the researchers found, often including direct quotes from people who were interviewed. Rather than summarizing what was learned with a statement like, "Many participants were apparently angry," detail is expected. What was said or done? Who said or did it? What was the context?

For instance, in the results section of a qualitative study of school climate, a direct quote like this one might be included: "I am just so tired of all the crap we have to deal with around here. They tell us one thing, then before we can put it into action, they change their minds and tell us to do the opposite. Sometimes I feel like just telling these decision makers that they should see what it's like to spend just a single day in my shoes. It just makes me crazy."

A tendency sometimes evident in qualitative reports is for the researchers to be verbose. Good qualitative research reports share characteristics with good novels. They provide sufficient detail so that the reader can feel a part of the experience. But as in cheap novels, the detail can become excessive. For example, in setting up the direct quote in the school climate study in the preceding paragraph, the researchers might say that interviews were conducted with selected teachers in the teachers' lounge at the end of a school day. However, we wouldn't need to know that the room was at the south end of the main building with windows facing east, a clock on the west wall, and a bulletin board made of cork. The challenge for the qualitative researcher, given the vast array of data that may have been gathered, is to present it in a manner that captures the essential themes and provides rich detail while not overwhelming the reader with inconsequential information.

Because detail, including direct quotes, is encouraged, it is tempting for the qualitative researcher to just report all of the data, leaving it to the reader to make the interpretation. This is clerical data gathering, not good qualitative research. In Example 5.2, you can see a poor illustration and a better illustration of analysis and interpretation in a qualitative study of coercion in a university department.

Example 5.2
Poor and Better Analysis and Interpretation in a Hypothetical Study of Coercion in a University Department

Poor Example

Interview responses from professors in the department showed that less than half of the faculty members in the department had any problems with feeling coerced.

Professor A: "I dislike everything about this department. The environment is toxic. I have no control over my work."

Professor B: "I have no control over my research or my teaching assignments. They just tell me what to do."

Professor C: "My work is supported by the administration, and I get to choose the assignments best suited for my expertise."

Professor D: "This is the most satisfying work environment that I have ever experienced. No one pressures me to take assignments that I don't want to do."

Professor E: "This isn't a perfect place, but I think the administrators are just trying to do their jobs."

Better Example

In interviews with faculty members, a pattern emerged suggesting that senior faculty members felt powerless while junior faculty were not especially concerned about administrative coercion.

Illustrative responses from interviews with senior faculty members included the following: "I have no control over my work," and "I have no control over my research or my teaching assignments."

The theme in interviews with junior faculty members was quite different, with responses such as these: "I get to choose the assignments best suited for my expertise," "No one pressures me to take assignments that I don't want to do," and "I think the administrators are just trying to do their jobs."

The primary difference in the two illustrations in Example 5.2 was that the better example included some attempt at interpretation of the interview data rather than just a simple division into satisfied and nonsatisfied categories. Notice also that in the better illustration, quotes were selected that directly focused on the question of coercion. The general dissatisfaction reported by Professor A in Example 5.2 might be relevant for other interpretation in the report, but did not directly involve the research question about coercion.

While evaluating the results, you are looking for balance. On one hand, you want enough information to be able to assess the adequacy of the findings; on the other hand, you don't want to be overwhelmed by extraneous information. A single qualitative research study may include data in the form of notes written by the researcher while observing, spoken words, written transcripts, documents, records, videos, photographs, and drawings. The core task of the qualitative researcher is to provide a written interpretation of those data in a manner that enables the reader to see how the data relate to the questions that emerged during the study.

The evaluation is usually quite a straightforward process. The researchers have identified what they found. They either did or did not provide enough detail for you to assess the adequacy of their analysis and interpretation and either did or did not provide the information in a clear and understandable format.

Quantitative Features

With the exception of looking for specific quotes and detailed examples, the general criteria for evaluating quantitative studies are essentially the same as those used when the report described a qualitative study. However, one additional question is essentially always a major element in quantitative studies: Were the results the researchers found likely to have occurred by chance alone? It's a simple and important question, because quantitative researchers usually want to extend their findings beyond the sample of participants used in the study. For example, the participants in a study of counseling strategies reported much more rapid progress when sessions were scheduled twice a week rather than weekly. Would that same outcome be evident with a different sample of participants, or was the difference just a chance outcome with these participants?

The results section in a quantitative study should focus on the research questions, and the findings should be clearly presented in sufficient detail to understand their context. Although quantitative researchers are not as prone to verbosity when presenting their findings, the information they provide is frequently presented in what appears to be a cryptic code.

The following is an excerpt from the results section of a study (Sapp, 1995) we've used in previous chapters (see Appendix A). The study compared different methods for teaching ethics to students in a counseling program.

> The ANOVA results were $F(3,53) = 26.26$, $p < .001$, indicating that the groups differ on the posttest or dependent variable. . . . The results of Analysis of Covariance (ANCOVA) support those of ANOVA. These results were $F(3,52) = 27.17$, $p < .01$ . . .

What they found is, of course, completely clear to all of you. (Just kidding!)

A great deal of information is provided in those three sentences. However, without a grasp of statistical concepts and/or terminology, the information in that excerpt is a mystery. The researcher may have identified something important to consider by anyone responsible for teaching ethics courses to graduate students. But unless you understand the language in which the results were presented, what was found remains unknown. If you were evaluating this study, would you have skipped over the results section or just given up on the whole thing?

Either of those alternatives, while certainly understandable, brings some risk. Skipping the material in the results section has the effect of giving the researchers free rein to draw conclusions and suggest implications of their findings. Researchers have invested a lot of time in doing the study, analyzing the results, and preparing the report; a tendency to perhaps overstate their findings would not be surprising. Your control for this tendency is to be able to read the results yourself and form your own conclusions before you read what the authors have to say about their findings. Just giving up on the article isn't necessarily a good answer either. Important information might be hidden in the article that could make a difference to you and those you work with.

Understanding some basic statistical concepts and terminology is a prerequisite for evaluating the results presented in essentially all quantitative research studies. Even if you might characterize yourself as "math phobic" or "not good with numbers," you will find that with a little effort and patience you may be able to forever banish these self-labels, at least in regard to basic statistics.

We do have a disclaimer. If you were not a statistician when you began this chapter, you will not be one when it is done. The content in this chapter will not teach you how to "do statistics." There are no formulas; there are no hand calculations of even basic statistics. Although these tasks are no less important, we have a much more limited agenda: simply to enable you to interpret the results of quantitative studies. The goal is to know what it means, even if you remain uncertain about exactly how they did it.

 ## BREAKING THE CODE

The numbers used to present results of a study come in two distinct "flavors." The **descriptive statistics,** as the name suggests, simply describe an outcome with numbers that summarize the results. There is no risk involved. It's like reporting the score of a sports event after the game is over. The others, **inferential statistics,** do include some risk. Their purpose is to make a judgment using a known outcome to predict one that is not known for sure. Using inferential statistics is like making a wager on the outcome of a ball game before the game begins.

Descriptive Statistics

Both qualitative and quantitative studies may use descriptive statistics in the results section of a report, and there are three primary categories of descriptive statistics. They are used to report typical performance (What was the average?), typical differences in performance (How close were most scores to the average?), and relationships (How did any of the variables seem to fit together?)

Measures of Central Tendency.   Three techniques are commonly used to describe central tendency: mean, median, and mode. Each is intended to provide a single numeral to identify what is typical among a group of numbers. The descriptive statistic you will see most often is the one you are probably already familiar with, the **mean,** typically labeled with an M. The mean is the average performance of some group on some measure and usually presents no problem in interpretation. When you see that label you know that the researchers just added some scores and divided the sum by the number of scores included. If several groups were used in a study and identified as Groups X, Y, and Z, their respective mean scores are usually labeled by just adding a subscript: M_X, M_Y, M_Z.

For example, a table in the study on teaching ethics to counseling students (Sapp, 1995) reported that the average posttest scores for the four groups in the study were 30.00, 27.93, 27.00, and 27.00 (see Appendix A). From that information alone, it is evident that overall the outcomes among the four groups were quite similar, with a remarkable difference evident in just one.

The other two measures of central tendency, the median and the mode, are less often reported in research studies. The **median** is the score in the middle after scores have been placed in rank order, and the **mode** is the score that occurs most often.

Researchers may, and probably should, report the median score when they have results in which the mean score is actually not descriptive of the actual results. For example, if there is an extremely high or an extremely low score, the mean will be pulled in the direction of the extreme score and may not provide an accurate description of the central tendency. Even without doing any calculation, it is evident that the mean of the scores 1000, 7, 6, 5, 4, 4, and 3 would not provide a good descriptor for those seven scores. The median (5) or even the mode (4) would be more descriptive of the typical performance represented by the scores. You can use Reflective Exercise 5.1 to check your understanding of central tendency.

That wasn't difficult. For the data in Exercise 5.1, the median and the mode were both 65. Without calculating, it is apparent that either would be more descriptive of these data than the mean, which is pulled in the direction of the high score. (The mean is $360/5 = 72$, but we promised that no calculations would be required.)

The following are the scores of five students on a midterm examination. What was the median and what was the mode for these scores? Would the mean, median, or mode be most descriptive of the performance of the class?

95
70
65
65
65

Measures of Variability.   Another descriptive statistic likely to be reported in the results of quantitative studies is the **standard deviation,** labeled as *SD,* which is used to describe how different the scores in the group were from one another. The standard deviation and some related descriptive statistics, including the **range** and the **quartile deviation,** are defined as *measures of variability.* The intent is to use a single numeral to identify the typical extent of differences within a set of scores.

The standard deviation is closely allied with the mean and is defined as the numeral that represents the average difference between each score and the mean. To illustrate the basic idea underlying the standard deviation, try to imagine a short column of numbers for which you calculate the mean score. Then, still in your imagination, create another column in which you subtract the mean from each number in the first column. You can refer to Table 5.1 if you need to, but just imagining them is much more fun and may help you resist the temptation to start calculating.

If the numbers you imagined for the first column were all very close together, the numbers in the second column would be rather small. Most numbers in the first column would be close to the mean. The standard deviation represents the average of your second column, the average distance between each score and the mean.

Table 5.1
Illustrating the Standard Deviation

Score	Difference between Score and Mean of Scores
9	+3
8	+2
8	+2
6	0
6	0
5	−1
5	−1
5	−1
4	−2
4	−2
($M = 60/10 = 6$)	($SD = 1.76$)

Actually calculating a standard deviation is a bit more complex because of a feature that requires us to keep saying *represents* the average instead of *is* the average. Technically, if you were to actually calculate the mean of your first column and subtract it from each score to get the numbers in the second column, you would have a serious problem if you then set out to calculate the mean of the numbers in column 2. When you added the scores in column 2, you would always get zero for an answer, as is evident in Table 5.1.

The differences in column 2 (differences between scores and mean of scores) will always add to zero, regardless of the scores in column 1. To avoid this, the actual calculation of the standard deviation involves first squaring the differences, adding the squared differences, dividing that sum by the number of scores, and then calculating the square root. However, this matters only if you are hand-calculating standard deviations (which we hope you never have to do). Just remember that the standard deviation is a descriptive statistic that represents the average difference and tells you how close the scores were to each other. Check your understanding of this concept with Reflective Exercise 5.2.

Reflective Exercise 5.2
Statistics to Describe a
Predicted Outcome

On a 40-item test, the instructor believes that almost all of the students will do well. If the instructor is correct, which outcome would be more likely?

a. $M = 35$, $SD = 2$
b. $M = 35$, $SD = 5$
c. $M = 25$, $SD = 2$
d. $M = 25$, $SD = 5$

(Answer is at the end of the chapter.)

Continuing with the measures of variability, the *range,* as you might guess, is simply the difference between the highest score and the lowest score.[1] The range for the scores in Table 5.1 would be 5 (the high score, 9, minus the low score, 4).

The *quartile deviation* is associated with the median and may be reported in situations where the mean is deemed inappropriate to identify central tendency because of a few extremely high or extremely low scores. The quartile deviation is defined as half of the difference between the high and low quartile points. This might sound a bit complicated, but it really isn't.

As shown in Table 5.2, the first step is to divide the distribution of scores into four parts, the quartiles. The median divides the distribution into top and bottom halves. In Table 5.2, the median is 5.5. Of the scores in

---

[1]Technically speaking, the range would be equal to the highest score minus the lowest score plus 1. That's because, using the data in Table 5.1, the highest score of 9 represents everything between 8.5 and 9.4999, and the lowest score, 4, represents everything between 3.5 and 4.4999. When you subtract 3.5 from 9.4999, you get 5.9999 or 6 (which is, of course, the same as 9 − 4 + 1). It's not that we think this is important (we don't); we just thought you might like to know.

Table 5.2
Illustrating the Quartile Deviation

Scores
9
8
8 ← **Median of top half is 8 (Q_3)**
6
6
← **Median of all scores is 5.5 (Q_2)**
5
5
5 ← **Median of bottom half is 5 (Q_1)**
4
4

the top half (9, 8, 8, 6, 6), the median is 8. The median of the scores in the bottom half is 5. The median is labeled Q_2. The upper and lower medians are labeled Q_3 and Q_1, respectively. Together, these are the quartile points.

The range of these quartile points is 3 ($Q_3 = 8$ minus $Q_1 = 5$). The quartile deviation is half of the quartile range—in this case, half of 3, or 1.5. Statisticians also refer to the quartile deviation as the *semi-interquartile range.* That name is a mouthful, but in fact quite accurately defines the process involved: half (semi) of the range between the interquartiles.

The information about the variability, most often the standard deviations, can at times become a fun, though not essential, "detective" activity to speculate about information the report did not provide. For example, in the study on teaching ethics, the standard deviations for the posttest scores reported for the four groups were 1.22, .73, .93, and 1.13. If you remember, the higher mean score was also found in the first group. So we know that the highest mean score (30.00) and the largest standard deviation (1.22) were in the same group. One might reasonably speculate that the higher mean might have been the result of a few very high scores by people in that group.

The mean and the standard deviation can be calculated to describe the performance of a group of participants if there is at least one measurement—for example, a test score. For the last of our descriptive statistics, at least two measurements on each participant are required.

Measures of Association. The descriptive statistic most often used to report the association between two sets of scores is the **correlation coefficient.** A correlation coefficient is a single numeral that describes the relationship between scores, in effect identifying how well you could predict one of the scores if you knew the other. For example, your professor might be interested in the relationship between midterm exam scores in your class and final grades in the class. How accurately could your final grade be predicted from your midterm exam?

This relationship is typically labeled as *r* if there are only two measures (such as midterm exam score and final grade) or as *R* if there are more than two (such as grade-point average, midterm exam score, and final grade). If there is no relationship between the scores/variables, the correlation coefficient is zero. If there is a perfect relationship between them, the correlation coefficient is 1.0. In real life, correlation coefficients of 1.0 are very rare because a perfect relationship between two variables would be quite unusual. For example, a perfect relationship between midterm exam score and final grade would mean that for everyone who took the test, the distribution of scores on the exam and the distribution of grades was a perfect match.

The primary caution in interpreting this descriptive statistic is that a correlation coefficient looks like a decimal fraction but is not. To interpret the correlation coefficient, you need to suspend what you learned back in elementary school about the number line.

Decimal Fraction Number Line

−1.00	−.75	−.50	−.25	.00	.25	.50	.75	1.00

← lower   higher →

Obviously, as a decimal fraction, the numeral .50 is higher than the numeral −.50. But, when these numerals instead are correlation coefficients, the interpretation is quite different, as in the following illustration.

Correlation Coefficients

high	1.00
	.75
↑	.50
	.25
low	.00
	−.25
↓	−.50
	−.75
high	−1.00

With correlation coefficients, the degree of the relationship is expressed by the numeral itself. The positive or negative sign that precedes the numeral indicates the direction, not the strength, of the relationship. When the sign is positive (which is assumed if it is not shown), as one score goes up, the other tends to go up as well. A negative sign indicates instead that as one measure goes up, the other tends to go down (such as number of hours worked each week in a part-time job and scores on exams).

When correlation coefficients are calculated between height and weight among adults, the value is approximately .60. This means that there is some, but not a perfect, relationship between how tall one is and how much one weighs. Correlation coefficients between scores on college admission tests and freshman grade point average are usually also in the .60s, with the same meaning: some, but not a perfect, relationship between how well one did on the admission test and how well one did in freshman classes. When the correlation coefficient is calculated between scores on the Graduate Record Examination (GRE) and graduate school performance, the results are often down in the .30s, low enough to suggest that GRE scores alone do not provide sufficient prediction of grades in graduate school.

A part of the reason for the latter has to do with technical characteristics of calculation when the predictor (GRE) has a small range. But in addition to reflecting that the range of ability among students who take the GRE is smaller than among those who take the undergraduate admission test, the lower correlation coefficient also reflects other characteristics of performance in graduate school. Your ability plays an important role, but haven't you found that motivation, available time, quality of instruction, and so forth are also very important determinants of how well you do in a course?

Be cautious also about the extent of relationship conveyed by the correlation coefficient. The difference between correlation coefficients and decimal fractions is more than just a difference in whether the numeral is positive or negative. For example, a correlation coefficient of .50 does not mean that scores on one measure could be predicted with 50% accuracy by scores on the other. Translating a correlation coefficient for a percentage-type interpretation requires first squaring the correlation coefficient (this is called a **coefficient of determination**). If, for example, the correlation coefficient between admission test scores and grade point averages is .30, this means that only 9% (.30 $\times$ .30 = .09) of the differences in grade point average could be explained by whatever is causing the differences in admission test scores.

Most of the correlation coefficients you will find in the results of quantitative studies are **product-moment correlation coefficients,** calculated with reference to the mean and standard deviation. However, there may be times when the nature of the data required the researchers to emphasize rank order (such as instances in which the median and quartile deviation are reported for central tendency and variability). This can happen, as noted previously, when a few scores are far above or below the others.

The quality of the measurement tool can also influence which descriptive statistics are reported. When the precision of the tool is sufficient only to put things in some rank order, medians and quartile deviations are better choices than means and standard deviations. A special form of correlation coefficient exists for such instances: the *Spearman rank correlation coefficient,* identified as r_s. The Spearman rank correlation coefficient, also referred to as *rho,* is calculated using rank order rather than means and standard deviations.

It is important to remember that a correlation coefficient only describes the relationship between variables and does not provide direct information about whether one of the variables is "causing" the other. For example, consider a study with results indicating a correlation coefficient of .80 between self-report of anxiety immediately after taking an examination and

Table 5.3
Related Descriptive Statistics

Measures of Central Tendency	Measures of Variability	Measures of Association
Mean	Standard deviation	Product-moment correlation coefficient
Median	Quartile deviation	Spearman rank correlation coefficient
Mode	Range	Not applicable

the number of errors made on the examination. Clearly there is a relationship between the two variables, but there are at least three possible causative interpretations. Elevated anxiety could have caused the errors on the examination. Making errors on the exam could have caused the elevated anxiety. Something else entirely (such as not studying for the exam) could have caused both the elevated anxiety and the errors.

Table 5.3 lists the typical descriptive statistics, including their relationship to one another.

Inferential Statistics

Inferential statistics, while occasionally found in qualitative reports, are almost always evident when there is a quantitative focus. The reason is that quantitative studies typically include the attention to the possibility of a chance occurrence that is not always a major concern in qualitative research.

Think about how this would work in real life. A counselor, for example, is concerned about whether group interventions are as effective as individual counseling in improving self-concept. The counselor designs a study with participants randomly assigned to participate in either group or individual counseling over a period of eight weeks. At the end of this period, each participant completes a measure of self-concept. Results for the individual counseling participants were $M = 31.4$ and $SD = 4.3$. The corresponding descriptive statistics for the group counseling participants were $M = 29.8$ and $SD = 4.4$. Remembering the information in the previous section, it is evident that the extent of differences within each of the groups was about the same (SDs of 4.3 and 4.4). But overall, there was a difference between the two groups in favor of the participants in individual counseling.

Does this study suggest that group counseling should be abandoned? Of course, many things would be involved in answering this question, but one of the more important factors to consider is associated with inferential statistics. Participants in individual counseling had higher average scores. That's *descriptive*. Was that difference likely to have been because of the type of counseling, or could this difference (31.4 versus 29.8) have been the result of chance? That's an *inferential* question.

There's a special way this question should be phrased, and it is important enough that we urge you to commit it to memory. Remember that the participants in the study were *samples* of people receiving individual or group counseling. As samples, they represented their corresponding *populations*, that is, all possible participants receiving one of these two forms of treatment. The appropriate inferential phrasing for the question is as follows:

What is the probability that the difference found between these samples would have occurred if there was really no differences in the total populations?

If the difference seems likely to have been the result of chance, the results would not provide support for abandoning what may be a viable treatment approach. If the question is phrased as, "Could this have occurred by chance?" little help will be provided because that answer is almost always *yes*. Essentially anything can occur by chance alone.

When the recommended phrasing for the question is used, those mysterious statistical inference tools actually produce a clear answer to the question. Knowing the probability of chance occurrence can be critically important when interpreting the practical implications of the findings.

Several tools are used by quantitative researchers to answer the inference question and then report it in their studies. While we will focus on only the most widely used methods, the underlying question is much the same: Do the differences between the samples reflect differences in the populations they represent, or were those differences likely to be the result of chance? Remember that our goal is to be able to readily comprehend, not calculate, the sometimes cryptic code in which results are presented.

The t Test. Before computer analysis became readily available, the *t test* was the most widely used and reported tool for answering the inferential statistics question. It is an old and rather simple inferential statistic used to determine whether the difference in mean scores between two groups is likely to have occurred by chance alone. The *t* test is still an appropriate tool when only two groups are being compared, and may be used as a follow-up when a more complex inferential statistic is the primary analysis tool.

Following is an example of the code used to provide the outcome of a *t* test:

$$t(49) = 1.34, p > .05$$

It's actually a very simple code, interpreted as follows:
The first letter simply identifies that it is a *t* test.

$$t(49) = 1.34, p > .05$$

The number in parentheses technically represents a statistical concept, the degrees of freedom.[2] The concept is important when calculating

---

[2]*Degrees of freedom* is the label used by statisticians to describe the number of values in the final calculation of a statistic that are free to vary. Detailed explanation of this concept is available in introductory statistics texts. For our purposes here, the material within the parentheses provides information about the number of participants in the research study (*t* test, ANOVA, and ANCOVA) and the number of mean scores being compared (ANOVA and ANCOVA).

statistics, but for interpretation you will find it much more helpful to think of it as simply as a number that tells you approximately how many people were involved in the study (in this case about 50).

$$t(\mathbf{49}) = 1.34, p > .05$$

The number after the equal sign is the result of the calculation of the *t* test. You don't have to do anything to interpret it because it is interpreted for you by the *p* value that immediately follows it.

$$t(49) = \mathbf{1.34,}\ p > .05$$

The letter *p* in this equation stands for *probability,* specifically the probability of getting the difference seen with the samples if the population difference is zero.

$$t(49) = 1.34, \boldsymbol{p > .05}$$

In this equation the probability of getting the observed score difference from two sample groups when the populations they represent are not different is greater than 5 in 100, or greater than a 5% chance. Researchers are a cautious group and will usually not reject a belief of no difference (null hypothesis) unless this probability is less than 5 in 100. So, if this *t* test had been conducted with the participants who received individual and group counseling, we could conclude from this equation alone that there were about 50 participants in the study. The difference in their posttest scores would have occurred more than 5 times in 100 if there were really no difference associated with whether group or individual counseling was used to enhance self-concept. In other words, the difference was probably not the result of a treatment effect of individual or group counseling, but just the result of chance. The probability in the equation is determined primarily by the extent of difference between the two scores (a larger difference would have a smaller probability that it occurred by chance) and by the number of people in the study (more people in the sample suggests a smaller probability that differences occurred by chance).

Researchers are now encouraged to report the actual probability value (for example, $p = .065$), rather than using the greater than/less than signs, but particularly in previous research studies you are likely to see something like this in the report:

- $p > .05$ (deemed likely to be a result of chance)
- $p < .05$ (not likely to be a result of chance)
- $p < .01$ (less likely to be a result of chance)
- $p < .001$ (even less likely to be a result of chance)

The smaller probability values indicate a smaller chance that the differences seen in the samples would have occurred if the population difference is zero. The probability level selected by the researcher as the boundary for identification of a chance level is called the **alpha level.** By convention it is usually set at .05, indicating that probability values equal to or less than .05 will be identified as unlikely to be the result of chance. These basic concepts for interpreting the *t* test will now become the foundation for a statistical method much more widely used because it offers a number of advantages.

Analysis of Variance.   The name of this tool may seem a bit off-putting, but it actually is very descriptive. When things differ from one another, they are said to vary. The total amount by which they vary is called the variance. Studying something in detail is analysis. Studying the difference in things in detail would thus be the analysis of variance.

ANOVA, an acronym for ANalysis Of VAriance, is a more useful inferential procedure than the *t* test because it can be used when researchers are comparing more than two groups. In fact, when more than two groups are being compared, the researchers should not begin by comparing each possible pair with the *t* test, but instead begin by comparing the groups with the ANOVA.

The study of methods for teaching ethics used four groups whose mean scores were to be compared. So, appropriately, the researchers began with the ANOVA and reported the result (the "mystery equation" on page 106) as follows:

$$F(3,53) = 26.26, p < .001$$

Interpreting this equation is very much like interpreting the *t* test equation.

The first letter, *F*, simply identifies that it is an analysis of variance (ANOVA):

$$F(3,53) = 26.26, p < .001$$

Notice that there are now two numbers inside the parentheses. These again are technically statistical degrees of freedom associated with this test. You can interpret the second number, as in the *t* test, as approximately the number of people in the study. To find out how many mean scores were compared, add 1 to the first number in the parentheses; in this case 3 + 1 = 4 identifies that there were four. (This first number isn't needed in the *t* test equation because the number of means being compared is always two).

$$F(\mathbf{3,53}) = 26.26, p < .001$$

The number after the equal sign is the result of the calculation of the *F* ratio. It again is interpreted by the *p* value that follows it.

$$F(3,53) = \textbf{26.26}, p < .001$$

The letter p in this equation still stands for *probability*, specifically the probability of getting the differences seen with the samples if the population differences are zero. In this example, the probability is less than 1 in 1,000, so the researcher appropriately concluded that the groups were different from one another.

$$F(3,53) = 26.26, \textbf{\textit{p} < .001}$$

With more than two groups, the p value less than .001 indicates that there are differences among the groups, but the equation does not identify which group(s) had differences in posttest scores unlikely to have occurred by chance alone. When the analysis of the combined differences produces a probability less than .05, the researchers can then choose one of several procedures, including the t test, to begin making paired comparisons between the groups. Figure 5.2 illustrates the comparisons that would be made in the four groups used in the ethics study.

Notice in Figure 5.2 that with four mean scores to compare, there will be six paired comparisons. In case you are wondering why the group with a mean of 30.0 has to be compared to both groups that had a mean of 27.0, the reason is that the analysis involves mean, standard deviation, and number of participants in the group. In the comparisons illustrated in Figure 5.2, one group was different enough from the others to have a less-than-5-in-100 chance that the difference was by chance. (It shouldn't be hard to identify this group as the one with a mean of 30.0.)

You will see the ANOVA much more often than the t test in the results section of research reports. While required when there are more than two comparisons to be made, the ANOVA can also be used when there are

FIGURE 5.2
Using Paired
Comparisons to
Follow Up an Analysis
of Variance

The researchers in the ethics study found means of 30.0, 27.93, 27.0, and 27.0 in the four groups taught with different instructional methods. The ANOVA indicated that the differences in those mean scores would have occurred by chance alone less than 1 time in 1,000 but does not indicate whether this applies to some or to all of the differences. The researcher's next step is to compare each pair of mean scores:

The group with a mean of 30.0 is compared to the group with a mean of 27.93.

The group with a mean of 30.0 is compared to one of the groups with a mean of 27.0.

The group with a mean of 30.0 is compared to the other group with a mean of 27.0.

The group with a mean of 27.93 is compared to one of the groups with a mean of 27.0.

The group with a mean of 27.93 is compared to the other group with a mean of 27.0.

The two groups with a mean of 27.0 are compared to each other.

only two mean scores to compare. In that case, the eventual p value is exactly the same as would have been evident if the t test had been used.

Analysis of Covariance. This is simply a special type of ANOVA, creatively labeled as ANCOVA. It can be used when there is some question about whether participants in the groups being investigated were sufficiently alike when the study began. When you see that an ANCOVA was used in the study, you know that the posttest scores being compared are not the ones actually made by the participants. Instead, the posttest scores have been statistically adjusted to account for differences on another variable, usually a pretest, before the analysis is done.

Suppose, for example, that researchers began with a belief that in a distance-learning environment, full-time students would have greater gains in performance than would part-time students. On the posttest the mean score for full-time students was 38 and the mean score for part-time students was 34. Since it was a large class, the difference was unlikely to have occurred by chance. Full-time students simply did better. However, there's more to this study. A pretest was administered at the beginning of the class to identify what students already knew about the content. On the pretest, the mean score of part-time students was 13; the mean score of full-time students was 15.

An ANCOVA creates new posttest mean scores to compare, taking into account the actual differences on both pretests and posttests and the correlation coefficients among the scores. The new posttest mean scores are statistically adjusted to compensate for differences between the groups in the pretest. With a set of sample data, this adjustment came out with a new mean posttest score of 37.8 for the part-time students and 36.9 for the full-time students. Now the part-time students actually have the higher score. Notice that without the adjustment, the researchers would have made an erroneous conclusion. Notice also that this is not the same as simply subtracting the pretest from the posttest to produce a gain score. The latter is not a recommended procedure because of issues associated with measurement error. The ANCOVA is often used when there is reason to believe that groups were not equivalent before the intervention began.

Interpretation of the ANCOVA equation is the same as with the ANOVA. For example, the ANCOVA equation in the ethics study was $F(3,52) = 27.17, p < .01$, again indicating that four $(3 + 1)$ mean scores were compared for about 50 participants with an outcome $(p < .01)$, suggesting that at least one group was different to an extent unlikely to have occurred by chance alone.

Comparing the ANCOVA equation with the ANOVA equation on the same participants, $F(3,53) = 26.26, p < .001$, suggests that the group with the higher posttest scores probably also had somewhat higher pretest scores as well. After the adjustment was made to account for pretest differences, the probability of a chance-alone occurrence went up from less than 1 in 1000 to less than 1 in 100—still indicating, though, a difference unlikely to have occurred by chance alone.

Chi-Square. Chi-square (χ^2) is an inferential statistic that can be used when the data are in a form that doesn't allow averaging, such as frequency counts in various categories (for example, how many students received an A, how many received an A−, how many received a B+, and so forth). The chi-square procedure compares the proportions found in a set of data with the proportions that would be expected by chance.

Both the *t* test and ANOVA are classified as **parametric.** They are inferential statistics that make assumptions about the nature of the data distribution (for example, a normal distribution of scores). Chi-square is one of the primary tools classified as **nonparametric.** That means that it can be used without assumptions about the shape of the data distribution. It can be very helpful in situations where using other techniques would make no sense because of the kind of data obtained. To illustrate, imagine that administrators at your school are considering changing the way evening classes are scheduled, so that all courses will have to meet at least twice per week. They conduct a survey using a sample of 120 current graduate students and get the results in Table 5.4.

From the first row in Table 5.4 it is clear that half of the respondents were not in favor of the scheduling change. But remember that this was a sample of graduate students, not the entire population of those who would be affected. The question then is, what is the probability of getting these results from the sample if there are really no differences in the preference of the population?

As you might guess, calculating mean scores to be compared through ANOVA is not feasible with these data. The chi-square inference tool is calculated by comparing the frequency obtained in each category (Row 1) with the frequency expected (Row 2). In this example, the outcome would be expressed as follows:

$$\chi_2(2, N = 120) = 12.39, p = .002$$

The format for this equation is slightly different, but the information conveyed is essentially the same as described with the *t* test and ANOVA. The first number inside the parentheses (2) is the degrees of freedom. In the chi-square equation the other number inside the parentheses (120) is exactly, rather than approximately, the number of participants. Again, this is followed by the outcome of the chi-square calculation (12.39) and then the key feature, the *p* value (.002). In this example, the probability of getting these results from a sample if the population had no preference is 2 in 1,000 or, said another way, the graduate students have expressed a preference, and it is to not have their classes meet twice per week.

Table 5.4
Chi-Square Responses to Schedule Change

	Favorable	Indifferent	Unfavorable
Responses	18	42	60
Expected	40	40	40

Correlation. The *t* test, ANOVA, ANCOVA, and chi-square all involve an inference question about whether some observed difference is likely to have occurred by chance. With just a minor change in wording, this same general concept is used to interpret correlation coefficients as well. For example, in a correlation study you might find something like "$r = .20$, $p > .05$" stated in the results. The interpretation would be that the probability is greater than 5 in 100 that a correlation this high (.20) would be found with this sample if the correlation between these variables in the population was zero. In other words, there does not appear to be a significant relationship between these two variables.

When the correlation coefficient is statistically significant and the researchers are conducting a study to determine whether one variable can be effectively predicted from another, the results will often include a **regression analysis.** The regression analysis is an extension of the correlation coefficient in which the correlation between the variables is combined with means and standard deviations of each variable to create an equation allowing direct prediction of one variable from the other.

For example, suppose that researchers were studying the relationship in college students between scores on a measure of an outgoing personality trait and number of hours per week spent in student government activities. They found a correlation coefficient of .70 between the two variables, a level of relationship unlikely to have occurred by chance alone. In order to actually make a prediction, a regression analysis would be completed to produce an equation such as:

$$Y = .35X + 2.50$$

in which Y is the predicted number of hours per week in student government activities and X is the score on the personality test. If the study involved the relationship between more than two variables—for example, including grade point average as another predictor—the process is called *multiple regression* and the equation might be something like

$$Y = .31X_1 + 3.42X_2 - 15.76,$$

in which Y is still the predicted number of hours per week in student government activity, X_1 is the score on the personality test, and X_2 is the grade point average.

This is an inferential procedure because there would of course be no need to predict the extracurricular activity of the participants in the study. Those data had to be available in order to calculate the correlation coefficient(s) and complete the regression analysis. The idea is that the results of the study could be used to predict the number of extracurricular hours for other students when only the personality test score and/or the grade point average were known.

The accuracy of the prediction is projected through the **standard error of estimate,** which is a number calculated from the standard deviation and the correlation coefficient and used to put an accuracy band around the prediction. If there is zero correlation, the standard error of estimate is equal to the standard deviation of the variable being predicted. As the correlation between two variables goes up, the standard error of estimate goes down—a logical outcome, since higher correlation coefficients allow better prediction.

Researchers often include calculation of a **confidence interval** when reporting regression analysis. In this context, the confidence interval, like the standard error of estimate, provides an accuracy band for the predicted scores. Levels of confidence comparable to the familiar .05 and .01 levels of significance are used to increase the standard error of estimate for greater certainty or confidence in the prediction. Figure 5.3 illustrates the outcome of a hypothetical study of college students in which personality test score and grade point average are used to predict the number of hours per week devoted to student government.

From Figure 5.3 you can see that a better prediction of the number of hours spent in student government is possible when grade point average is included along with the personality score ($R = .84$) than if the personality test score was used alone ($r = .70$). From the multiple-regression equation, a student with a personality test score of 70 and a grade point average of 3.5 would be predicted to spend approximately 18 hours per week in student government activities. To be approximately 95% certain

FIGURE 5.3
Illustration of
Regression Analysis

Variables

Y is the number of hours per week spent in student government activities
X_1 is the personality test score
X_2 is the grade point average

Product-Moment Correlation Coefficients

$r = .70$: correlation between Y and X_1
$r = .60$: correlation between Y and X_2
$r = .20$: correlation between X_1 and X_2

Multiple Correlation Coefficient

$R = .84$: multiple correlation with Y as dependent variable, X_1 and X_2 as independent variables

Regression Equation

$Y = .31X_1 + 3.42X_2 - 15.76$

Standard Error of Estimate

$SE_{est} = 2.71$

Confidence Intervals

$CI_{95} = 5.3$ +/− predicted score: 95% confidence interval
$CI_{99} = 6.99$ +/− predicted score: 99% confidence interval

Example:

Personality test score is 70; grade point average is 3.5

Predicted number of hours per week in student government activity is 17.91
$(.31 \times 70) + (3.42 \times 3.5) - 15.76 = 17.91$

95% confidence interval = 12.61 to 23.21
99% confidence interval = 10.92 to 24.9

Table 5.5
Correlation Coefficients among Selected Study Variables

	Trait Anxiety	Procrastination	Age
Self-efficacy average	−.37**	−.39**	.16
Trait anxiety		.23*	.08
Procrastination			.04

*$p < .05$ **$p < .001$

of the prediction, the number of hours would be projected in the range between about 13 (12.61) and 23 (23.21). To be even more certain, there has to be an even larger range (10.92 to 24.9).

In previous chapters you've evaluated components of a study (Haycock, McCarthy, & Skay, 1998) involving procrastination, self-efficacy, and anxiety in college students (see Appendix C). Table 5.5 is an excerpt from their results.

Three of the correlation coefficients were sufficiently high to suggest a probability of less than either 5 in 100 (trait anxiety and procrastination) or 1 in 1,000 (self-efficacy and trait anxiety; self-efficacy and procrastination) of that result if the correlation between these variables in the population was zero.

Remember that the minus signs indicate the direction of the relationship. Higher self-efficacy scores went with lower anxiety scores (−.37); higher self-efficacy scores went with lower procrastination scores (−.39). Higher anxiety scores went with higher procrastination scores (.23). The relationship between age and self-efficacy was also in a positive direction, with older students getting higher self-efficacy scores. But the analysis indicated that this correlation coefficient (.16) in this sample could have occurred by chance more than 5 times in 100 if there was no correlation between age and self-efficacy in the population.

Other Inferential Tools. The inference tools presented in this chapter were selected because they are the ones most likely to be found in the studies you read and because they provide the foundation for most of the other tools you might encounter. However, there seems to be almost no end to the subtypes and extensions of these procedures. For example, *t* test analysis includes one type of calculation if a pretest is compared to a posttest in a single group and another type of calculation if two different groups are compared on one test. A special form of ANOVA, called MANOVA (Multiple ANalysis Of VAriance), is used when there is more than one dependent variable in the study. The simple correlation coefficient can be extended to more-involved techniques such as factor analysis and structural modeling, or latent trait analysis.

The good news, though, is that essentially all of these techniques culminate at the same place: identification of a *p* value to communicate the likelihood of a chance occurrence. That information will usually be most valuable to you when attempting to glean the essence of the results. More important, the thought process regarding what is meant by the probability value remains the same in all of these methods. The researchers appear to have found "something" with this sample. What's the probability of this happening if there's really "nothing" in the population?

Statistical Significance.   In research reports, when a difference is found that appears unlikely to have occurred by chance, that difference is identified as being *statistically significant.* By convention, if the probability value obtained from one of the analyses described earlier is less than or equal to .05, the associated result is identified as statistically significant. The modifier *statistically* is essential, because the finding may or may not be really important, critical, momentous, or any of the other semantic implications associated with something being significant.

A statistically significant difference is simply one that is unlikely to have occurred in a sample (would have occurred less than 5 times in 100) if there was really no difference in the population. Remember that the likelihood of an analysis producing a statistically significant result mostly depends on two factors: the size of the difference (or the relationship, if it's a correlation coefficient) and the number of participants in the study.

For example, a correlation coefficient of .20 found in a sample of 200 participants would be identified as statistically significant. But, remembering the squaring principle, this actually means that only 4% of the differences in one of those variables could be accounted for by differences in the other one. That doesn't seem very momentous. Or consider a study of two teaching methods in a sample of 5,000 students in which one method produced a mean score of 70.8 and the other produced a mean score of 71.4. With a sample this large, that difference would probably be statistically significant. But a difference that small could hardly be described as one that really matters. The "Does it matter?" question will be examined in the chapter that follows by adding other modifiers.

Remember also that finding a statistically significant difference doesn't alone provide direct information about what caused that difference. Even if the observed difference is quite large, suggesting both statistical and practical significance, identifying the cause of a difference is more a function of how the research was designed than how the data were analyzed. The concern would be about the extraneous variables discussed in the previous chapter—in essence, what else might have caused the difference?

Of course, indirect information about cause is provided when a finding is evaluated as not statistically significant. If the difference in outcome from using two different teaching techniques is so small as to be evaluated as probably a result of chance alone, it is usually safe to assume that teaching method is not causing an important difference.

Consider the following:

- Study 1: Control group: $M = 65$ Treatment group: $M = 75$
- Study 2: Control group: $M = 65$ Treatment group: $M = 66$

If you were given this information and asked to identify which difference was more likely to be statistically significant, you would want to be very careful before you answered. A crucial piece of data is missing. What would that be?

The answer is that you couldn't make a good prediction about which of those results would be more likely to be statistically significant without knowing how many participants were included in each of the studies. If the number of participants in Study 1 was quite small and the number of participants in Study 2 was quite large, it's possible that only the small difference between mean scores found in the second study would reach statistical significance. That is one reason why quantitative researchers like to use the largest samples that they can possibly afford and have time to study.

To compensate for this interpretive limitation with statistical significance, most journals recommend and some require that an additional statistic called the **effect size** be provided in the results. Effect size is a standardized difference between groups, calculated in its simplest form by subtracting the mean of one group from the mean of another and dividing the answer by a standard deviation.

There are several ways to calculate the effect size, and experts do not yet completely agree about which is best. But regardless of the specific calculation procedure, the effect size gives you additional information about how important any observed differences may be. The most popular of the current techniques is called *Cohen's d*, with a general recommendation that small, medium, and large differences correspond to *d* values of .20, .50, and .80, respectively.

The tools we've considered thus far all deal with whether a difference is likely to have occurred by chance alone. The effect size is an attempt to identify whether the difference is large enough to be important. To illustrate, earlier we suggested that a control group mean score of 65 and a treatment group mean score of 66 might be evaluated as statistically significant if the number of participants in the study was quite large. But even if that occurred, the effect size would probably be rather low. For example, if the standard deviation was 4, the calculated effect size would be only .25 (66 − 65/4).

Statistical significance and effect size are related but clearly not identical. As you would guess, quantitative researchers usually hope to find that differences in scores are statistically significant, and that the effect size is large.

Null Hypotheses.   Quantitative researchers are expected to begin their studies with some prior belief about the probable outcome. You may remember from Chapter 2 that the prior belief can be classified as either directional, nondirectional, or null.

Most often, regardless of the classification, in the results section the data will be analyzed using the null form. Researchers who believe that Treatment A would be more effective than Treatment B (directional hypothesis) or who believe that one of the two treatments will be more effective but are not sure which one (nondirectional hypothesis) can find the answer to their question using a null form of hypothesis test. If the nondirectional hypothesis is correct, the null hypothesis will be rejected because there will be a statistically significant difference between the two treatments. If the directional hypothesis is correct, the null hypothesis will be rejected *and* the difference between mean scores will be in the predicted direction. In either case, testing of the null hypothesis serves perfectly well in answering the question.

From the information in the results section, the researchers can either reject or fail to reject the null hypothesis. A null hypothesis is *never* accepted. The difference between "failing to reject" and "accepting" when applied to the null hypothesis may seem to be just a choice of words, but the difference is important. By not accepting a null hypothesis, researchers always allow for the possibility that the hypothesis could be rejected if more data were available.

FIGURE 5.4
The Wisdom of the
Null Hypothesis: Two
Views

"Use of the null hypothesis for all analyses is not an unreasonable approach," Paul said casually in his lecture voice.

"That's what you think," Jeffrey said under his breath.

"Excuse me?"

"Nothing," Jeffrey muttered.

"No," Paul encouraged, "go on. What were you going to say to the readers?"

"Just that I have never considered this null hypothesis custom to be all that reasonable."

"What do you mean?" Paul pressed defensively.

"Well, come on! If you've got something to say, something you want to predict, why not just come right out with it and say what you think is going to happen? What's all this business of saying that there is going to be no difference between the two groups studied, and then try so hard to find that difference that you're pretty sure is going to be there?"

"Jeffrey," Paul said, in his most pedantic voice, "the null hypothesis was developed . . ."

Jeffrey isn't finished. "And another thing, while we are on the subject, this language related to statistical significance: A statistical difference is one that is unlikely to have occurred if there really was no difference in the population. I mean, why can't you just say that you are about 95% certain that you found something that is beyond chance? And another thing: what was that nonsense about how it's okay to say that you fail to reject a null hypothesis, but it's not okay to say that you accept a null hypothesis. It's the same thing."

"Listen to me, Jeffrey," Paul implored, "we can't say those things to our readers, because they are not the same thing."

"Seems like almost the same thing to me," Jeffrey said, with more than a little sarcasm in his voice.

"With all due respect, my friend, you are missing the point. Words like *almost* and *about* do not belong in quantitative research. I know there are limitations in this approach, but don't try to take away the major advantage. Quantitative studies rest on a foundation of precise language. We are just about to explain how testing with the null hypothesis clearly can demonstrate when there is actually a difference. And immediately after that, how researchers can avoid the null hypothesis if they choose. And the reason why quantitative researchers 'fail to reject' instead of 'accepting' a null hypothesis is that the first way leaves open the possibility of a different outcome if more data are gathered—and we quantitative researchers always want to gather more data."

Jeffrey, still unconvinced, said, "Why don't you stop lecturing and show me?"

"Okay," said Paul, "try to pay attention."

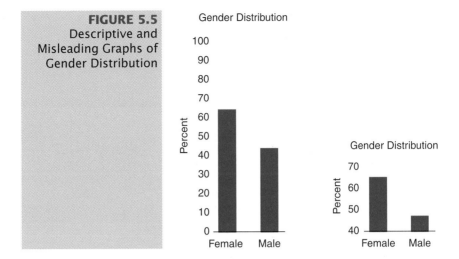

FIGURE 5.5
Descriptive and
Misleading Graphs of
Gender Distribution

Does this seem inconsistent, perhaps even inappropriate? It's actually not, but before going further you might enjoy the conversation about this topic between the authors of this text in Figure 5.4.

Not all researchers use the null hypothesis when testing a directional hypothesis. You would know they did not if in the results section you find the term *one-tailed test*. When a directional hypothesis is being evaluated with a one-tailed test, the probability value is a function of both the difference between the mean scores and which score was higher. For example, with a hypothesis that Treatment A is more effective than Treatment B, the outcome will not be reported as statistically significant even if Treatment B is far more effective.

Interpreting Graphs.   We've all heard that a picture is worth a thousand words, and graphs presented in the results section can often clarify the words and numbers provided by the researchers. Unfortunately, pictorial information can also be highly misleading, so caution is warranted when you form impressions from graphs unless you also give careful attention to the numbers they are representing. One concern, well illustrated in Darrell Huff's classic 1954 text, *How to Lie with Statistics*, is the effect of truncating the graph to save space. The two graphs in Figure 5.5 actually portray

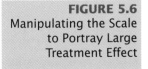

FIGURE 5.6
Manipulating the Scale
to Portray Large
Treatment Effect

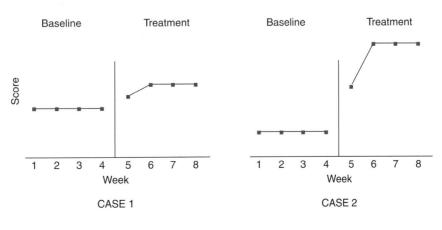

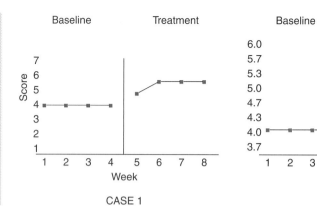

exactly the same information about gender distribution of students enrolled in a university college of education: 60 percent female, 40 percent male. But a quick glance at the graph on the right side magnifies that difference to an extreme. The visual impression is different to the point of clearly exaggerating the disparity.

Still another area of concern is the visual effect of adjusting the units in the scale. Figure 5.6 describes two cases in which self-confidence was measured once a week for eight weeks. No intervention was provided during the first four weeks, the baseline. Weeks 5 through 8 show what happened to the self-confidence measurements during counseling. It would appear from Figure 5.6 that the intervention was somewhat helpful for the first case but very effective in the second.

Look carefully though at those same data as portrayed in Figure 5.7 when the actual scores are included. The two cases in fact had exactly the same outcome. The only difference is in how that outcome was illustrated.

Always remembering to attend to the numbers in a scale and not just the visual impression is usually sufficient to avoid being misled when evaluating the content in the results section. We would also note, by the way, that it is not always reasonable to assume that the researchers alone are responsible for the visual displays. Journals are expensive to print, and things done to save space may come from the journal itself and not the authors.

SUMMARY AND CLOSING THOUGHTS

Evaluating the results in a research report involves only two key questions: Did the researchers provide enough detailed information to enable you to understand what they found, and did they present the information with sufficient clarity so that you did understand their findings?

When you are evaluating a qualitative study, the findings will not necessarily be located under a heading of "Results." For example, a qualitative report might, instead provide headings for data interpretation associated with each of the research questions. Qualitative researchers often amass a vast amount of information in a variety of different forms. Their task is to integrate and summarize the data to address their research questions, providing extensive detail about what they found but not overwhelming you with information. Your task is to evaluate whether they accomplished their task. After reading the sections devoted to analysis and interpretation, do you truly understand what they found?

The findings in a quantitative research report will, most often, be located in a section headed "Results," and the findings typically include descriptive statistics. A summary of each variable often appears in the form of a measure of central tendency: the mean, median, and/or the mode. The differences within a variable are reported in the form of measures of variability: the standard deviation, quartile deviation, and/or the range. Relationships between and among the variables may be reported in the form of measures of relationship: the correlation coefficients.

Measures of central tendency, variability, and relationship are called descriptive statistics because that is what they do: They describe the data. Descriptive statistics are sometimes used in qualitative studies as well. But because quantitative researchers are usually interested not only in reporting what they found but also in whether the findings would be likely to occur with other participants, they often add the use of inferential statistics. Tools such as the t test, analysis of variance, and chi-square are inferential statistics that go beyond what was found, adding a prediction of whether the finding was likely to represent something real or was instead just a chance outcome. The interpretation of the coded outcome of the inferential analysis rests primarily on the probability value at the end of the code. That probability value (for example, $p = .0234$) is the "best bet" about whether the differences and/or relationships found in this participant sample would have emerged by chance if there were really no differences or relationships. The lower the p value, the better the odds that an observed finding was not a function of chance alone.

When the p value is sufficiently low (usually .05 or lower is the standard), the researchers can reject the null hypothesis of no difference or no relationship. When this occurs, the difference or relationship is labeled as statistically significant.

Portraying the findings using graphs and pictures is often helpful in understanding the findings of a research study. Pay attention to the numbers associated with the graphic: A picture may be worth a thousand words, but that picture can lead to an erroneous conclusion.

We won't pretend that it will usually be easy to make one's way through the results reported in either qualitative or quantitative studies. Feeling a bit overwhelmed by the amount of information presented is not an unusual response. Staying afloat, especially while reading the results of quantitative studies is made much easier by remembering the following:

- Much of the information is simply descriptive statistics: numbers used to identify average performance of a group, how large the differences were within a group, and sometimes relationships between variables used in a study.

- The inferential statistical analysis, regardless of the specific tool, ultimately produces a probability, the p value, to simply address the likelihood of getting the difference or the relationship found in the sample if there was truly no difference or relationship in the population represented by that sample.

While the journey may at times be difficult, the destination can be important. Qualitative and quantitative studies each provide information that is not usually part of the findings of the other. Because, by definition, almost anything can happen by chance, one might often want to consider whether the outcome of a research study was just a chance outcome before changing a professional practice because of information found in a research study. Quantitative studies provide that information directly and explicitly.

Qualitative studies, on the other hand, provide an important dimension not always evident in the quantitative approach. For example, in the study we've cited about different methods for teaching ethics to counseling students, you might not know at the end of a qualitative study whether the differences found between the groups were the result of chance. You would, however, know a great deal more about what really happened in the groups during the study, much more than just their posttest scores. That information can also be crucial in evaluating the importance of a study, particularly in regard to whether a change in your own professional practice is warranted.

To restate the obvious, qualitative and quantitative studies can each provide essential, though different, types of information. And don't forget that you may be reading a study that identifies itself as having used mixed methods, intentionally combining elements of both quantitative and qualitative approaches in the same study. In all cases, the results presented can be evaluated in regard to the following:

1. Clarity: Did the researchers clearly report their findings?
2. Completeness: Did the researchers report all of what they found that might be relevant for the objectives they identified? If something possibly relevant isn't evident, did they explain the omission?

AN EXERCISE FOR REVIEW

It may be helpful to check your comprehension of the material in this chapter using the following questions:

1. The results section of a research article includes the following: $t(25) = 2.49, p < .05$. How many mean scores were compared?
   a. 2
   b. 4
   c. 25
   d. cannot tell from the information provided

The correct answer is (a). The t test always compares just two mean scores.

2. Researchers compare the mean scores and find that students who were taught in large classes had lower scores than comparable students who were taught in smaller classes, and had lower scores than students who were taught in midsize classes. The difference found by the researcher would be expected to occur less than 1 time in 100 if the real difference was zero. There were 60 students in each group. Which of the following summarizes this finding?
    a. $F(2, 60) = 4.49, p > .05$
    b. $F(2, 177) = 4.49, p = .01$
    c. $F(2, 60) = 4.49, p < .01$
    d. $F(2, 177) = 4.49, p = .05$
    e. $F(2, 177) = 4.49, p < .01$

This one is a bit more challenging. The answer would have to be either (c) or (e) to meet the criteria of a finding expected to occur less than 1 time in 100. You may have been tempted to select (c) because of the number 60, but (e) is the correct answer. Remember that there were 60 students in each group (a total of 180) and that the second number inside the parentheses is only the approximate total number of participants.

3. A researcher obtained social security numbers and phone numbers from 30 participants and then correlated the last four digits of the social security numbers with the last four digits of the phone numbers. The researcher reported the following result: $r = .15$, $p > .05$. Which of the following statements best describes this finding?
    a. The researcher must have made a mistake. There couldn't be a correlation between the last four digits of the social security number and the last four digits of phone number.
    b. The probability is greater than 5 in 100 that a correlation of .15 would have been found with this sample if there was actually zero correlation in the population.

The correct answer is (b) While there is obviously no correlation between social security numbers and phone numbers, remember that in a sample, anything can happen by chance.

ANSWER FOR REFLECTIVE EXERCISE

Reflective Exercise 5.2

On a 40-item test, the instructor believes that almost all of the students will do well. If the instructor is correct, which outcome would be more likely?

The correct answer is (a). Higher average performance (do well) is evident in (a) and (b) with the higher mean scores of 35 out of 40. Less variability (almost all) is evident in (a) with the smaller standard deviation of 2. Choice (c) also has a standard deviation of 2, but its mean of 25 is lower.

6

So, Now What?
Evaluating the Discussion Section

CHAPTER OUTLINE

BASIC CONCEPTS

Clinical significance
Conclusions
Implications

Limitations
Practical significance
Statistical significance

Summary
Theoretical significance

Quite often, first we do something, and then we talk about it. So it is with research reports: Investigators follow a logical process of saying what they intend to do (providing background and proposing hypotheses), how they intend to do it (method), report what they discovered (results), and then talk about what they think it all means. All components in Figure 6.1 are now shaded. We've finally arrived at the last stage in the process, the discussion section.

The last section of a research report is significantly different in style and content from the sections that preceded it. Ideally, the information in the results section is independent of any preconceived notions of the researchers; they simply report what they found. In contrast, the discussion section provides the opportunity for the researchers to go beyond their actual findings, to speculate about the implications of their results.

We know that it is tempting to read the abstract of an article, and then, if it seems interesting, skip right to the discussion section to find out "the bottom line" and its implications. In fact, this is a practice of many professionals. We have pointed out some dangers in doing this, since it would reflect a level of trust and uncritical judgment that is often not warranted.

The discussion section is informed by the data generated in a study, and there is room for speculation, inference, and reflection. If, for example, a study found that children who present discipline problems in school tend to come from lower-socioeconomic-status homes, this could mean any number of things, all of which may be discussed in this section of the report. The authors, for example, might suggest that the misbehavior stems from inadequate diet and overconsumption of preservatives in food. However, readers might draw other conclusions from the results presented—that diet may be a contributing variable but not the main factor (which, they claim, is the economic deprivations associated with poverty). In any case, the discussion section is the place in the report where the authors have a chance to tell the story of what they believe the results mean.

In different journals, this last section may be under one of several headings: "Summary," "Conclusions," "Implications," or "Discussion and Implications." Regardless of the specific heading used, it will be the last section,

FIGURE 6.1
Evaluating the Discussion

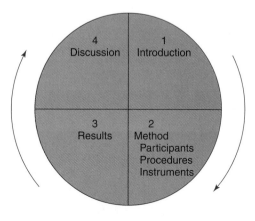

and there should be a clear demarcation between it and the results of the study. This boundary signals that a different narrative voice will be employed to "discuss" rather than merely to "present" information. One reason why many professionals jump right to this section is that the writing style is most consistent with a conversational interaction. Therefore, it may be the easiest section of a report to digest; however, in some ways it presents you with the largest challenge—determining whether the authors have overstepped their bounds.

HOW PRIOR BELIEFS MAY INFLUENCE YOUR EVALUATION

Before we look at some of the specific tools you can use to evaluate the final section (and decide whether the commentary is sound and reasonable based on the data collected), think about the context from the viewpoint of the reader. After convincing you that the topic was important, that they had sufficient understanding of the topic to conduct the study, and that they had sufficient skill to design an appropriate study, the researchers have just finished telling and/or showing you what they found. Now they are about to tell you what they think it means. To what extent will you agree with them?

Obviously, your first response would probably be that the answer depends on what the researchers say in the discussion. Remember, though, that you don't come to the table with empty hands. If you decided to take the time to read the article, that is evidence that you probably have some interest in and knowledge about the topic. Because you are likely to have some prior knowledge, our caution is that what you already know or believe may often predispose you to be overly critical (or overly accepting) of the conclusions drawn by the researchers.

For example, suppose that today you picked up an article in which the primary hypothesis was that spending one's time in graduate school does not improve the quality of a person's life, nor even advance one's career. In fact, it harms relationships, creates long-term stress disorders, and wastes money. It's likely that just the act of reading those words elicits some emotional response. And, most important in this context, that response can make it difficult to read the results and discussion with an objective eye. It's likely that instead you will be looking for evidence to support your existing beliefs (that the money and time you are spending are not being wasted).

To further illustrate the concern, suppose that you have just finished reading a report in which the results were in sharp contrast to a belief that you, and perhaps most people in your field, hold quite sacred. For example, in the field of counseling, the results of the study may have found that the relationship between the client and the counselor had no effect whatsoever on whether a positive treatment outcome was obtained. In leadership and school administration, let's pretend a study showed that an authoritarian style was shown to be far more effective than a democratic one. Or, perhaps the results in a study of the factors that are most important in instruction indicated that rote memorization was the only instructional strategy that produced positive results. Using one of these, or something comparable from another specialization, spend a few minutes in a small-group discussion of the questions in Reflective Exercise 6.1.

Reflective Exercise 6.1
Prior Beliefs

> 1. How strong would those results have to be in order for you to even consider changing your prior belief?
> 2. Would *any* evidence be sufficient to keep you from simply discounting the findings?
> 3. Would you be more likely to be critical of the design, the sample, and so forth than you would if the findings had supported the common belief? If so, could you justify such a response?

To be critical of findings counter to prior beliefs is, of course, quite a normal response. Assuming that the prior belief was supported by a foundation of previous research, drastically modifying that belief on the basis of just one study would be foolhardy. But it's not hard to picture the outcome if all results inconsistent with earlier beliefs were simply ignored or were subject to intense criticism simply because they didn't agree with an earlier notion. Simply said, you would be stuck in the mud.

So when you begin to read what the researchers feel are the implications of their findings, we urge you to be aware of the following:

1. We are tempted to approach with disdain anything inconsistent with what we already believe and think we know.
2. Our prior beliefs may have been based on studies with even more design flaws than the one now being read.

A ROSE BY ANY OTHER NAME: RECOGNIZING SIGNIFICANCE

In discussing the results of their studies, researchers frequently use the term *significant*. The study itself may be described as providing significant new perspectives on a given problem. Differences between two variables may be defined as significant. The researchers may report that they had significant difficulty in finding a large sample of participants. The term *significant* occurs with such frequency in the discussion section of research reports, particularly when a quantitative approach was used, that it requires some special attention. The differentiation among three types of significance summarized by Bloom, Fischer, and Orme (2003) may be especially helpful. They suggest the following three categories:

1. Statistical significance
2. Practical significance
3. Theoretical significance

Statistical Significance

The first of the three, *statistical significance,* was our focus in the preceding chapter. Researchers find a difference in two groups after one receives a treatment not offered to the other. That difference is evaluated as statistically significant if it appears unlikely to have occurred by chance alone. For example, an instructor assigned to teach two sections of a research methods course decides to use group discussion as the primary instructional modality in one class and focus on lecture presentations in the other. Both classes take the same 100-item final examination. The mean score on the exam was 81.3 in the lecture class and 79.4 in the class that emphasized group discussion. Thus there was a difference in performance on the examination. Was that difference likely to have occurred by chance alone? To answer that question, an inferential statistic was used. The probability value that resulted from the calculation was .045.

The probability value estimates the likelihood of finding the observed difference (81.3 versus 79.4) in these two classes if choice of lecture and group discussion modalities really had no effect on final examination performance. In this case, the probability value was less than 5 in 100, so by tradition the outcome would be identified as statistically significant. Statistical significance does not mean the difference was important. It just means that it was unlikely to have been only a chance effect.

Practical Significance

There is no universally agreed procedure for calculating the *practical significance* of a research finding. Instead it will usually be a function of personal and/or societal standards and addressed in reference to implications in the discussion section of the research report.

To illustrate, consider again the hypothetical study of group discussion versus lecture methods while teaching a research methods course. The mean score for one method was 81.3. The mean score for the other was 79.4. The probability value of .045 suggested that this difference was unlikely to have occurred by chance, so the difference was identified as statistically significant. But given the actual data generated by this study, this difference is not large enough to have any practical significance. The best the researcher should probably say in describing this finding is that one of the methods seemed to work almost equally well as the other when the criterion was the score on the final exam.

If a finding is not statistically significant, it would seem safe to assume that it will not have practical significance either. Statistical significance could, in fact, be identified as a necessary but not sufficient condition for implications citing some practical significance of the researchers' results.

FIGURE 6.2
Excerpt from a Study
of Procrastination

Brief Summary
The results of a regression analysis indicated that cumulative efficacy strength was a significant and inverse predictor of procrastination. Individuals with strong efficacy expectations tended to report less procrastination. Cumulative efficacy strength was defined as the sum of participant confidence ratings that they could accomplish 31 behaviors necessary to complete a major project.

Practical Implication
. . . [P]rocrastination encompasses more than poor study habits and a lack of time management. It involves a complex interaction of behaviors, cognitions, and affect. The current results suggest the need for expanding interventions to include the cognitive component of efficacy expectations. An efficacy intervention could be accomplished by first explaining self-efficacy theory to clients. Next, a graduated set of tasks that will produce client success should be identified and executed to increase clients' success experiences and, thus, strengthen efficacy expectations. . . .

A study we've referred to in previous chapters involved factors associated with procrastination among college students (Haycock, McCarthy, & Skay, 1998; see Appendix C). In their results they reported a statistically significant relationship between self-efficacy and procrastination. Excerpts in Figure 6.2 from their discussion section illustrate the presentation of a brief summary of the results and presentation of a practical implication of their findings.

Depending on the context of the study, terms such as *clinical significance* and *social validation* may be used instead of *practical significance* for discussion of whether the study found differences large enough to have real-life significant impact. Whichever term is used for the label, remember that this is not identical to a finding of statistical significance.

Theoretical Significance

One more area of significance may be presented somewhere in the final section: the *theoretical significance* of the results. A finding is identified as having theoretical significance when the outcome of the study was consistent with what would have been predicted from some theory.

To illustrate, suppose that your two authors have proposed a new model to effect positive change in counseling. The theory underlying this model might be that two distinct stages are necessary for the positive change to occur. In Stage 1, the counselor builds an empathic relationship with the client. In Stage 2, the counselor prepares a detailed prescription for the client to follow and then verbally praises the client in weekly sessions when the prescription is followed. Our theory assumes that both stages are essential.

We then set out to do a study to test our theory. The control group received a traditional form of counseling. Counseling for the experimental group was based on our new approach. When the study is completed, we find both good news and bad news in the results. When the study began, it appeared that our random assignment to treatment and control groups had worked well. The average level of symptoms of distress was essentially the same between the two groups. After just two weeks, the clients in our new treatment group reported significantly fewer symptoms of distress than did their peers in the other group, and the difference remained constant throughout the rest of the study. What could we report as implications of the study?

Let's assume that we had a relatively large sample of participants—for example, 25 in each group—and that the difference in symptoms was dramatic. Thus, in the results section we could report a statistically significant difference in favor of the experimental group that occurred early in the treatment and remained evident throughout the period of the study. As implications in the discussion section we could, after acknowledging any limitations in our study and recommending further research with other samples and/or other problems, suggest that the difference in favor of our counseling strategy was sufficiently strong to indicate a practical or clinical significance as well. So there was good news (especially for the participants in the experimental group).

But assume that the stage of establishing a relationship was a two-week process—and remember that our theory was that both stages were essential to effect positive change. In the discussion we would also have to report that these results did not support our theory. The positive change took place after just one of what we thought were two required stages, and there was no evidence in the results to indicate that the second stage was even necessary.

We found differences that were *statistically significant* and were large enough to warrant identification as having *practical significance.* But we did not find *theoretical significance* in reference to our initial hypothesis.

Whether there is any reference to theoretical significance in a report depends on the specific objectives of the study. But, when relevant, it provides a quite different frame of reference for conclusions and implications of the findings.

Figure 6.3 summarizes the three primary categories of significance.

The results section told you what the researchers found. Now, in the discussion section, with the cautions about your prior beliefs and the various meanings of significance, you should expect to find several features specifically addressed, including the following:

- A summary of the findings (restating the findings)
- Conclusions (what the findings mean)

FIGURE 6.3 Categories of Significance		
	Statistical significance	Were the results beyond what might be expected as outcomes from chance alone?
	Practical significance	Were any differences large enough to make a difference in real-life applications?
	Theoretical significance	Were the findings consistent with predicted outcomes from a theory?

- Implications (what the findings might mean)
- Limitations of the study
- Suggestions by the authors for further research

SUMMARY OF FINDINGS

Not surprisingly, the final section of the report will often include a brief summary of the findings presented in the results section of the report (perhaps in recognition that the discussion sometimes is the only part of the publication that will be read). Be very cautious as you read the summary, because it is more than just a little tempting for the researchers to stretch a bit in this presentation. There should be clear differentiation in style between paragraphs in which the outcomes are presented and paragraphs that elaborate on those findings. Elaboration is allowed and even expected in this section, but should be clearly identified as going beyond the actual findings.

Figure 6.4 illustrates how the words selected by the researchers to summarize their findings may overstate the actual outcomes.

FIGURE 6.4
Well-Written and Exaggerated Summaries

Actual Data (average scores on a client satisfaction scale)

32.4 Face-to-face interaction
31.2 Online interaction
33.1 Online interaction with video

A Satisfactory Summary

A higher satisfaction score was found in the group with online interaction including video, but the average satisfaction scores were quite similar among the three conditions.

A Summary That Goes Too Far

The results clearly support the belief that online interactions with video are superior in outcome to both standard online and even face-to-face interactions.

The content identified in Figure 6.4 as a satisfactory summary is consistent with the data in the left column. Notice that the exaggerated summary, though factually accurate, misrepresents the data through omission (failing to note how close the scores were to one another) and by the use of the value-laden terms *clearly* and *superior.*

CONCLUSIONS

The primary caution for you in evaluating the conclusions is to be sure that they flow logically from the results. The researchers do have some freedom to speculate about the ultimate meaning of their findings, but you will want to assess whether lines of separation are evident between the summary and the conclusions.

The summary identified in Figure 6.4 as satisfactory was, in essence, simply a restating of the findings of the study. In reporting what those findings mean, the authors might add a sentence along these lines: "The responses of these participants did not suggest a particular advantage for any one of the three modalities used for interaction in this study." This would be a *conclusion* from the findings.

IMPLICATIONS OF FINDINGS

We readily acknowledge that the distinctions between summaries and conclusions can be very subtle and may not always warrant a great deal of your attention. That is most likely one of the reasons why the content is often presented under a single heading.

The researchers' presentation of implications, however, is another story. While there obviously should be some connection to the specific results of the study, the researchers have extensive latitude to speculate about how far the results can be extended.

In their recommendations for preparing the final section of a qualitative research report, Bogden and Biklen (2003) suggest the importance of providing a broader context for the specific outcomes. They recommend reminding the reader that the results are only one piece of the puzzle and providing the reader with a broader societal perspective to which the specific results might contribute. This recommendation applies equally well in the implications of quantitative studies.

In a description of the "Seven Deadly Sins of Qualitative Research," Shank (2002) suggests that researchers should vigorously avoid timidity when speculating about the importance of their findings. Extreme caution certainly reduces the chances of being criticized for going too far, but unfortunately also reduces the chances of doing something important both in the design of the study and in the presentation of its outcomes. Again, this recommendation for qualitative research is equally applicable for quantitative studies.

To illustrate the difference between conclusions and implications, let's return to one of the studies we've been following through this section of our text. Sapp (1995) investigated techniques for teaching ethics to mental health counseling students, comparing the outcomes of three different teaching methods and a control group (see Appendix A). The following is an excerpt from the discussion section of the report. Would this statement be better classified as a conclusion or an implication?

> This study demonstrated that a direct lecture presentation of ethics combined with a student-led presentation of teaching ethics was a more effective method of presenting ethics . . . than was a direct lecture presentation of ethics, a student-led presentation of ethics, or an attentional control group.

This sentence is a conclusion rather than an implication because it is simply a direct interpretation of the findings of the study. Notice that there is no direct reference suggesting that instructors should change the way ethics is presented in their courses. Observe that, as a conclusion, the interpretation is presented in the past tense: "demonstrated" and "was a more effective method." Later in the discussion section of this study, there is an example of an implication with a statement that the combination of lecture and discussion "is an effective method of teaching ethics to . . . students." The demarcation between conclusion (what the findings mean) and implication (what the findings might mean) is clear.

 ## LIMITATIONS OF THE STUDY

While it's safe to predict that the researchers will emphasize the significance of their findings in the last section of their research report, somewhere in the section your attention should be directed to what cannot be found because of the way the study was designed. Nobody (as far we know) has ever designed and completed the perfect study, either qualitative or quantitative. Even though your own previous analysis of the report has identified some possible problems (perhaps even more than the researchers would want to admit), the researchers themselves are expected to specifically acknowledge some limitations in their results. We think you'll agree that this is quite a lovely tradition in which researchers are expected to identify, label, and own the things they may have missed or didn't address in their study. It's sort of like asking someone who is trying to make an important point to take the counterview of things and shoot holes in his or her own case.

Limitations often focus on the specific sample used for the study. Researchers who conducted a qualitative research study, for example, might note that all of the participants came from a school located on a university campus where teachers and students might have attitudes specific to that setting. Or, quite often in quantitative studies, the researchers remind the reader that the sample was drawn from students in university classes, who may not reflect the general population.

Possible concerns about the sample are easy for the researchers to identify and thus are frequently included as limitations. But other things may be mentioned as well, including how the information was gathered. In Sapp's (1995) study, mentioned earlier, the author noted that the findings rested on the validity of the posttest and also noted that the study did not have a follow-up component, so there was no way to check whether the higher level of performance by the combined technique was maintained (see Appendix A).

In the report itself you would not expect the researchers to dwell at length on the limitations. But if no limitations are included, you are left with the possibility that the researchers either were unaware of them or thought that they were so well masked that they could be ignored. In either case, bad idea!

NEED FOR FURTHER RESEARCH

Near the end of the discussion section, expect the researchers to tell you that more research is needed on this topic. You can count on it. Researchers always tell you that more research is needed because no study will be sufficient to provide the ultimate answer.

Look for more than just the simple statement that more research is needed (this is like saying you could use a little more money). There should be specific suggestions about how those studies could be designed to complement the findings of the current study. For example, suppose a research study found a higher level of achievement in elementary school classrooms with small enrollment compared to those with larger enrollment. A prescription for additional research could include a different standard for classifying large and small classes, a comparable study done in a different district, or a different way to define achievement level. Again, this part of the discussion section will probably not be long, but some specificity should be provided.

Including suggestions for further research is one of the beautiful things about the research process: It is as if all the educational practitioners and scholars in the world (or the universe) stand together as collaborators, each of us building on the work that has been completed previously. Each of us experiments with new practices, or tests the ones already in use, notes the outcomes, and then tells the community (through publication or conference presentations) about what we discovered. Others are then able to use our efforts to continue advancing the educational knowledge base a small step forward. Each of us is a collaborator with the giants of the past, building on their ideas with the work of our own. No matter how significant our contributions, we should always end with a statement that others need to follow up what we found, to apply the concepts to other settings, to replicate our efforts to see if they were not a fluke, and to take the ideas to the next level.

TEMPLATE FOR EVALUATION

There are no hard-and-fast rules about the order in which information should be provided in the discussion section, and you will often find information about implications, limitations, and conclusions interspersed throughout this section. The *Publication Manual of the American Psychological Association* (2001) does, however, suggest that this section should open with a clear statement about how the findings relate to the overall objective of the study. For example, if the objectives were stated in the form of hypotheses, did the results indicate support or nonsupport for the beliefs that guided the study? Regardless of form, a brief summary statement about the findings can be expected to begin this section.

To evaluate the discussion section of a research report, use a checklist with these questions:

1. Is the discussion clearly written?
2. Is the discussion focused on how the findings are related to the objectives of the study?
3. Do the conclusions follow logically from the results?
4. Are implications, limitations, and recommendations for further research included?

SUMMARY AND CLOSING THOUGHTS

In both qualitative and quantitative studies, the last section in a research report serves more than one purpose. The information in this section summarizes the findings of the study and provides the opportunity for the researchers to go beyond what they found.

How the information is organized will vary, but somewhere in the last section of the report you can expect to find (1) a summary of the findings of the study, (2) the researchers' conclusions about how those findings relate to the objectives of their study, and (3) the implications of their findings. You should also find attention given to (4) limitations of the study and (5) recommendations by the researchers about what should come next.

Using a criterion of what is read most often, the last section of research reports would probably be the clear winner. Busy professionals often scan the abstract and, if interested, go directly to the section where the results are summarized. This response is easy to understand, but we urge you to be especially cautious about the risks.

For example, it would be extremely unlikely for researchers to devote time and effort to designing, conducting, and writing the report of a study, and then conclude that the findings were anything other than important (researchers are human, too). Their definitions of an important outcome might or might not agree with yours.

The choice of words used in the final section is another area of concern. We've encouraged you to be especially cautious about the word *significance* and to watch for the difference between a finding that is statistically significant—that is, a finding that is unlikely to have occurred by chance—and a finding that has some practical significance or theoretical significance. Practical significance, also referred to as clinical significance or social validation, is certainly an "eye of the beholder" phenomenon; it is up to you to make the judgment about whether the outcome of a study warrants a change in your own professional practice.

The best way to control for the possibility of researchers' overestimating the importance of their findings is simply to read the entire study. What were the questions? Who answered them and under what conditions? What exactly were the findings? At the very least, if you choose to go directly from the abstract to the final section and think you've found something important, be sure that you then go back to the details in the study before you change something in your practice based on the findings.

Finally, while these cautions are consistent with the skeptical mindset we've been encouraging throughout this book, don't forget that you're not likely to be reading any study with a completely open mind. It is much easier to find significance in a study whose findings agree with what you already thought. That's a human response. But the quality of the services we provide to others can improve only when we remain open to the possibility that some of our prior beliefs may be less than perfect. When we remain open to embracing new ideas and new practices, particularly when those changes are supported by research, we are in the best possible position to improve our professional (and personal) effectiveness.

7 Not the Last Chapter

CHAPTER OUTLINE

 ONE MORE THING

It's been a long journey, but we've finally reached a destination. Chapter 6 covered the elements needed to evaluate the final section of a published research report. The only thing left in the report is the references section and perhaps some appendixes. We now have a job for you that will help you determine the extent to which you've mastered the art of evaluation. But before you begin this task, we want to explain why we selected this particular title for a chapter that certainly appears to be the last one in the book.

Now that you are reasonably competent (even if perhaps still not completely comfortable) as a critical consumer of research, your next mission will be to try doing research yourself. You've learned to evaluate the work of others. But until you are willing—and able—to conduct your own studies, there will be limits to what you can learn.

Actually, you've probably already been a researcher all this time and just didn't know it. We feel quite certain that on some, actually many, occasions you've awakened with a decision along the lines of, "Today, I'm going to try something different in my work."

If you are an elementary school teacher, for example, this could have been something as simple as giving the weekly spelling test on Thursday rather than on Friday, or the first thing in the morning rather than just before lunch. A school administrator might decide to begin the day by informally visiting with staff in the lounge area, rather than responding to e-mail. A school psychologist or counselor might want to try completing notes immediately after each session rather than doing all of the paperwork at the end of the day.

There's a common feature in each of these examples: doing things one way, and then deciding to try another way. Whether the motivation was seeking a better solution or merely avoiding the boredom of routines, some automatic monitoring of the outcome is inevitable.

Something in your daily activities was intentionally changed. That's an *independent variable.* You observed what happened after making the change. Were the scores on the spelling test better, worse, or about the same? Did starting the day with the staff help in any way to communicate their importance? Was it easier to write good case notes when the task wasn't postponed until the end of the day? Those are *dependent variables.* And where did you get the idea in the first place? Most certainly your idea emerged as a result of something you heard or read—in other words, a *review of the literature.*

We'll freely admit that doing good research involves far more than just avoiding the mistakes you've learned to identify in the work of others. Nevertheless, while learning to evaluate research studies conducted by others, you've already mastered many of the basic skills needed to conduct your own research. With that foundation, we hope that evaluation isn't the last chapter in your research travels. Instead, our hope is that this is just a beginning point for a new journey that involves conducting your own research to enhance your professional practice.

 ## BEFORE WE LEAVE

The time has come to put into practice everything you have learned about evaluating research reports. It is one thing to read about evaluating; it is quite another to apply the skills you have learned to an actual real-life case example. We are now going to ask you to use all your new evaluative concepts and critical reading skills; in fact, we are going to ask you to do it twice.

We've included two full research reports for your review, one qualitative and one quantitative. So you won't have to keep thumbing back through the chapters to locate the evaluation templates that we have provided as guides, we've put the guides together for you here.

AN EXERCISE FOR REVIEW

Template for Evaluating the Research Report

Introduction
- ☐ Significance—Does the topic appear important to society? Is it personally relevant?
- ☐ Language—Is the presentation clear and objective? Is the language consistent with the approach used by the researchers?
- ☐ Literature Review—Is there balance in the point of view found in the citations? Is there an appropriate time frame, with some older and some more current references? Is there a coherent theme? Are primary sources emphasized?
- ☐ Research Questions—Are the questions/objectives clearly identified?
  - ☐ If the study is qualitative, are the questions/objectives supported by the literature review and/or by the data that emerged during the study?
  - ☐ If the study is qualitative, are the questions/objectives open-ended to facilitate theme exploration?
  - ☐ If the study is quantitative, are the questions/objectives limited to those with direct foundation in the literature review?

Methods
Participants
- ☐ What—Can you identify the target population?
- ☐ Who—Is sufficient detail provided about the participants to judge if they are consistent with the target?
- ☐ Where—Did the researchers identify the setting, and is that setting appropriate?
- ☐ When—Did the researchers identify the time period during which the study was conducted?
- ☐ How—Did the researchers specify how participants were selected, and did the selection procedure appear to be appropriate?
- ☐ Why—Was there explanation for why these participants were chosen, and is there reason to suggest a bias in selection that would influence the findings?

Procedures
- ☐ Completeness—Was sufficient detail provided about the procedures so that the study can be replicated?
- ☐ Appropriateness—Do the procedures appear relevant for the research questions/objectives identified for the study?

Instrumentation
- ☐ Identification—Were the tools used to gather information clearly identified?
- ☐ Quality—Do the instruments used to gather information appear appropriate and sufficient to define and describe the variables that were being studied?

Results
- ☐ Clarity—Were the findings clearly reported?
- ☐ Completeness—Were there indicators of an incomplete analysis, and, if so, was the reason explained?

Discussion
- ☐ Style—Is the discussion clearly written?
- ☐ Relevance—Is the discussion focused on how the findings are related to the objectives of the study?
- ☐ Conclusions—Do the conclusions follow logically from the results?
- ☐ Completeness—Are implications, limitations, and recommendations for further research included?

Selected Content for Evaluation

Qualitative Research Study

D'Cruz, P. (2002, September). Caregivers' experiences of informal support in the context of HIV/AIDS. *The Qualitative Report, 7*(3). Retrieved March 16, 2003, from http://www.nova.edu/ssss/QR/QR7-3/dcruz.html*

Caregivers' Experiences of Informal Support in the Context of HIV/AIDS: A Comparative Study

P. D'Cruz

Social support is an important buffer for family caregivers of people living with HIV/AIDS (PLWHIV/AIDS). With limited formal support options, these caregivers have to rely increasingly on informal networks. Yet, accessing this avenue is also fraught with difficulty due to the stigmatising nature of HIV infection.

Author Note: Premilla D'Cruz, Ph.D., has a Ph.D. in social science from the Tata Institute of Social Sciences, Mumbai, India. She currently teaches behavioural sciences at the Indian Institute of Management, Kozhikode, India. Her areas of interest include family psychology, gender studies, creativity, emotion, health studies and qualitative research methods.

She can be contacted at IIM Kozhikode, P.O. Kunnamangalam, Calicut 673 571, Kerala, India. Her e-mail addresses are Premillaruth@yahoo.com and Pdcruz@iimk.ren.nic.in.

An Exercise for Review   **151**

Research in this area is not just not sparse, but focusses largely on sources of support and the circumscribing effects of stigma. To further our understanding, a qualitative study was conducted using various concepts from social support theory. Twelve family caregivers in Mumbai, India, were interviewed, using the in-depth interview method. An iterative, thematic analysis was done through which themes and major themes were identified. Major themes included sources of support, types of support received, spontaneous support, soliciting support, caregivers' perceptions of support experiences and reciprocity. The findings raised several issues for intervention.

INTRODUCTION

An extensive body of literature underscores that providing care to an ill family member is a stressful experience for the entire family (See, for example, Baider, Cooper, & De-Nour, 1996; Chesler & Parry, 2001; Chilman, Nunally, & Cox, 1988; D'Cruz, 2002; Hilbert, Walker, & Rinehart, 2000; Kuyper & Wester, 1998; Mailick, Golden, & Walther, 1994; Northouse, Dorris, & Charron-Moore, 1995; Radina & Armer, 2001). Within the family, caregivers, who have a greater degree of involvement in the caregiving process, are subject to more adverse outcomes. These include experiences of objective and subjective burden, and detrimental effects on physical and mental health (Berg-Weger, McGartland Rubio, & Tebb, 2000). While caregiving research has disproportionately focussed on negative caregiver outcomes (D'Cruz, forthcoming), it has devoted limited attention to the role of social support in buffering them (Jankowski, Videka-Sherman, & Laquidara-Dickinson, 1996). Studying this aspect is of significance because social support has been shown to be positively related to good health. It is associated with better health outcomes, better coping and less negative effects of stress (Cohen & Syme, 1985).

Explorations of this aspect of caregiver experiences are particularly relevant in the context of HIV/AIDS. The progressive, long-drawn and terminal nature of the infection compound the stress engendered by the caregiving role but the stigmatising nature of the virus circumscribes caregivers from seeking and receiving much needed support. Indeed, the limited research available in the West provides evidence of this. For example, Jankowski et al. (1996), in a study of male and female confidants of PLWHIV/AIDS, reported confidants' networks to be constricted in contact and size. Confidants had diminished "weak social ties", namely, those with acquaintances, co-workers and neighbours, and relied primarily on "strong social ties" with family members and close friends. While limiting contacts resulted in fewer questions and lower likelihood of having to divulge the diagnosis, using misrepresentations of the diagnosis such as maintaining a veil of pretense or a diagnostic charade, though an important means of coping, made interaction more stressful and reduced the support available. Confidants reported that having at least one person with whom they could share the truth served as a safety valve for their emotional burdens. Yet, disclosure of diagnosis resulted in outright rejection in several cases. Moreover, where confidants provided care to PLWHIV/AIDS, the ensuing time constraints resulted in less social interaction and hence, less support. In these various circumstances, professionals played an especially important role in providing support.

Poindexter and Linsk's (1998) study of older, female, African-American caregivers pointed out that while respondents experienced reciprocal support from their care receivers as well as support from spiritual sources, external support came largely from relatives. Friends were rarely resorted to, partially due to the experience of discrimination and ostracism following disclosure of the HIV diagnosis, and partially because respondents did not wish to disclose their HIV caregiving to persons outside the family. Though they manifested the need for additional social interaction and support, respondents felt that they could not trust anyone to receive the truth and power of their stories. With their choices for accessing the external support limited, they could not enjoy the stress buffering effects of social support and were losing their community at the most trying and painful times of their lives.

Poindexter and Linsk's other (1999) study of a similar population found that because of the anticipation of HIV related stigma, caregivers of HIV positive individuals did not widely disclose the HIV diagnosis, if at all. Consequently, they neither experienced overt HIV related stigma nor received support that acknowledged their struggles as HIV affected caregivers. The study reported that although church participation and spirituality were important sources of social support for the respondents, they varied in their disclosure patterns to churches. While eleven of those who attended church had disclosed to no one in their churches, two had told only the pastor, and another two had told the pastor and a few church members. There were two others who had gone public in their churches, but their disclosures were received with different responses—one noticed no ramifications, and one was disappointed that none of the church members provided support.

While the aforementioned studies provide valuable insights into caregiver experiences of social support in the context of HIV/AIDS, a closer look at them from the point of view of social support theory highlights their limited foci. That is, these studies examined sources of support, and the circumscribing effects of stigma on support seeking and the consequent loneliness. But social support is a multidimensional concept and its study must necessarily touch upon aspects such as solicited versus spontaneous support, types of support solicited versus those received, positive versus negative support, actual versus perceived support, and reciprocity (See, for example, Boyce, Kay, & Uitti, 1988; Cohen & Syme, 1985; Cooke, Rossmann, McCubbin, & Patterson, 1988; Erickson, 1989; House & Kahn, 1985; Revenson, Schiaffino, Majerovitz, & Gibofsky, 1991; Sherbourne & Stewart, 1991; Unden & Orth-Gomer, 1989; Williams, 1993). Moreover, in the case of HIV/AIDS, an exploration of the process of accessing support and its relationship with disclosure is also relevant. With these objectives in mind, a study of caregiver experiences with the informal support system in the context of HIV/AIDS, was undertaken in Mumbai, India.

METHOD

Design

The study adopted the qualitative approach. A phenomenological orientation was incorporated since the objectives were to explore subjective meanings and experiences from the respondents' points of view. In-depth interviews were employed as the method of data collection, and in order to facilitate this process, an interview guide was developed (See appendix). Observations made during the course of the interview were recorded.

Sample

Public, private and voluntary health sector organisations working in the field of HIV/AIDS in the city of Mumbai, India, were contacted for the study. The researcher knew about these organisations either because of her personal contacts with the organisations themselves or with people who knew them; or because she had heard about their work from other professionals or the media. Agreement of these organisations to assist the researcher was on a voluntary basis. Respondents from these organisations were chosen through purposive sampling (Morse, 1991). Caregivers with past or present experience of caring for male and/or female positive people, infected through the sexual and/or parenteral modes, who had moved beyond the asymptomatic stage and who had shared their serostatus with the caregiver were included in the study, regardless of whether the caregiver-care receiver relationship was based on blood or marital ties or whether the familial form was traditional or not (See Macklin, 1987, for a discussion on forms of family). Co-residence of the caregiver and care receiver was not a necessary criterion for participation.

Of the 12 caregivers who participated in the study, 7 (6 women and 1 man) were seropositive caregivers and 5 (2 men and 3 women) were negative. Their ages ranged from 27 to 60 years, and all but 1 caregiver resided with their care receivers. Six positive caregivers and 4 negative caregivers cared for one positive person. Of these, 6 looked after a spouse who had passed away before the study; 2, their sons; 1, a brother; and 1 was an adopted daughter who was deceased at the time of data collection. One male positive caregiver had cared for his positive mother-in-law and positive wife (both of whom had died prior to the interviews) and was currently caring for his positive son, while one negative male caregiver was looking after his positive father and positive brother. Six caregivers belonged to the lower income group (Table 1).

Table 1
Socio-demographic Profile of Respondents

	Gender	Age	Serostatus	Class	Number of care receivers	Co-residence with care receiver(s)	Relationship with care receiver(s)
1	Female	27	Positive	Lower middle	1	Yes	Wife
2	Female	36	Positive	Lower middle	1	Yes	Wife
3	Female	40	Positive	Lower	1	Yes	Wife
4	Female	30	Positive	Lower	1	Yes	Wife
5	Female	38	Positive	Lower	1	Yes	Wife
6	Female	33	Positive	Lower	1	Yes	Wife
7	Male	37	Positive	Lower	3	Yes	Husband Son-in-law Father
8	Female	40	Negative	Middle	1	Yes	Mother
9	Female	60	Negative	Upper	1	Yes	Mother
10	Female	55	Negative	Lower	1	Yes	Adopted mother Father
11	Male	36	Negative	Upper	2	Yes	Brother
12	Male	33	Negative	Lower middle	1	No	Brother

Procedure

In keeping with ethical considerations in HIV research, the researcher did not approach potential participants directly. Instead, the staff of the organisations from where the sample was being drawn identified respondents who matched the specified criteria and introduced the idea, and explained the purpose of, the research to them. Only after they agreed and were comfortable enough, the researcher was introduced to them. Following rapport building and soliciting their co-operation, respondents signed a consent form, informing them of details of the study and their rights as participants. These included voluntary and informed participation, freedom to withdraw at any point of time without giving any explanation, and confidentiality. They decided the location of the interview, as also the possibility of tape-recording the interviews. Nine respondents were interviewed in the organisation premises while 3 were interviewed in their homes. Seven respondents consented to tape recording the interviews while for the remaining five, the researcher maintained detailed notes. While interviews were conducted in Hindi, the national language (7 respondents), Marathi, the regional language (3 respondents) and English (2 respondents), all notes were kept in English. Thus, interviews recorded on audio cassettes were translated into English during transcription and those which were kept as field notes were also written in English. There were 3 interview sessions with 1 caregiver, 2 sessions with 6 caregivers and 1 session with 5 caregivers.

Interviews were informant directed in that they started at points which respondents wished to discuss. Nonetheless, they covered the various areas of the interview guide as well as explored issues emerging from the data. Probes and prompts were used judiciously thereby allowing an open-ended interview structure to be maintained.

Data Analysis

During the period of data collection, the researcher read the transcripts and field notes carefully and repeatedly, 'immersing' herself in the data (Crabtree & Miller, 1992). Immersion allowed the researcher to identify themes, categories and patterns emerging from the data (Marshall & Rossman, 1999). This process was facilitated through the use of various tools such as charts, matrices, event lists, causal networks and memos (Miles & Huberman, 1994). Linkages, if any, with social support theory were made at this juncture. Miles and Huberman's (1994) tools were then used to examine the linkages between themes, patterns and categories and thereby initiate interpretation (Patton, 1990). Proceeding in this manner, she developed various understandings (such as concepts, causal linkages, processes, and so on) of the phenomena under study. These understandings were used to inform further data collection, through which they were tested and challenged. Based on newer data, they were further developed, thereby feeding back into the analysis (Marshall & Rossman, 1999). Iteration thus formed an integral part of the research process.

When all the data were collected, the researcher immersed herself further in the transcripts and the preliminary findings. Through the use of Miles and Huberman's tools and memoing, she not only identified more patterns, themes and categories in the data and [looked] for interpretations at this level, but also subsumed under major themes, those themes, patterns and categories and their linkages within and across respondents that held together in a meaningful yet distinct way (Guba, 1978). Interpretations based on this level of analysis were made.

Methodological rigour was maintained through prolonged engagement (Lincoln & Guba, 1985), and consensual validation (Eisner, 1991)/peer debriefing (Lincoln & Guba, 1999). Prolonged engagement led the researcher to spend a lot of time in the organisations where the data were collected. This gave her a chance to observe patients accessing services from there and to discuss her observations with the staff. Particular importance was given to rapport building with the respondents—it was opined that making the respondents feel comfortable and establishing their trust would play a critical role in helping them to share their stories. During the course of the interview, the researcher used probes and cross-checks to better her understanding of respondents' narratives. Immersion in the data during the process of analysis helped the researcher gain insight into respondent experiences and ensure the rigour of the findings. For peer debriefing and consensual validation, the researcher shared her analysis procedures and outcomes with academicians and practitioners. Academicians working in the areas of HIV/AIDS, family care and qualitative research methods as well as practitioners working in the field of HIV/AIDS care and support reviewed the researcher's methods, interpretations and findings, providing critical evaluations, suggestions and feedback. The incorporation of their inputs strengthened the analysis. This process continued till most, if not all, the academicians and practitioners agreed on the analysis and its outcomes.

It is important to note that social support theory partially guided the formulation of the interview guide so that the researcher could holistically explore all aspects of social support, as subjectively experienced by the respondents. But data collection was in no way limited by theory and the in-depth nature of the interview ensured that the understanding of social support was furthered through respondent narratives. In keeping with the phenomenological tradition, the experiences of the researcher were not allowed to interfere with the inquiry—the researcher suspended her own points of view (Creswell, 1998) allowing respondent perspectives to prevail. During the analysis, respondents' narratives were examined for themes, patterns and categories, and if these related to existing social support theory/concepts, they were used to deepen knowledge of the same. Other findings emerging from the data were used to expand the understanding of social support.

FINDINGS

Sources of Support

Caregivers defined the informal support system as close relationships from which they derived social support. As a group, caregivers' informal support network comprised the extended family/relatives and friends, though the composition of individual caregiver support systems varied. A support system comprising only extended family/relatives was described by 5 caregivers, whereas 6 caregivers spoke of extended family/relatives and friends constituting their supporters. Among these, 2 specified that their friends included religious people, and 1 included religious leaders and professional colleagues. One caregiver had only friends as her support network.

Types of Support Received

Caregiver descriptions of the kind of support received pointed out to seven broad categories. These included emotional support (11), material support (9), financial support (8), medical support (1), informational support (2), network support (3), and physical support in the execution of caregiving tasks (4).

Spontaneous Support

Eight respondents reported that all or some of the members of their informal support systems responded to their observable needs.

> "I have not told my (natal) family about his (my son's) HIV, nor have I asked them for help. But they know how hard things are for us. They know that he has thalassemia, that he is not keeping well of late. They know that we are not well off, and that now we have lots of tension and problems because of money, his health, and so on. So on their own, they help us."

This was even though in some cases, the support system did not know the care receivers' serostatus. There were a few instances where spontaneous support was given only for a limited period of time, either because the support system was unable to help out for a longer duration or because knowledge of care receivers' serostatus made the support system withdraw.

Respondents perceived the spontaneous support as reassuring, but at the same time, mentioned that since it was based on observation alone, it could not fulfil all their needs.

Soliciting Support

Soliciting support involved behavioural and affective dimensions. Behaviourally, caregivers described a process involving a series of complex decisions that they made, contingent on their circumstances, while affectively, numerous competing feelings were reported.

The Behavioural Dimension.   Accessing support from the informal support system was an easy, taken for granted process prior to the knowledge of the care receiver's seropositive diagnosis. Caregivers would frequently approach their relatives and/or friends for assistance as and when required, being inhibited only by a desire not to trouble others and a feeling of shame to be dependent. Knowledge of the infected family member's HIV diagnosis, however, because of its stigmatising nature, changed their approach.

When support was required after the HIV infected person's serostatus was diagnosed and the support system was not aware of the diagnosis, the decision to solicit support did not come easily. Deep deliberation and careful thinking preceded the decision. Caregivers meticulously weighed the pros and cons of whether they should seek out help. Firstly, they evaluated their need to see if it demanded immediate attention or could be postponed. In other words, they were willing to put off attending to their needs until they became absolutely unavoidable. Once this was resolved, then based on what they actually needed, they considered possible sources of support. Of these, they shortlisted those who were in the best position to help them out and from whom they were comfortable receiving support. The next thing to decide upon was whether support seeking should involve disclosure of the seropositive diagnosis or not. Depending on the need and/or who they were accessing support from, caregivers decided what exactly they should tell and whether they should disclose their care receiver's seropositive status during the process of accessing. More than anything else, the need they were seeking to satisfy dictated the necessity for disclosure. Some needs necessitated the disclosure of the care receiver's HIV status and caregivers had no choice but to comply.

"We (my wife and I) were looking for a place where we could keep him (the positive care receiving brother) till his TB (tuberculosis) subsided. We felt that though HIV does not spread, TB does and since our children are small and the house is tiny, if he lives with us, they may get it. But we knew of no such place, so we decided to contact Father _____ (a priest known to the family) and Sister _____ (a nun known to the family), as they were the only ones who could help us. And since we were looking for something specific, we had to tell them that he had HIV. Even to tell them we felt bad. But what to do? That way they are such great people, we knew that they would never turn against us and they did not. Of course not. That is why we did not mind approaching them, but still we felt bad."

Where the need was not so specific and could be fulfilled by a number of persons, a different process operated. If families could trust the person from whom they were seeking support with the secrecy of the diagnosis and be sure that he/she would help them without being judgmental, soliciting support was accompanied by disclosure, even if it was not needed or asked for and could have been avoided. If, on the other hand, they were not sure how the person would react, they would cover up their need for support with a plausible excuse, refusing to take the risk of being truthful. A process of discerning was thus apparent.

"See, I will approach those who I will benefit from. And I will ask them for help. Now whether I tell them the diagnosis or not, depends. My family will help in looking after, but I will not tell them the diagnosis because they will collapse, they may refuse to care. But I'll tell them such that they will take precautions. With my professional friends, I can rely on them for medical and emotional support, and they will keep it confidential. So I can tell them the diagnosis. With my religious friends, I go for emotional support and I'll tell them it is a deadly illness. That would suffice."

Reluctance to solicit support and fear to disclose the care receiving family member's HIV seropositivity were very clearly seen even in instances where the care receiver was said to be "innocently" infected and was not seen as personally responsible for acquiring the HIV infection. One caregiver, looking after a thalassemic seropositive adolescent who had been parenterally infected through blood transfusions, was hesitant to access support from the support network and did not see disclosure as an option.

"We (my husband and I) have not told anyone, except household members, about his HIV infection. Even our extended family members do not know. People may or may not understand, you never know. And if we tell and by chance, it slips from their mouths to others, then our entire community will come to know, and not everyone will be good and understanding. Even though he has been infected due to a blood transfusion, and everyone knows he is a thalassemic, once they are told he has this AIDS, one never knows how people's minds will work—they may just insist that he has done something wrong and then reject us. So instead of having that tension, it is better to keep it to ourselves and manage on our own. Of course, I feel it—the loneliness and pain are so acute, it would be a relief to share them. But the risk always remains, so we feel it is better to stay silent. What I tell you so easily and in the process, experience so much relief, I cannot tell anyone."

Another caregiver, a doctor whose HIV positive father had been infected through infected intravenous (IV) equipment, decided that soliciting support and disclosure of his father's serostatus would be only with his medical friends whom he was sure would understand and could be counted upon to support and maintain confidentiality.

The Affective Dimension.   Caregivers reported that soliciting support was accompanied by a plethora of feelings. Besides feeling bad that they were in a position of dependency where they needed support and could not manage on their own, they approached their support system with both the hope of things improving and with the fear of being rejected, and if there was disclosure of the care receiver's HIV status, then the fear of the information being spread, and of inviting stigma and isolation. There was also a feeling of helplessness and lack of choice that led one to seek out the support in the first place. Shame, humility and hope thus coexisted.

The emotional turmoil that accompanied the decision to, and the process of, accessing support got exacerbated when these requests were met with refusal. Caregivers received these negative responses with great disappointment and a sense of rejection, compounding their feeling of isolation.

> "I went to the village with such hope. I felt that his (my husband's) brothers (who were there) would do something for us. Here (in the city), there was no one to help and I had to see to him, the children and the house. So we felt it was better to go there to them. But they did not help. They said, 'We have no money, we have our own families, so we cannot help you.' But I did not need money. Basically, it was because of AIDS that they did not wish to come near. So they did not help. My brothers saw to us. I felt very, very bad, but if they did not wish to help, but what can be done?"

Such feelings were true even in cases where the refusal came from only a part of the support network, while the rest continued to support. Moreover, the intensity of the feelings multiplied when soliciting support involved disclosure of the care receiving family member's HIV positive status, and the support system, in addition to refusing to help, spread the serostatus within the social network. The caregiver not only had to cope with less support than desired, but also with the negative reactions of the social network.

> "His (my husband's) brothers refused to help. But as if that was not bad enough, they told everyone. So people would not come near. They told the doctors, so they refused to treat. They would not touch or examine him. I felt totally alone and helpless. At least my brothers stood by me."

Yet, the decision not to access support and/or to maintain the secrecy of the care receiver's serostatus from the informal support system precipitated acute loneliness in caregivers. This feeling of loneliness coexisted with the receipt of spontaneous support, because such support could address only their observable needs, leaving the rest unfulfilled.

Overall, all caregivers reported receiving some support, either spontaneous and/or solicited, from at least a part of their support system, for at least some period of time.

> "I told my (natal) family that we had AIDS. They understood what it meant but still, they behaved with us as before and they helped us out as before. If they saw that we needed help, they would at once respond. Or if I asked them, they never refused."

Caregiver Perceptions of Support Experiences

Caregiver perceptions of their experiences with their informal support networks varied along a continuum of satisfaction-dissatisfaction, and were based on three factors, namely, the content of support, the extent to which their needs were met and their perceptions of the availability of support.

The content of support referred to the presence of positive and negative components. Fulfillment of needs moved through various degrees, from complete fulfillment to no fulfillment at all. The perception of the availability of support was linked to the willingness and ability (in terms of time, resources, geographical proximity/distance, and so on) of the support system to support.

At one extreme were 2 highly satisfied caregivers receiving positive support that fulfilled many of their needs and was perceived as easily available.

> "With her (my sister) by my side, I needed no one else. She went out of her way to help, and never once a mean or hurtful word . . . no reproach or taunts . . . Her behaviour was such that I knew that she was there, I only had to ask for what I wanted, and she would never hesitate or hold back. It was like . . . guaranteed."

At the other end of the continuum were 2 caregivers who were deeply dissatisfied. Though their support networks were geographically proximate and capable of helping, their reluctance to do so led caregivers to feel that support was only somewhat available. Support system reluctance arose from their anger towards the HIV infected individuals for their lifestyles and for inviting problems into the family, and from their negative perceptions of HIV infection and not from a lack of resources. Moreover, since support often was inadequate and inappropriate, it failed to meet the needs of caregivers and left a feeling of dissatisfaction. One elderly mother looking after a seropositive son in a joint household where her other son and his wife controlled family resources stated:

> "She (my other son's wife) is so angry with him (my seropositive son) for getting this AIDS that, though they (my other son and his wife) have enough money, she just refuses to give me anything much to spend for him. Instead, when I ask, she keeps grumbling that they have to do . . . and gives me the bare minimum. It becomes really difficult for me to look after him with this kind of an attitude but what to do?"

Between these two extremes lay two sets of caregivers. In one group were caregivers in receipt of only positive support that fulfilled many of their needs and was seen as somewhat available. A satisfied feeling was apparent.

> "Sister _____ (a nun) and Father _____ (a priest) have done alot for us (my family and my positive brother)—whenever we need something, whatever they can do, they do. And they never make us feel bad about it, they never point out that they are doing so much for us. But finally, how much can one expect—they have to help others too, so we ask only when there is no other alternative."

In the other group, four caregivers expressed mixed feelings where both satisfaction and dissatisfaction coexisted. In one case, the caregiver was receiving positive support from one part of her support system, which was perceived as somewhat available and as meeting some of her needs. She was happy with this. But the other part of the support system refused to support her and evoked dissatisfaction in her.

In another instance, a female seropositive caregiver who had looked after her seropositive husband had received high levels of positive support from her natal family. She knew that despite their limited resources, if ever she needed anything, she only had to ask them and they would do their best for her. The support that she received helped her satisfy many of her needs. Yet she felt that her natal family should have done more for her. Thus, though she praised all that they had done for her and acknowledged their constraints, dissatisfaction was also concomitant.

> "My people (natal family) supported us a lot when he (seropositive husband) was alive—they used to come, inquire if I needed anything, or I would phone and tell them . . . money, food, coming to the hospital, looking after _____ (child), everything . . . so much they have done . . . even when he died, my people saw to everything. They have their own families, their own homes and jobs, and we are not well off people, but still, they always accommodated my needs. Yet, I feel that they should have been with me more—I used to be by myself in the hospital, they would come for a few hours only. When he was admitted near by, I had to go to their place to pick up the food and all, for every meal. I feel that they should have come with it. But how I can tell them— they should understand on their own, right? After all, they could see that I was all by myself . . . I am ill too—so they should come over here more often. If people are really around one, one feels much better . . . And how can I keep asking them? I feel that they know my condition, so they should do on their own. If I ask, they will surely do. But why should I ask? . . . naturally I feel so alone."

This woman also reported anger over the indifference of her in-laws.

> "And those people (in-laws) even after knowing that he (husband) was so ill, didn't ask a single word. Once they knew he had this illness, they hardly came and never, ever bothered. Their own son . . . but they did not care at all. Everything was left to me. Don't even speak to me about them—they fill me with such fury."

Reciprocity

Negative feelings associated with being in a position of dependency led caregivers' need, and ability, to reciprocate taking on greater significance, in an attempt to compensate for their predicament. Yet given their meagre economic resources and role overload, most caregivers (8) could reciprocate only emotionally.

> "I want to give her (my sister) back something in return, for all that she has done for me. After all, how much can one keep taking from others—it is not a nice feeling— one should give also. But I have nothing so all I can do is show her my concern and affection."

Reciprocating in tangible terms, either through role performance or provision of economic resources, was possible only for four caregivers.

> "My (natal) family has helped me out alot, given us so much. When he (my husband) was ill, and before that also. But we were never able to repay them, because we had absolutely nothing. Now at least (after his death), with his provident fund/PF and my earnings, I have paid off the debts and I can think of giving them something. In fact, I definitely will, because they have done so much, and I feel so ashamed that we used to keep taking, taking, asking, asking, without giving back."

Nonetheless, being able to give back even a little bit, in whatever form, restored some sense of dignity in caregivers.

> "Even though I can give her (my sister) only my concern and affection, it makes a difference. At least, I am giving something back, and not only taking. So I feel good about it. By showing her my concern and appreciation, I ease her strain. She also feels that I am thinking of her, and not just selfishly taking from her all the time."

IMPLICATIONS

In this age of structural adjustment, decreased social welfare and reductions in health sector allocations, community care has become the watchword for secondary and tertiary health care interventions (Duggal, 1998). But community care is a mere euphemism for family care (McCann & Wadsworth, 1992). In HIV/AIDS, these policies are promoted by the adoption of the continuum of care model as the globally recognised and recommended ideal form of intervention to deal with the infection (See Global Programme on AIDS/GPA, 1995). The result is that family caregivers have to bear the bulk of the responsibility for the care and support needs of their sick members, experiencing considerable burden and adverse health effects in the process (See D'Cruz, 1998, 2000). That caregivers need support to cope with the demands and outcomes of their role requires no reiteration. But contemporary policies have left very limited options from formal sources and have augmented the roles and responsibilities of the informal support system. Unfortunately, the study of caregiver support in relation to informal networks has remained a largely unexplored area. To this end, the present study has extended our understanding in the context of HIV/AIDS.

The findings have implications for intervention. First, they underscore the necessity for the development of various caregiver services. These include counselling services, the provision of material and financial assistance, support groups and respite care services. In the case of an infection like HIV/AIDS, such services assume significance because the stigmatising nature of the infection limits support seeking from informal sources and consequently, caregivers are left to fend for themselves. At the same time, the extent to which these needs would be taken cognisance of and responded to remains questionable in the light of structural adjustment policies, cutbacks in health sector expenditure and reduced social welfare. Nonetheless, their relevance should not be overlooked.

Second, the findings of this study suggest the importance for members of the informal support system to be educated about and sensitised to HIV/AIDS. Such endeavours could incorporate a two-pronged strategy. They could provide knowledge about the infection, thereby dispelling myths and misconceptions; and also descriptions of its demands and impact, thereby bringing home the predicament of the caregiver. With this information, members of support systems would be less likely to withdraw from the caregiver and to provide negative support, but instead would be more likely to rally around him or her.

Finally, the study points out to the urgency with which public awareness about HIV/AIDS should be created. Building up awareness would have two advantages. Firstly, the community would be sensitised to the experiences of caregivers and instead of discriminating against them, they would reach out to them. Inappropriate support would also be eliminated. Secondly, caregivers, being reassured of an understanding response, would come forward and seek support.

References

Baider, L., Cooper, C. L., & De-Nour, A. K. (1996). *Cancer and the family.* Chichester: John Wiley.

Berg-Weger, M., McGartland Rubio, D., & Tebb, S. S. (2000). Depression as a mediator: Viewing caregiver well-being and strain in a different light. *Families in Society, 8,* 162–173.

Boyce, W. T., Kay, M., & Uitti, C. (1988). The taxonomy of social support: An ethnographic analysis among adolescent mothers. *Social Science and Medicine, 26,* 1079–1085.

Chesler, M. A., & Parry, C. (2001). Gender roles and/or styles in crisis: An integrative analysis of the experiences of fathers of children with cancer. *Qualitative Health Research, 11,* 363–384.

Chilman, C. S., Nunally, E. W., & Cox, F. M. (1988). *Chronic illness and disability.* Newbury Park, CA: Sage.

Cohen, S., & Syme, S. K. (1985). *Social support and health.* Orlando: Academic Press.

Cooke, B. D., Rossmann, M. M., McCubbin, H. I., & Patterson, J. M. (1988). Examining the definition and assessment of social support: A resource of individuals and families. *Family Relations, 37,* 211–216.

Crabtree, B. F., & Miller, W. L. (1992). *Doing qualitative research: Multiple strategies.* Newbury Park, CA: Sage.

Creswell, J. W. (1998). *Qualitative inquiry and research design: Choosing among five traditions.* Thousand Oaks, CA: Sage.

D'Cruz, P. (1998). *The family context of a terminal illness: The case of HIV/AIDS.* Unpublished M.Phil. dissertation. Mumbai: Tata Institute of Social Sciences (TISS).

D'Cruz, P. (2000). *Family care in HIV/AIDS and its interface with support systems.* Unpublished doctoral dissertation. Mumbai: Tata Institute of Social Sciences (TISS).

D'Cruz, P. (2002). Engulfing darkness: The impact of HIV AIDS on the family. *Families in Society, 83,* 416–430.

D'Cruz, P. (forthcoming). Family caregiving revisited. *Radical Journal of Health (New Series).*

Duggal R. (1998). Health care as human right. *Radical Journal of Health (New Series), 3,* 141–142.

Eisner, E.W. (1991). *The enlightened eye.* New York: Macmillan.

Erickson, C.A. (1989). Negative perceptions of social support: Satisfaction with support from family versus friends. *Family Perspective, 23,* 85–97.

Global Programme on AIDS/GPA. (1995). *1992–93 Progress report: Global programme on AIDS.* Geneva: World Health Organisation (WHO).

Guba, E. (1978). *Toward a methodology of naturalistic inquiry in educational evaluation.* Los Angeles: University of California, Los Angeles (UCLA), Centre for the Study of Evaluation.

Hilbert, G. A., Walker, M. B., & Rinehart, J. (2000). In the long haul: Responses of parents caring for children with Sturge-Weber syndrome. *Journal of Family Nursing, 6,* 157–179.

House, J. S., & Kahn, R. L. (1985). Measures and concept of social support. In S. Cohen & S. L. Syme (Eds.), *Social support and health* (pp. 83–108). San Diego, CA: Academic Press.

Jankowski, S., Videka-Sherman, L., & Laquidara-Dickinson, K. (1996). Social support networks of confidants to people with AIDS. *Social Work, 41,* 206–213.

Kuyper, M. B., & Wester, F. (1998). In the shadow: The impact of chronic illness on the patient's partner. *Qualitative Health Research, 8,* 237–253.

Lincoln, Y., & Guba, E. (1985). *Naturalistic inquiry.* Newbury Park, CA: Sage.

Lincoln, Y., & Guba, E. (1999). Establishing trustworthiness. In A. Bryman & R. G. Burgess (Eds.), *Qualitative research* (Vol. 3) (pp. 397–444). Thousand Oaks, CA: Sage.

Macklin, E. (1987). Non-traditional family forms. In M. B. Sussman & S. K. Steinmetz (Eds.), *Handbook of marriage and the family* (pp. 317–353). New York: Plenum.

Mailick, M. D., Holden, G., & Walther, V. N. (1994). Coping with childhood asthma. *Health and Social Work, 19*, 103–111.

Marshall, C., & Rossman, G. B. (1999). *Designing qualitative research.* Thousand Oaks, CA: Sage.

McCann, K., & Wadsworth, E. (1992). The role of informal carers in supporting gay men who have HIV-related illness: What do they do and what are their needs? *AIDS Care, 4,* 25–34.

Miles, M. S., & Huberman, A. M. (1994). *Qualitative data analysis: A sourcebook of new methods.* Thousand Oaks, CA: Sage.

Morse, J. M. (1991). Strategies for sampling. In J. M. Morse (Ed.), *Qualitative nursing research* (pp. 127–145). Thousand Oaks, CA: Sage.

Northouse, L. L., Dorris, G., Charron-Moore, C. (1995). Factors affecting couples' adjustment to recurrent breast cancer. *Social Science and Medicine, 41,* 69–76.

Patton, M. Q. (1990). *Qualitative evaluation and research methods.* Newbury Park, CA: Sage.

Poindexter, C. C., & Linsk, N. L. (1998). Sources of support in a sample of HIV-affected older minority caregivers. *Families in Society, 79,* 491–503.

Poindexter, C. C., & Linsk, N.L. (1999). HIV-related stigma in a sample of HIV-affected older female African-American caregivers. *Social Work, 44,* 46–61.

Radina, M. E., & Armer, J. M. (2001). Post-breast cancer lymphedema and the family. *Journal of Family Nursing, 7,* 281–299.

Revenson, T. A., Schiaffino, K. M., Majerovitz, S. D., & Gibofsky, A. (1991). Social support as a double-edged sword: The relation of positive and problematic support to depression among rheumatoid arthritis patients. *Social Science and Medicine, 33,* 807–813.

Sherbourne, C. D., & Stewart, A. L. (1991). The MOS (medical outcomes study) social support survey. *Social Science and Medicine, 32,* 750–714 [*sic*].

Unden, A. L., & Orth-Gomer, K. (1989). Development of a social support instrument for use in population surveys. *Social Science and Medicine, 29,* 1387–1392.

Williams, H. A. (1993). A comparison of social support and social networks of black parents and white parents with chronically ill children. *Social Science and Medicine, 37,* 1509–1520.

APPENDIX
INTERVIEW GUIDE

Sociodemographic profile of respondent:
Gender
Age
Household income per month
Serostatus
Number of care receivers
Relationship with care receivers
Co-residence with care receivers

1. Composition of the caregiver's informal social support system.
2. Caregiver perception of the availability of social support.
3. Types of social support received by caregiver.
4. Caregiver opinion on manner in which social support is given.
5. Caregiver evaluation of social support received. Impact of social support on caregiver's life.
6. Process by which caregiver seeks social support and its relationship with disclosure of care receiver's serostatus.
7. Caregiver's reciprocity to the informal social support system.

Quantitative Research Study

Lemieux, P., McKelvie, S. J., & Stout, D. (2002, December). Self-reported hostile aggression in contact athletes, no contact athletes, and non-athletes. *Athletic Insight—The Online Journal of Sport Psychology*, 4(3). Retrieved March 16, 2003, from http://www.athleticinsight.com/Vol4Iss3/SelfReported Aggression.htm*

Self-Reported Hostile Aggression in Contact Athletes, No Contact Athletes, and Non-Athletes
A Comparative Study

P. Lemieux, S. J. McKelvie, and D. Stout

To investigate the relationship between athletic participation and off-field hostile aggression, Buss and Perry's (1992) Aggression Questionnaire (AQ) was completed by two groups of 86 university athletes in either contact or no contact sports and two control groups of 86 non-athletes who were matched to the athletes in physical size. In general, bigger participants scored higher on hostile aggression and reported more fighting than smaller participants, but athletes and non-athletes did not differ. These results contradict the learning and catharsis theories of aggression in sport, and undermine the media image of the belligerent off-field athlete.

INTRODUCTION

Theoretical Considerations

Vigorous athletic activity can be classified as assertive behavior, instrumental aggression, or hostile aggression[1] (Tenenbaum, Stewart, Singer, & Duda, 1997; Wann, 1997). In assertive behavior, the player employs legitimate force within game rules. In instrumental aggression, the player tries to inflict physical damage as a step towards the higher goal of winning. In hostile aggression, the player is angry and primarily bent on physically harming an opponent. Although such behaviors have been linked to team success (Caron, Halteman, & Stacy, 1997; Huang, Cherek, & Lane, 1999), hostile aggression is particularly controversial. It is not clear if it improves performance by increasing arousal to an optimal level or causes it to deteriorate by distracting the player from the task at hand (Cox, 2002).

Because hostile aggression involves physical harm (Buss & Perry, 1992), it is likely to be more frequent in contact than in no contact sports. Contact sports may attract people who are already aggressive or engaging in contact sports may

---

Author Note: Send correspondence to Stuart J. McKelvie, Department of Psychology, Bishop's University, Lennoxville, Québec J1M 1Z7.

[1]Recently, the dichotomy between hostile and instrumental aggression has been questioned by Bushman and Anderson (2001), who argue that it is confounded with automatic-controlled processing and does not take account of aggression stemming from more than one motive. However, the framework is retained here, because the focus was on physical aggression with angry/hostile feelings, which is captured by the concept of hostile aggression.

promote aggression (the selection and developmental hypotheses respectively, Cox, 2002). Furthermore, and of particular concern, hostile aggression may occur not only on but also off the field, where it has consequences for everyday life. Indeed, according to *social learning theory* (Bandura, 1973), aggressive behavior can occur via modeling the behavior of others or even oneself. In the latter case, it has a circular effect, one act of aggression leading to another. Applying this reasoning to sport, contact sport athletes may be more aggressive off the field than no contact sports athletes because their actions on the field have a cumulative effect. Furthermore, aggression is often rewarded in contact sport, increasing its frequency on the field and making it more likely in other situations (Zillman, Johnson, & Day, 1974). As Bandura (1973, p. 59) puts it: "A culture can produce highly aggressive people . . . by valuing aggressive accomplishment, furnishing successful models, and ensuring that aggressive actions secure rewarding effects." A similar view has been expressed by the Seville Statement on Violence (1986), which argues that aggression is not genetically programmed but is largely a function of cultural factors. This statement refers to aggression in general, and therefore outside sport, but similar sentiments have been expressed about aggression inside sport [Tenenbaum et al.'s (1997) ISSP Position Statement on Aggression and Violence]. Contact sports such as football and rugby are thought to be particularly likely to provoke aggression off the field (Arnold, 2001).

The idea that aggression breeds aggression is also part of *cognitive neoassociation theory,* according to which venting of aggression activates aggressive thoughts and primes angry feelings, thereby increasing the possibility of further aggressive behavior (Bushman, 2002). This theory is related to the classic *frustration-aggression hypothesis* as modified by Berkowitz (Wann, 1997). Inability to attain a goal leads to frustration with triggers an aggressive drive [*sic*], and the likelihood of aggressive behavior is enhanced by cues in the environment. Contact sports are particularly likely to provoke aggression because they provide many aggressive cues.

Although athletes in contact sports may display more off-field hostile aggression than no contact athletes and non-athletes, there is also a popular belief that vigorous sporting activity is healthy because it allows participants to "let off steam" in acceptable ways, thereby *decreasing* aggressiveness in everyday life. In other words, sports participation serves a protective function. (Bushman, Baumeister, & Stack, 1999). This is *catharsis theory,* according to which aggression is a basic instinctive drive that builds up and must be released directly in behavior (Bushman, et al., 1999, Cox, 2002). Catharsis theory actually comes in two forms (Zillman, et al., 1974). In *the motor-discharge model, any* vigorous activity releases pent-up aggression. In *displacement theory,* the activity must consist of hostile or perhaps instrumental aggression. Officials in the National Hockey League seem to endorse this notion (Jones, Stewart, & Sunderman, 1996), holding that violence on the ice is acceptable because it permits the cathartic release of frustrations brought on by the game itself. Similarly, some educators have supported interscholastic football as a healthy outlet for natural childhood aggression (Bennett, 1991; Martin, 1976).

In summary, off-field hostile aggression might be higher in contact than in no contact athletes or in non-athletes due to selection or development (learning). However, if displacement catharsis theory is correct, aggression might be lower in contact athletes than in the other two groups. Alternatively, if the motor-discharge model is correct, aggression might be lower in both groups of athletes compared to non-athletes.

Evidence for Off-field Aggression

Media Reports. Examples of off-field hostile aggression are not difficult to find. Boxer Mike Tyson was indicted for ear-biting inside the ring, but was also convicted of rape outside the ring (Oates, 1992; Springer, 1998). Hockey and football players have been in court for sexual assault, for fighting, and for destruction of property ("Nedved Charged with Sexual Assault," 1996; "Three College Football Players Charged with Rape," 1998; "3 North Carolina Players Convicted in Brawl," 1998), often with alcohol involvement (e.g., "Illinois State Players Charged in Frat Fight," 1998). Indeed, a survey of 200 college police departments showed that assaults by athletes were reported on the average every 18 days (Caron et al., 1997). Such reports create the image of athletes as belligerent drunks.

Such cases and statistics reflecting off-field aggression seem compelling, but they may distort the true picture. On the one hand, the media may give greater coverage to criminal acts by people who are well known than by those who are unknown. In other cases, they may play down the misbehavior of celebrities, in order to protect them (Arnold, 2001; Caron, et al., 1997). Rarely do they report comparative statistics for crime rates in athletes and non-athletes. In fact, for male university students who participated differentially in college sports, there was no significant relationship between sport involvement and either rape-supportive attitudes or aggressive sexual experiences (Caron et al., 1997). Although sexual aggression was predicted by competitiveness, it was not connected directly to athletic participation per se.

Laboratory Experiments. Contradicting popular opinion, experimental research has not supported catharsis theory. For example, Zillmann, Katcher, and Milarsky (1972) exposed participants to a high or low level of aggressive instigation, then placed them in either a high or low state of arousal via physical exercise (threading discs or vigorously riding a stationary bicycle). Subsequently, they were allowed to shock their instigator. Contrary to the motor discharge theory of catharsis, strenuous physical activity did not reduce aggressive shocking. Recently, Bushman (in press) invited angered participants to punch a bag while they thought about the instigator (rumination condition) or about becoming fit (distraction condition). Compared to a control group who did not punch at all, ruminators felt more angry and delivered more aversive noise to their instigator. This contradicts displacement catharsis theory and supports cognitive neoassociation theory. Furthermore, distracted participants who punched and thought about fitness did not deliver different noise intensities compared to control or ruminating participants, contradicting motor discharge catharsis theory.

These experiments tested catharsis theory by manipulating exercise directly. However, Zillmann et al. (1974) compared groups of contact sport varsity athletes, no contact sport varsity athletes, and non-athletes. Under the no-provocation condition, delivery of obnoxious noise did not differ among the three groups, contradicting motor-discharge catharsis theory, which predicts lower aggression in athletes. Under provocation, aggression again did not differ between contact athletes and the other two groups, contradicting both the displacement catharsis theory and learning theory, which respectively predict less and more aggression in contact athletes than in non-athletes. However, under provocation, aggression was *lower* in *no contact* athletes than in non-athletes. Zillman et al. argue that participation in no contact sports serves a protective function by preparing people to cope with provocation.

However, Huang, et al. (1999) conducted another laboratory study in which they found more aggression after provocation in high contact than in low contact high school athletes. They also administered self-report questionnaires measuring verbal and physical aggression in everyday life. Physical aggression scores were slightly higher for the high than for the low contact athletes but, as the authors note, the small sample sizes ($n = 8$) meant that the study had low power. Although they conclude that the results are consistent with a learning theory of aggression, they are also consistent with a cathartic effect of *low* contact sport. In the absence of a non-athlete control group [which Zillman et al. (1974) had], it is difficult to distinguish these two possibilities.

In summary, the studies with experimentally-manipulated exercise contradict the motor discharge and displacement catharsis theories, but support the cognitive neoassociation/learning theories. The studies with athletic participation as a subject variable are less clear, with evidence against all three theories (Zillman et al., 1974), but also evidence in favour of learning theory (Huang et al., 1999) and of coping theory (possibly Huang et al., 1999; Zillman et al., 1974).

Self-Reported Hostile Aggression.   Laboratory studies have the advantage of control over the experimental task, but they do not bear directly on the relationship between athletic activity and off-field aggression in everyday life. One way of obtaining this information is to administer an inventory containing questions that cover angry feelings and behaviour in a variety of situations. Huang et al. found some suggestive evidence with this method, but their study lacked power.

In other studies, it has been found that college athletes in general are more aggressive and more dominant than non-athletes (males, Fletcher & Dowell, 1971; males and females, Valliant, Simpson-Housley, & McKelvie, 1981), and that both male college baseball and tennis players scored higher than the college norms for aggressiveness. A group of male and female college athletes also reported more criminal behavior (including hitting a significant other) than non-athletes (Young, 1990). These findings indicate that participation in *any* sporting activity is associated with trait aggression.

On the other hand, it has been suggested that football players, who are contact sport athletes, are more aggressive than no contact athletes such as golfers or tennis players (Cox, 2002; Singer, 1975). Indeed, one study found that hostile aggression scores increased over the season for university football players, but not for physical education students (Patterson, 1974). Elsewhere, football players were more dominant than non-athletes, but not different from baseball players or track athletes (Aamodt, Alexander, & Kimbrough, 1982). University football players have also been found to be higher than other athletes in narcissism (Elman & McKelvie, 2002), which involves anger and aggressive behavior (Ruiz, Smith, & Rhodewalt, 2001). However, male varsity football players have scored in the average range on an aggression test (Lowe & Sani, 1972), and male varsity boxers have scored *lower* than wrestlers and cross-country runners (Husman, 1955). In addition, within a football team, it has been reported that active football players were less aggressive than redshirted (inactive) players (Nation & LeUnes, 1983). These findings do not show a consistent relationship between contact sport (football) and hostile aggression.

The Present Study

The purpose of the present study was to examine hostile off-field aggression in athletes and non-athletes. The theoretical goal was to test predictions from learning theory and catharis [sic] theory. The practical goal was to evaluate the media image of the violent athlete, particularly from contact sports.

Although no clear picture emerges from the self-report descriptive studies, we adopted the inventory method, but we also incorporated elements of control that are sometimes found in experimental studies. Hostile aggression was measured for varsity athletes in a variety of contact and in no contact sports. However, a unique feature of the present research was that each group of athletes was compared to a corresponding control group of non-athletes which was matched to the athletes on a number of variables. Special care was taken to match on physical size (height, body weight), which may be related to aggressiveness. For example, if contact athletes reported more hostile aggression than no contact athletes or than a general group of non-athletes, it might reflect the fact that they were bigger.

On the basis of the three major theories of the relationship between athletic participation and aggression, our expectations were as follows. If learning theory was correct, aggression would be greater for contact than for no contact athletes, and also greater for contact athletes than for their non-athlete counterparts. If the motor-discharge model of catharsis was correct, aggression would be similar for contact and no contact athletes, but lower than for non-athletes. If the displacement catharsis theory was correct, aggression would be lower for contact than for no contact athletes, and also lower for contact athletes than for their non-athlete counterparts.

Following previous studies (Huang et al., 1999; Zillman et al., 1974), football was classified as a contact sport, and both track and baseball were classified as no contact sports. Rugby was added as a second contact sport, and golf and volleyball were added as no contact sports. However, basketball has been classified as both a contact sport (Huang et al., 1999) and a no contact sport (Zillmann et al, 1974). Although the degree of contact in basketball is somewhat less than in football or rugby because players cannot deliberately hit to bring each other down, physical clashes are frequent, and athletes must be strong enough to deal with it. Similarly, in soccer, direct kicking of an opponent is prohibited, but there is frequent and vigorous contact when players tackle for the ball. Consequently, we added basketball and soccer to the contact group.

To measure hostile aggression, Bush and Perry's (1992) Aggression Questionnaire (AQ) was employed. It is an updated version of their widely-used hostility inventory, and has been employed by other researchers examining trait aggression (e.g., Wann, Shelton, Smith, & Walker, 2002). Because there has been criticism of bias in self-reports of aggression (Kirker, Tenenbaum, & Mattson, 2000), we added a second control feature, which was a measure of socially-desirable responding. Although the earlier hostility inventory was not related to social desirability (Govia & Velicer, 1985), the present version has been, at least with women (Harris, 1997). The Eysenck Personality Inventory (EPI; Eysenck & Eysenck, 1968) was also administered to help conceal the main purpose of the study.

METHOD

Participants

Male undergraduates were recruited from two local universities, one English-speaking and one French-speaking. A total of 96 athletes and 98 non-athletes completed the questionnaires. Athletes represented their university in one of eight sports: football, rugby, basketball, soccer, baseball, volleyball, track, and golf. The non-athletes did not participate in sport at the varsity level but could have played intramural sports, engaged in recreational activity, or may not have exercised at all. For each athlete, a corresponding non-athlete was matched in university attended, age, year of study, height and weight. For the last two variables, matching was acceptable if height was within 2 inches and weight was within 10 pounds.

This procedure resulted in a final sample of 86 athletes and 86 non-athletes. For athletes, the number in each sport was: 15 football, 16 rugby, 10 basketball and 5 soccer (46 contact); 7 baseball, 9 volleyball, 12 track and 12 golf (40 no contact). For each sport, there was an identical number of matched non-athletes. Thus, the design of the study had two variables (physical size, athletic participation), each with two levels: bigger, smaller (physical size) and athlete, non-athlete (athletic participation). The contact and no contact athletes fell into the cells for the bigger athletes and smaller athletes respectively.

Materials

Buss and Perry's (1992) Aggression Questionnaire (AQ), which is a revised version of their earlier Hostility inventory (Buss & Durkee, 1957), was used. It consists of 29 items, distributed unequally among physical aggression, verbal aggression, anger and hostility. It measures hostile aggression, because it contains items for aggressive behavior and for angry/hostile feelings. For the total score, internal consistency (alpha) was .89 and 9-week test-retest reliability was .80 (Buss & Perry, 1992; Harris, 1997). Validity is supported by acceptable correlations with other self-report measures of aggression and with peer nominations of aggressive behavior (Buss & Perry, 1992; Harris, 1997).

Social Desirability was measured by the Balanced Inventory of Desirable Responding (BIDR; taken from Robinson, Shaver, & Wrightsman, 1991), which consists of 40 statements. The total score reflects both self-deception, the tendency to overrate oneself, and impression management, the tendency to create a positive social image. Robinson et al. report that alpha is .83, test-retest reliability is .65 or better, and that criterion validity coefficients with other self-report measures of social desirability are .71 or better.

Items for the AQ and BIDR were combined into a single questionnaire of 69 true-false items entitled "Personality Inventory." BIDR items were kept in their original order and randomly mixed with AQ items, which were themselves randomly mixed among the 4 subscales as recommended by Buss and Perry (1992). Because Huang et al. (1999) found a difference between high and low contact athletes on a direct question about physically-aggressive behavior, a final yes/no question was added at the end of the Personality Inventory: "Since coming to university, have you ever been an active participant in a fight?" If the answer was in the affirmative, the participant was asked how many times they had fought, and how many times alcohol was involved.

The Eysenck Personality Inventory (EPI; Eysenck & Eysenck, 1968) consists of 24 extraversion items, 24 neuroticism items and 9 lie items, all answered with either yes or no. Because these scores were not analyzed, no further psychometric information is given here.

All questionnaire items were translated into French by the first author, then proof-read and corrected by another bilingual individual. The English versions were given at the English-speaking university and the French versions were given at the French-speaking university.

Procedure

Athletic participants were tested individually or in groups, in some cases via campus mail. Non-athletic participants were tested individually in the same manner. Participants filled out a consent form, provided demographic information (age, weight, height, year of study), then completed the Personality Inventory and EPI in counterbalanced order. No names were attached to questionnaires and confidentiality was assured.

RESULTS

Preliminary Analyses

For all 172 participants combined, the AQ scores were correlated with other scores as follows: $-.080$ (age), $.186$, $p = .015$, (weight), $.003$ (height), $-.023$ (year of study), $-.506$, p .001, (L), and $-.457$, p .001 (BIDR). Aggression scores were positively related to weight, and negatively related to social desirability (BIDR). There were also two significant positive relationships between self-reported number of fights and the other variables: $.206$, $p = .007$ (weight) and $.189$, $p = .013$ (year of study).

To check the matching of athletes and non-athletes in the two physical size conditions, 2 X 2 (Physical Size X Athletic Participation) factorial ANOVAs were conducted on age, year of study, height and weight. For age and for year, neither main effect or their interaction was significant. For both height, $F (2, 166) = 7.03$, $p = .009$, and weight, $F(2, 166) = 20.85$, $p < .001$ (see Table 1), the main effect of physical size was significant. Contact athletes and their non-athlete counterparts were both taller and heavier than those no contact athletes and their non-athlete counterparts. The lack of significant effects of athletic participation, and of the physical size X athletic participation interactions, shows that the contact (bigger) and no contact (smaller) athlete groups were successfully matched to their non-athletic control groups on all variables.

Major Analyses

For aggression scores (see Table 1), a 2×2 (Physical Size $\times$ Athletic Participation) factorial ANOVA gave only a significant effect for physical size, $F (2, 168) = 5.23$, $p = .024$. Bigger participants (athletes and non-athletes combined) scored higher than smaller participants (athletes and non-athletes combined). The standardized effect size d (Cohen, 1977) was 0.45. The effect of athletic participation ($p = .116$) and of the physical size $\times$ athletic participation interaction ($p = .628$) were not significant.

Because AQ scores (hostile aggression) were significantly correlated with BIDR scores (social desirability), a 2×2 (Physical Size $\times$ Athletic Participation)

Table 1
Mean Scores on the Aggression Questionnaire

Size	Athletes				Non-athletes				Total			
	n	M	SD	M_c	n	M	SD	M_c	n	M	SD	M_c
Bigger	46	12.35	5.57	12.46	46	13.20	5.12	12.69	92	12.77	5.34	12.58
Smaller	40	10.20	5.02	10.90	40	11.80	4.42	11.55	80	11.00	4.77	11.23

Note. Maximum score = 29, M_c = adjusted means from covariation analysis.

ANCOVA was run with BIDR scores as a covariate. The results were the same as above, with the exception that the effect of physical size was now marginally significant, $F(1, 167) = 3.71, p = .056$.

Finally, because a learning (developmental) account of greater hostile aggression in contact compared to no contact athletes implies that scores would increase over time for the contact athletes whereas a selection account implies that they would not, a $2 \times 2 \times 4$ (Physical Size $\times$ Athletic Participation $\times$ Year of Study) ANOVA was conducted on the AQ scores. Again, the only significant effect was physical size, $F(1, 156) = 4.20, p = .042$. The effect of year of study ($p = .190$) and its interaction with other variables did not approach significance ($ps = .740, .698, .948$).

The data for the reported number of fights were also analyzed. A 2×2 (Physical Size $\times$ Athletic Participation) factorial ANOVA gave a significant effect of physical size, $F(1, 168) = 10.34, p = .002$. The mean number of fights was greater for bigger than for smaller participants ($d = 2.08$). The effect of athletic participation ($p = .254$) and of the interaction between the two variables ($p = .409$) did not approach significance. These data were also analyzed with year of study as a factor, but it did not alter the results. The only significant effect was physical size, $F(1, 156) = 7.92, p = .006$. The effect of year of study ($p = .498$) and its interaction with other variables did not approach significance ($ps = .525, .758, .966$).

Although the number of people reporting that they had fought was highly variable across conditions, and very small in some cases (see Table 2), an ANOVA was run on the proportion of cases in which alcohol was stated to be a factor in fighting behavior. There was a significant main effect of physical size, $F(1, 41) = 5.65, p = 002$, [*sic*] and of athletic participation, $F(1,41) = 4.23, p = .046$. Alcohol was reported to be involved more often by bigger than by smaller participants (.70, .40). Athletes reported less alcohol involvement than non-athletes (.52, .80).

DISCUSSION

Matching of Athletes and Non-Athletes

The purpose of this study was to compare self-reported hostile aggression between contact and no contact athletes, and between each group of athletes and matched control groups of non-athletes. The matching was successful in that each group of non-athletes was similar to their athletic counterparts on age, year of study, height, and weight. The analyses also showed that contact athletes and

Table 2
Mean Number of Reported Fights and Proportion of Fights Involving Alcohol

Size	Athletes			Non-Athletes			Total		
	N	M	SD	N	M	SD	N	M	SD
Number of Fights									
Bigger	46	1.28	1.97	46	0.82	1.96	92	1.05	1.97
Smaller	40	0.32	0.94	40	0.25	0.71	80	0.29	0.83
Proportion of Fights Involving Alcohol									
Bigger	23	.58	.43	12	.21	.29	35	.70	.41
Smaller	5	.27	.43	5	.53	.51	10	.40	.47
Total	28	.52	.44	17	.80	.39	45	.63	.44

their matched non-athlete controls were taller and heavier than no contact athletes and their matched controls. Other studies have either compared contact and no contact athletes without any non-athlete control group (e.g., Huang et al., 1999) or, if there were non-athletes, they were not systematically matched to each athlete group (e.g., Patterson, 1974; Zillman et al., 1974).

Theoretical Implications

The results were clear. Self-reported hostile aggression on the AQ was higher for participants who were bigger in stature than those who were smaller, and it did not differ between athletes and non-athletes. So, although contact athletes reported more hostile aggression than no contact athletes, the corresponding group of bigger non-athletes also reported more hostile aggression than the corresponding group of smaller non-athletes. This means that present differences in self-reported hostile aggression can be attributed to differences in physical stature. The effect size of $d = 0.45$ is close to Cohen's (1977) standard of 0.50 for medium.

When the negative correlation between AQ scores and the BIDR (social desirability) was accounted for with ANCOVA, the effect of physical size remained, although statistical significance was slightly greater than the traditional .05 level. However, self-reported fighting was not correlated with social desirability, and it was also greater for bigger than for smaller participants. Moreover, this effect size was $d = 2.08$, which is much greater than Cohen's (1977) standard of 0.80 for large. This indicates that lower AQ scores may be somewhat contaminated by social desirability responding, but this bias did not seriously distort the main finding that hostile aggression was a function of physical size and not athletic participation.

The higher aggression in contact than in no contact athletes is consistent with learning theory. However, this theory also demands that aggression should be greater for contact athletes than for their bigger non-athlete counterparts, and similar for bigger and smaller non-athletes. In fact, aggression did not differ between contact athletes and their non-athlete counterparts and it was greater for bigger than for smaller non-athletes.

According to the motor-discharge catharsis theory, aggression would be generally lower in athletes than in non-athletes, but it was similar in both cases. In addition, displacement catharsis theory predicts that aggression would be lower in contact athletes compared to both non contact athletes and bigger non-athletes, but neither of these outcomes occurred. Clearly, the present results contradict the learning theory of aggression and both versions of the catharsis theory of aggression, at least as applied to sport.

On the other hand, this study provides some support for the selection hypothesis over the developmental hypothesis of athlete aggression. Aggression was a function of size, which means that it was higher for contact (bigger) athletes compared to smaller non-athletes but was similar for contact athletes and bigger non-athletes. This implies that bigger people are more likely to be attracted and more likely to be chosen for high contact sport than for no contact sport. In addition, for contact athletes, AQ scores and reported number of fights did not increase over the four years of study compared to the other groups, as would be predicted by the developmental hypothesis.

Other Implications

Bearing in mind the unequal and sometimes limited sample sizes for the number of people in each condition who reported fighting, the proportion who stated that alcohol was involved was significantly higher for bigger than for smaller participants. This may mean that alcohol is more likely to fuel fighting in bigger than in smaller people, or that bigger people drink more.

Although athletic participation was not associated with overall hostile aggression or with reported frequency of fighting, the proportion of people reporting that alcohol was a factor in fighting was significantly smaller for athletes than for non-athletes. This could mean that athletes simply drink less than non-athletes, but surveys have shown that athletes actually drink more or similar amounts (Higgs, McKelvie, & Standing, 2001). Whatever the reason, the results belie the media image of athletes engaging in alcohol-fueled fighting (e.g., "Illinois State Players Charged in Frat Fight," 1998).

Furthermore, the most important practical implication of the findings from the aggression questionnaire and from the fighting reports is that they contradict the media image of the aggressive *contact* sport athlete. The fact that both measures of hostile aggression were higher for bigger than for smaller participants whether or not they were athletes highlight the fact that such reports fail to examine whether other people of similar size might also be aggressive.

Finally, although the results of the present study contradict the ideas that athletic activity fosters aggression in everyday life or provides a release from it, there may still be good reasons to be concerned about the level of aggression and violence both on and off the field. In particular, Tenenbaum et al. (1997), in their ISSP Position Statement on Violence inside sport, make nine recommendations for reducing violence in the athletic domain.

CONCLUSION

Scores on the aggression questionnaire (reflecting general levels of aggressive behavior and feelings), reported incidents of actual fighting, and reported frequency of alcohol involvement in fighting, were all higher contact [*sic*] than for no contact athletes. However, these differences also occurred with matched control groups of non-athletes, indicating that they were a function of physical stature rather than type of sport[.] Overall, there was no support for the learning or catharsis theories of aggression in sport, although they are consistent with the idea that size is a factor in the selection of contact athletes. Together with the fact that alcohol was stated to be a factor in fighting less often for athletes than for non-athletes, the results undermine the media image of the aggressive, drunken athlete, at least for university students.

Future research should obtain systematic information about off-field aggression in athletes at various levels of expertise in various events, perhaps comparing team vs. individual as well as contact vs. no contact sports. Because the media has profiled cases of aggression in professional athletes, this group is of particular interest. Given that the present matching technique was successful in revealing the relationship between size and aggression, it should be employed to control for physical variables and others such as social background and level of education.

References

Aamodt, M. G., Alexander, C. J., & Kimbrough, W. W. (1982). Personality characteristics of college non-athletes and baseball, football, and track team members. *Perceptual and Motor Skills, 55,* 327–330.

Arnold, J. (2001). Researchers say some athletes prone to domestic violence due to aggressiveness, socialization. http://www.uwire.com/content/topsports021601003.html.

Bandura, A. (1973). *Aggression: A social learning analysis.* Upper Saddle River, NJ: Prentice-Hall.

Bennett, J. C. (1991). The irrationality of the catharsis theory of aggression as justification for educators support of interscholastic football. *Perceptual and Motor Skills, 72,* 415–418.

Buss, A. H., & Durkee, A. (1957). An inventory for assessing different kinds of hostility. *Journal of Consulting Psychology, 21 (4),* 343–349.

Buss, A. H., & Perry, M. (1992). The aggression questionnaire. *Journal of Personality and Social Psychology, 63 (3),* 452–459.

Bushman, B. J. (2002). Does venting anger feed or extinguish the flame? Catharsis, rumination, distraction, anger, and aggressive responding. *Personality and Social Psychology Bulletin, 28,* 724–731.

Bushman, B. J., & Anderson, C. A. (2001). Is it time to pull the plug on the hostile versus instrumental aggression dichotomy? *Psychological Bulletin, 108,* 273–279.

Bushman, B. J., Baumeister, R. F., & Stack, A. D. (1999). Catharsis, aggression, and persuasive influence: Self-fulfilling or self-defeating prophecies? *Journal of Personality and Social Psychology, 76,* 367–376.

Caron, S. L., Halteman, W. A., & Stacy, C. (1997). Athletes and rape: Is there a connection? *Perceptual and Motor Skills, 85,* 1379–1393.

Cohen, J. (1977). *Statistical power analysis for the behavioral sciences (rev. ed.).* New York: Academic Press.

Cox, R. H. (2002). *Sport psychology: Concepts and application (5th ed.).* Boston: WCB/McGraw-Hill.

Elman, W., & McKelvie, S. J. (in press). Narcissism in football players: Stereotype or reality? *Athletic Insight.*

Eysenck, H. J., & Eysenck, S. B. G. (1968). *Manual for the Eysenck Personality Inventory.* San Diego: Educational and Industrial Testing Service.

Fletcher, R., & Dowell, L. (1971). Selected personality characteristics of high school athletes and nonathletes. *The Journal of Psychology, 77,* 39–41.

Govia, J. M., & Velicer, W. F. (1985). Comparison of multidimensional measures of aggression. *Psychological Reports, 57,* 207–215.

Harris, J. A. (1997). A further evaluation of the aggression questionnaire: Issues of validity and reliability. *Behavioral Research and Therapy, 35 (11),* 1047–1053.

Higgs, S. R., McKelvie, S. J., & Standing, L. G. (2001). Students' reports of athletic involvement as predictors of drinking: A pilot study. *Psychological Reports, 89,* 487–488.

Huang, D. B., Cherek, D. R., & Lane, S. D. (1999). Laboratory measurement of aggression in high school age athletes: Provocation in a nonsporting context. *Psychological Reports, 85,* 1251–1262.

Husman, B. F. (1955). Aggression in boxers and wrestlers as measured by projective techniques. *Research Quarterly of the American Association for Health, Physical Education, and Recreation, 26,* 421–425.

Illinois State players charged in frat fight. (1998) [Online]. *The Associated Press.* [1998, October 28].

Jones, J. C. H., Stewart, K. G., & Sunderman, R. (1996). From the arena into the streets: Hockey violence, economic incentives and public policy. *American Journal of Economics and Sociology, 55 (2),* 231–243.

Kirker, B., Tenenbaum, G., & Mattson, J. (2000). An investigation of the dynamics of aggression: Direct observations in ice hockey and basketball. *Research Quarterly for Exercise and Sport, 71,* 373–386.

Lowe, R., & Sani, R. (1972). An investigation of the athletic personality type hypothesis. *The Journal of Psychology, 82,* 167–169.

Martin, L. A. (1976). Effects of competition upon the aggressive responses of college basketball players and wrestlers. *The Research Quarterly, 47 (3),* 388–393.

Nation, J. R., & LeUnes, A. (1983). Saturday's heroes: A psychological portrait of college football players. *Journal of Sport Behavior, 5,* 139–149.

Nedved Charged with sexual assault. (1996) [Online]. *The Associated Press,* Nando.net. [1998, October 28].

Oates, J. C. (1992, February 24). Rape and the boxing ring. Newsweek [Online]. [1998, October 28].

Patterson, A. H. (1974). Hostility catharsis: A naturalistic quasi-experiment. *Personality and Social Psychology Bulletin, 1,* 195–197.

Robinson, J. P., Shaver, P. R., & Wrightsman, L. S. (1991). *Measures of Personality and Social Psychological Attitudes; Volume 1 in Measures of Social Psychological Attitudes Series.* San Diego: Harcourt Brace Jovanovich, Academic Press.

Ruiz, J. M., Smith, T. W., & Rhodewalt, F. (2001). Distinguishing narcissism and hostililty: Similarities and differences in interpersonal complex and five-factor correlates. *Journal of Personality Assessment, 76,* 537–555.

Seville Statement on Violence (1986). http://www.unesco.org/human_rights/hrfv.htm

Singer, R. N. (1975). *Myths and truths in sports psychology.* New York: Harper & Row.

Springer, S. (1998). Tyson rolls out a new image. http://www.msnbc.com/news/222034.asp

Tenenbaum, G., Stewart, E., Singer, R. N., & Duda, J. (1997). Position Statement on Aggression and Violence in Sport: An ISSP Position Stand. http://www.issponline.org/

Three college football players charged with rape. (1998). [Online]. The Associated Press, Nando.net. [1998, October 29].

3 North Carolina players convicted in brawl. (1998). [Online]. The Associated Press, Nando.net. [1998, October 28].

Valliant, P. M., Simpson-Housely, P., & McKelvie, S. J. (1981). Personality in athletic and non-athletic college groups. *Perceptual and Motor Skills, 52,* 963–966.

Wann, D. L. (1997). *Sport Psychology.* Upper Saddle River: Prentice Hall.

Wann, D. L., Shelton, S., Smith, T., & Walker, R. (2002). Relationship between team identification and trait aggression: A replication. *Perceptual and Motor Skills, 94,* 595–598.

Young, T. J. (1990). Sensation seeking and self reported criminality among student-athletes. *Perceptual and Motor Skills, 70,* 959–962.

Zillmann, D., Johnson, R. C., & Day, K. D. (1974). Provoked and unprovoked aggressiveness in athletes. *Journal of Research in Personality, 8,* 139–152.

Zillmann, D., Katcher, A. H., & Milavsky, B. (1972). Excitation transfer from physical exercise to subsequent aggressive behavior. *Journal of Experimental Social Psychology, 8,* 247–259.

Teaching Ethics to Mental Health Practica Students at the Master's Level
A Comparative Study

Marty Sapp
Department of Educational Psychology
University of Wisconsin-Milwaukee

This study compared three methods of presenting ethics to mental health practica students at the master's level. Fifty-seven mental health practica students at the master's level were randomly assigned to the following four experimental conditions: (1) direct lecture presentation of ethics, (2) student-led presentation of ethics, (3) direct lecture presentation of ethics combined with a student-led presentation, and (4) attentional control group. A one-way analysis of variance (ANOVA) indicated that the four groups differed in the degree to which they learned ethics, F(3,56) = 26.26, p < .001. These results were supported by an analysis of covariance (ANCOVA).

Dewayne, Gordon, Joyce, and Maureen (1991) defined ethics as the process of making moral decisions that are designed to protect the rights and welfare of clients. In terms of practice guidelines, both the American Psychological Association (1981; 1992) and the American Counseling Association (1988) have established a set of principles to guide the ethical behavior of counseling professionals. Welfel and Lipsitz (1984) pointed out that research is needed to determine the impact of formal coursework in ethics upon actual practice. Also, Corey, Corey, and Callanan (1993) noted that the literature is sparse in supporting the premise that ethics courses have a positive impact on students in actual practice. Similarly, it is not known from empirical research the impact that ethics courses have upon the actual behaviors of mental health counselors with clients. Moreover, there are no data to determine whether ethics is better taught in a separate course or integrated within existing courses. In addition, Welfel and Lipsitz (1984) also questioned if ethical training translates into actual practice.

Many articles on ethics in counseling and psychology have appeared in academic journals (Adair, Linsay, & Carlopio, 1983; Britton, Richardson, Smith, & Hamilton, 1983; Dalton, 1984; Handelsman, Rosen, & Arguello, 1987; Korn, 1984; McGovern, 1988). This article differs in that its purpose is to describe and evaluate three methods of presenting ethics to mental health practica students at the master's level.

Various models have been proposed for teaching ethics, three of which seem quite distinct. First, Kitchener (1986) recommends the integration of psychological

Sapp, M. (1995). Teaching ethics to mental health practica students at the master's level: A comparative study. *College Student Journal, 29,* 333–339.

processes and educational goals. In fact, Kitchener believes that counseling programs can equip counselors with the critical thinking skills needed to evaluate and interpret ethical codes. Moreover, according to Kitchener, mental health counseling programs can also provide counselors with the ability to evaluate their own behavior during ethical dilemmas. In summary, the foregoing author suggested that ethical training should involve four components: 1) sensitizing students to ethical issues, 2) stimulating the ability of students to reason about ethical issues, 3) encouraging in students a sense of moral responsibility to act ethically, and 4) instructing students how to tolerate the ambiguity involved in ethical decision making.

Second, Pelsma and Borgers (1986) proposed an experience-based developmental model of teaching ethics. Their model integrates the learning process formulated by Kolb (1976) and a developmental scheme of ethical reasoning proposed by Van Hoose (1980). Essentially, this model has four components: 1) concrete experience with feelings that involve ethical concerns, 2) reflective observations about ethical dilemmas, 3) abstract conceptualization—the ability to generalize from concrete ethical principles to abstract ethical dilemmas, and 4) active experimentation—the use of complex strategies to reason out ethical concerns. In summary, this is an integrated model of teaching ethics. As students experience new ethical dilemmas, their new reflections and observational skills result in novel perceptions and a solid basis for the formulation of ethical behavior.

Finally, Strom and Tennyson (1989) developed a problem-posing model for teaching ethics, stressing critical reflective thinking. They emphasize that students develop the capacity and inclination to make rational, defensible, practical, and moral judgments through a problem-posing model. This can be done by presenting students in Fieldwork or Practicum with potential ethical dilemmas that can occur in actual practice. Then, students are allowed to reflect critically upon how they would respond to various ethical issues.

The purpose of the project covered herein was to assess the ethical knowledge of mental health practica students at the master's level who had previous exposure to the ethical principles of ACA and APA and to determine if students' reactions to three different methods of presenting ethics differed from those of students in an attentional control group.

METHOD

Subjects

Fifty-seven mental health practica students at the master's level were randomly assigned to four experimental conditions: (1) direct lecture presentation of ethics, (2) student-led discussion of ethics, (3) direct lecture presentation of ethics combined with a student-led presentation, and (4) attentional control group.

This study occurred at a midwestern university where mental health counseling, school counseling, and rehabilitation counseling are subareas of an educational psychology program at the master's level. Although this is an accredited program, it does not meet the standards for the Council for Accreditation of Counseling and Related Educational Programs (CACREP) endorsement.

Before students enroll in Practicum, they complete at least three courses (12 semester hours): Counseling-Theories and Issues, Essentials of Counseling Practice, and Fieldwork in Counseling. Each of these courses exposes students to ethical issues.

Counseling Theories is a student's first exposure to ethical issues. Essentials of Counseling Practice is the first skills-building course that a student takes. Corey, Corey, and Callahan (1993) is introduced at this point of a student's training. By the time students enroll in practicum, they have been exposed in some detail to the ethical principles of both ACA and APA. This is a standard procedure in our program. Practicum meets weekly for an entire semester. While enrolled in Practicum, students learn about and receive detailed feedback about their skills development.

Students spend a minimum of 10–15 hours a week at a field site for both Fieldwork and Practicum; however, Practicum is a more advanced course than Fieldwork. On a weekly basis, during both Fieldwork and Practicum, students receive four hours of supervision (i.e., one hour on site and three hours in class). In sum, within our program, we have attempted to make Fieldwork and Practicum as uniform as possible.

To summarize, this field experience involved 57 students, all of whom were community or mental health master's level counseling majors. Forty-nine of the students were female and eight were male. All students were community counseling majors. The author explained the purpose of this project to all students and obtained informed constent. Any students choosing not to participate were excused.

In order to assess the subjects' prior knowledge of ethics, the author used a multiple choice classroom test to pretest students at the beginning of the semester. It took eight semesters to complete this study. Pretest results indicated that the four groups of students were statistically equivalent, $F(3,53) = .31, p = .82$. This demonstrated that they had a similar amount of ethical knowledge. Towards the end of the semester in which they were enrolled, all students were posttested using the same instrument.

Evaluation

To measure pre-post changes in ethical knowledge, the author constructed a crierion-referenced questionnaire. This questionnaire consisted of [a] 34-item multiple choice test based on the nine principles of APA and the eight sections of ACA. Vignettes were employed to test the APA and ACA principles. Each item of the instrument had four distractors. Below is an example of one of the items from the instrument that was designed to measure principle 4 of APA and section F, part 2 of ACA ethical principles.

> Dr. Jones is a Ph.D. counselor and psychologist in private practice at an agency. He decides to advertise his services by mailing brochures to prospective clients. The brochures contains Dr. Jones membership status in both APA and ACA. In addition, it uses the title "Dr." and does not list Dr. Jones' Ph.D. in counseling psychology. Moreover, the brochure contained a quotation that was included in an article Dr. Jones had accepted for publication by a professional journal. Did an ethical violation occur in this situation?
>
> a. Yes, it is unethical for psychologists and counselors to advertise.
> b. Yes, it is unethical for mental health professionals to mail brochures to prospective clients.
> c. An ethical violation has not occurred in this situation.
> d. *Yes, it is unethical to advertise by using the title "Dr.," which may be misleading.

Since this was a criterion-referenced questionnaire, a validity coefficient was not calculated; however, a split-halves reliability coefficient comparing even-numbered and odd-numbered item responses produced a reliability coefficient of .88. The high split-halves reliability coefficient shows that the criterion-referenced question-naire consistently measured the characteristic it was constructed to measure.

In addition, the average item difficulty index was 59%. The ideal difficulty index from an item analysis is 50% (Anastasi, 1988). The results of this instrument came close to the ideal recommended measure. In terms of item discrimination, the ability of test items to differentiate between students who have a command of elements being tested, and those who lack that ability, an item analysis produced an average index of discrimination equal to .82. This indicated that students who had mastered ethical principles were able to answer test items correctly, whereas those who had not mastered the principles found the incorrect distractors attractive.

Teaching Methods

Direct lecture presentation of ethics. In order to ensure that participants received uni-form methods of instruction, three manuals were used to standardize this process. The direct lecture presentation involved the author providing six, three-hour lec-tures covering the ethical principles of APA and ACA. During these six Practicum class lectures, the author discussed the principles of APA and specifically the evolu-tion of ethical principles. Distinctions were made between ethics and the law, with attention being given to possible penalties that can occur when ethics are violated. In addition, the following substantive areas of APA principles were discussed in de-tail: the preamble and the principles of responsibility, competence, moral and legal standards, public statements, confidentiality, welfare of the consumer, professional relationships, assessment techniques, and research with human participants.

Similarly, during lectures this author discussed the preamble of ACA and the following sections of ACA ethical principle Section A: General; Section B: Coun-seling Relationship; Section C: Measurement and Evaluation; Section D: Research and Publication; Section E: Consulting; Section F: Private Practice; Section G: Per-sonal Administration; and Section H: Preparation Standards. Students asked questions at the end of each lecture.

Student-led triadic discussion of ethics. Students in the triadic group discussion method of teaching ethics were given the following instructions:

> The purpose of this triad is to discuss the ethical principles of APA and ACA. This process will take six class periods, a total of eighteen hours of discussion. During session one, you will discuss the ethical principles of APA. This will be done in systematic manner by having a student serve as a reader of the nine ethical prin-ciples and the other two students writing down issues they perceive as important while the principles are read aloud. After each principle is read aloud, discuss the issues from your notes relating to that principle. You will have only three hours to cover all nine principles, so use your time wisely. During session two, you will follow exactly the same procedures used during session one. That is, one group member will read aloud the ethical principles of ACA and the other two group members will write down ideas that occur as the principles are read. After each principle is read aloud, you are to discuss the important issues raised.

During this period, the author observed each triad. Observations provided qualitative data on how studentsx employ this method.

Combinational method of teaching ethics. The combinational method of teaching ethics was similar to the two previously discussed methods and was essentially a blend of these two approaches. This combinational method covered the same length of time (six Practicum class periods) as the other methods, which was six class periods for two individual sessions. During session one, the author lectured directly on the principles of APA for 1 and 1/2 hours, while students were instructed to take detailed notes. Afterwards, students were put into triads to discuss issues that were raised from the lecture. This triadic discussion took place for 1 and 1/2 hours. During this period, the author visited each triad to clarify any issues that were not clear.

Each of the class periods was started in a standardized fashion. First, the author lectured directly on the ethical principles of ACA for 1 and 1/2 hours. Next, students were put into triads to discuss those principles for 1 and 1/2 hours. During each session, the author visited each group to clarify any issues that were unclear. In summary, during each lecture of this blended approach, in contrast to the direct lecture approach, the author encouraged students to process ethical issues and to arrive at personalized methods of deliberating about ethical concerns.

Attentional Control Group

While other groups received various methods of learning ethics, this author interacted with the attentional control group. The attentional control group was asked to discuss issues related to practica sites as well as to discuss and summarize information from their weekly logs. The author observed this process. Once this study ended, members of the attentional control group were presented with the combinational method of presenting ethics and were met with individually to ensure that the ethical material was processed. These students in this group reported that they felt they were learning about ethical issues even while discussing information from weekly logs.

RESULTS

As a frame of reference for this section, the means and standard deviations for pretests and posttests measures are found in Table 1. Table 2 shows the results of a one-way Analysis of Variance (ANOVA), and Table 3 shows the results of a one-way Analysis of Covariance (ANCOVA).

The ANOVA results were $F(3,53) = 26.26$, $p < .001$, indicating that the groups differ on the posttest or dependent variable. ANOVA was followed by Tukey post hoc procedures. Tukey post hoc procedures indicate that the attentional control group, direct lecture presentation group and student-led triadic discussion group all differ from the combinational group at the .05 significance level.

Pretests and posttests means for the combinational group were 23.62 and 30.00, respectively. For the student-led triadic discussion group, the respective pretests and posttests means were 23.36 and 27.93. In terms of the direct lecture presentation group, the respective pretests and posttests means were 23.20 and 27.00. For the attentional control group, the respective pretests and posttests means were 23.53 and 27.00. The results of Analysis of Covariance (ANCOVA) support those of ANOVA. These results were $F = (3,52) = 27.17$, $p < .01$, which indicate that the experimental groups differ on the posttest when statistical adjustments are made on the posttest.

DISCUSSION

This study demonstrated that a direct lecture presentation of ethics combined with a student-led presentation of teaching ethics was a more effective method of presenting ethics to master's level mental health counseling practica students at the master's level than was a direct lecture presentation of ethics, a student-led presentation of ethics, or an attentional control group. The results of an ANOVA and ANCOVA both supported these contentions. An ANOVA and ANCOVA were both performed. The assumptions of these statistical tests can be found in Sapp (1993, p. 79, p. 115) and Stevens (1990, p. 41, p. 166). Assumptions from both statistical tests were tenable; therefore, the results from this study are accurate.

Pretest scores obtained from this study suggested that master's level mental health counseling practica students at the master's level because of gained ethical knowledge exposure to ethical principles throughout counselor training. The grand mean for pretest scores was 23.42 or approximately 68.88% correct. This indicated that all students had a reasonable grasp of ethical principles; however, statistically significant gains only found were for the direct lecture presentation of ethics combined with a student-led presentation. This combinational group obtained a score of 88.24% correct on the posttest; therefore, it appears that student-led presentations, direct lecture presentations, and an attentional control group were equally effective in helping students to increase mastery of ethical principles. This study suggests that it is important for trainers or educators of mental health counselors to maintain constant involvement with students' development of ethical principles. Similarly, another implication of this study is the necessity for educators of mental health counselors to repeatedly cover ethical principles throughout students' training so as to ensure that the students will understand and master these principles.

Some potential limitations of this study should be discussed. First, follow-up data were not obtained, which makes it impossible to determine if students maintained their positions on the dependent variable after the study ended. Another limitation of this study was use of a criterion-referenced measure of ethical principles. Even though this instrument had adequate reliability, it was not possible to report validity measures. Since this was a classroom test designed to measure ethical principles, standardized validity coefficients may not be an adequate method to evaluate such an instrument. Nevertheless, item analyses indicated that this instrument did accurately discriminate among groups, but as Ebel (1979, pp. 272–273) pointed out, indices of item analyses obtained from criterion-referenced tests tend to be inflated because of two factors. First, criterion-referenced tests are often short, as was the case of the instrument used in the current study, hence making them less reliable. Second, sampling error, which also existed in the current study, can inflate indices of item analyses obtained from criterion-referenced tests.

In summary, this study suggested that educators and supervisors of mental health counselors can be an integral part of these practica students' learning of ethical principles. Moreover, it appears that a direct lecture presentation of ethics combined with a student-led presentation of ethics is an effective method of teaching ethics to practica students. This study suggested that the method of instruction employed can affect the learning of ethics by mental health counseling students in practica classes. Finally, as Welfel and Lipsitz (1984) suggested, research is needed to determine if mastery of ethical principles results in the applications of ethical reasoning during actual situations.

References

Adair, J. G., Lindsay, R. C. L., & Carlopio, J. (1983). Social artifact research and ethical regulations: Their impact on the teaching of experimental methods. *Teaching of Psychology, 10,* 159–162.

American Association for Counseling. (1988). Ethical standards (rev. ed.). Alexandra, VA: Author.

American Psychological Association. (1981). *Ethical principles of psychologists.* Washington, DC: Author.

American Psychological Association. (1992). *Ethical principles of psychologists.* Washington, DC: Author.

Anastasi, A. (1988). *Psychological testing* (6th ed.). New York: Macmillan.

Britton, B. K., Richardson, D., Smith, S. S., & Hamilton, T. (1983). Ethical aspects of participating in psychology experiments: Effects of anonymity on evaluation, and complaints of distressed subjects. *Teaching of Psychology, 10,* 146–149.

Corey, G., Corey, M. S., & Callanan, P. (1993). *Issues and ethics in the helping professions* (3rd ed.). Pacific Grove, CA: Brooks/Cole Publishing Company.

Dalton, J. H. (1984). Discussing ethical issues in practicum courses. *Teaching of Psychology, 11,* 186–188.

Dewayne, K., Gordon, G., Joyce, L., & Maureen, C. (1991). Ethical issues in supervising counseling practitioners. *Counselor Education and Supervision, 31*(1), 48–57.

Ebel, R. L. (1979). *Essentials of educational measurement* (3rd ed.). Upper Saddle River, NJ: Prentice-Hall.

Handelsman, M. M., Rosen, J., & Arguello, A. (1987). Informed consent of students: How much information is enough? *Teaching of Psychology, 14,* 107–109.

Kitchener, K. S. (1986). Teaching applied ethics in counselor education: An integration of psychological processes and philosophical analysis. *Journal of Counseling and Development, 64*(5), 306–310.

Kolb, D. (1976). *Learning style inventory.* Technical manual. Boston: McBer and Co.

Korn, J. H. (1984). Coverage of research ethics in introductory and social psychology textbooks. *Teaching of Psychology, 11,* 146–149.

McGovern, T. V. (1988). Teaching the ethical principles of psychology. *Teaching of Psychology, 15*(1), 22–26.

Pelsma, D. M., & Borgers, S. C. (1986). Experience-based ethics: A developmental model of learning ethical reasoning. *Journal of Counseling and Development, 64*(5), 311–314.

Sapp, M. (1993). *Test anxiety: Applied research, assessment, and treatment interventions.* Lanham, MD: University Press of America.

Stevens, J. P. (1990). *Intermediate statistics: A modern approach.* Hillsdale, NJ: Lawrence Erlbaum Associates.

Strom, M. J., & Tennyson, W. W. (1989). Developing moral responsibleness through professional education. *Counseling and Values, 34,* 33–42.

Van Hoose, W. H. (1980). Ethics and counseling. *Counseling and Human Development, 13,* 1–12.

Welfel, E. R., & Lipsitz, N. E. (1984). The ethical behavior of professional psychologists: A critical analysis of the research. *The Counseling Psychologist, 12*(3), 31–42.

Table 1
Means and Standard Deviations for Pretest and Posttest Measures

		Pre	Post
n=13	Combinational Method	23.62(1.04)	30.00(1.22)
n=14	Student-led Triadic Discussion	23.36(1.50)	27.93(.73)
n=15	Direct Lecture Presentation	23.20(1.66)	27.00(.93)
n=15	Attentional Control	23.53(.52)	27.00(1.13)

Note: Standard deviations are in parentheses.

Table 2
Results of One-way Analysis of Variance

Source	D.F.	Sum of Squares	Mean Squares	F Ratio	F Prob.
Between Groups	3	81.6328	27.2109	26.2556	.0000*
Within Groups	53	54.9286	1.0364		
Total	56	136.5614			

*Denotes statistical significance at the .001 level.

Table 3
Results of Analysis of Covariance (ANCOVA)

Source of Variation	SS	DF	MS	F	Sig of F
Within Cells	53.04	52	1.02		
Regression	1.89	1	1.89	1.86	.179
Constant	152.14	1	152.14	149.17	.000
GPID	83.12	3	27.71	27.17	.000*

*Denotes statistical significance at the .01 level.

Segregated Classrooms, Integrated Intent

How One School Responded to the Challenge of Developing Positive Interethnic Relations

Appendix

Rosemary C. Henze
ARC Associates Oakland, California

Children who feel unsafe in school because of threats of violence or verbal abuse based on race, ethnicity, or language cannot focus on the learning and achievement goals that the U.S. educational system has placed before us in the form of national standards. A primary need for some schools is to create a safe and secure environment and to ensure that children and adults of different backgrounds feel respected. Yet this raises an interesting question: Can schools be vehicles for improving race relations? In this article, I draw on a case study of 1 elementary school, Cornell,[1] to examine this question in depth. Many would answer that, given historical inequities such as segregation and tracking, schools are unlikely places for improvements in race or ethnic relations to take place. On the other hand, schools do create cultures and norms of their own that may deviate in some ways from the national culture, and in this sense they represent a potential site for change in race relations, at least locally.

During the past 3 years, several colleagues and I have carried out a research project called Leading for Diversity to document proactive approaches that school leaders are using to reduce racial and ethnic conflict and to promote positive interethnic relations (Henze, Katz, Norte, Sather, & Walker, 1999). One of the assumptions underlying this work is that schools can indeed make a positive difference in race relations, and therefore the activities they engage in to do so are worth documenting so that others can learn from them.

In the process of visiting many of the 21 schools participating in the study, I was from time to time challenged to look critically at this assumption. Can schools really be vehicles for improving race relations? On what basis can we answer this positively? What evidence is there to suggest that schools, as currently configured, cannot serve this function, or can only serve it partially? This article explores these questions in the context of one particular elementary school, Cornell, which served a diverse population of vibrant, hopeful children from low-income homes.

Henze, R. C. (2001). Segregated classrooms, integrated intent: How one school responded to the challenge of developing positive interethnic relations. *Journal of Education for Students Placed at Risk*, 6(1&2), 133–155.

[1]The school and individuals mentioned in this article have been assigned pseudonyms to protect the confidentiality of information shared.

Kozol (1991) wrote that "Most of the urban schools I visited were 95 to 99 percent nonwhite" (p. 3) and "reminded me of garrisons or outposts in a foreign nation" (p. 5). He questioned why, in a country that calls itself a democracy, "we would agree to let our children go to school in places where no politician, school board president, or business CEO would dream of working" (p. 5). What emerges from his analysis, and from that of others such as McDermott and Varenne (1995), is the flip side of the traditional risk equation. These scholars, rather than focusing on factors in families and children that may predict school failure, asked instead how schools fail students and families, and indeed how our school system is structured so tightly around the label of "at riskness" that there is a necessary corollary: In addition to children acquiring at-risk factors, the at-risk label has to acquire children. We have, according to McDermott and Varenne, developed a culture that requires some of its members to be disabled, poor, illiterate, and low achieving.

Although many schools work hard, often against great odds, to address risk factors such as poverty, limited English proficiency, racial minority group membership, and others, a few take the brave step of beginning to look at how the school system itself structures inequality and how school staff, school policies, school curriculum, and so on, are part of the problem. An example is Hollinger Elementary school in Arizona, where teachers worked with a group of applied anthropologists to implement an approach called "funds of knowledge." Key domains of change in this approach are as follows: "(1) the development of teachers as qualitative researchers; (2) the formation of new relationships with families; and (3) the redefinition of local households as sites containing important social and intellectual resources for teaching" (González et al., 1995, p. 445). By recasting low-income, Latino households from sites that are culturally deprived to sites where valued knowledge and skills are transmitted from one generation to the next, González and her colleagues fundamentally shifted the way we think about schools and communities. Another example of schools seeking to examine their own part in creating student failure are those that try to eliminate or reduce tracking. Recognizing that the practice of grouping students by presumed ability has resulted in low-ability and high-ability tracks that too often become permanent pathways with no exit, "detracking" schools are moving toward less rigid and hierarchical grouping practices, high academic standards for all students, and the provision of supports that enable all students to reach their highest potential (Oakes, Wells, & Associates, 1996).

In the process of reaching this understanding that the structures, policies, and practices of school systems often create or reinforce existing societal inequalities, schools may question specifically how they help or hinder the development of positive intergroup relations. Given that the society in which U.S. schools are nested has a historical legacy of racism that still affects us today (Banks, 1997; Sleeter, 1991), schools are in a position to reinforce racial and ethnic inequality and stereotyping, which are primary causes of racial and ethnic conflict (Kreisberg, 1998). Schools can also ignore racial inequality and stereotyping or take actions to counter them. The nature of schools as partially bounded cultures within the larger national culture gives them this potential to shape a particular, local culture that may deviate somewhat from the norms and practices of the larger society. In a volume appropriately titled *Shaping School Culture: The Heart of Leadership,* Deal and Peterson (1999) pointed out that school cultures are "shaped by the ways principals, teachers, and key people reinforce, nurture, or transform underlying norms, beliefs, and assumptions" (p. 4).

If we want all children to grow and learn to their fullest potential, then certain basic elements have to be in place in schools. Children who feel physically unsafe because of threats of violence, or who constantly fear verbal abuse such as racial slurs or mockery of their language, are not going to be ready to learn (Bolman & Deal, 1991; Maslow, 1954; Norte, in press). Schools that do not safeguard these basic human needs place children at great risk of school failure. For this reason, it is vital that we consider what schools can do to constructively alter the societal conditions of racial inequality and stereotyping, to nurture a positive racial and ethnic identity among students as well as adults, and to create a strong sense of shared community in which differences are respected and valued.

Several models have been proposed in the literature for the enhancement of interethnic relations. The first of these in Allport's (1954) equal status contact theory, which asserts that positive intergroup relations will develop when the following conditions are present: (a) Groups have equal status within the context, (b) there is one-to-one personal interaction among individuals of different groups, (c) cooperative activities encourage people to work together on superordinate tasks, and (d) there is explicit support for and modeling of intergroup relations by relevant authority figures.

Building on and extending Allport's (1954) theory, Fine, Weis, and Powell (1998) wrote about three high schools that ranged along a "continuum from desegregated but racially separate to integrated communities of difference" (p. 248). However, Fine et al. found equal status contact theory to be inadequate by itself to explain what they saw in the one "integrated community of difference." They suggested that in addition to Allport's four conditions, schools need to "(1) build a sense of community among students; (2) demonstrate a commitment to creative analysis of difference, power, and privilege; and (3) invest in democratic practice with youth" (p. 249).

The reasoning behind these suggestions is that, even though many schools are technically desegregated, there is also tremendous resistance to inclusion. Fine et al. (1998) cited research by Braddock, Dawkins, and Wilson (1995), which showed that over time, sites that purportedly have equal status contact devolve into sites where inclusion and interaction barriers such as differential expectations, or subtle forms of social exclusion, counter the move toward positive intergroup relations. It is worth noting that the three conditions Fine et al. suggested are predicated on work with high school students, and that a "creative analysis of difference, power, and privilege" might look and sound quite different at the elementary level, as would an investment in "democratic practice with youth" (p. 249).

Similar conditions are part of what Tatum (in press) called the ABCs of intergroup relations: (a) affirming identity, (b) building community, and (c) cultivating student leadership. What is different in Tatum's set of conditions is the notion of affirming identity. This grows out of her understanding of the stages of racial identity development that individuals of different racial groups experience (Cross, 1978; Helms, 1990). For somewhat different reasons and at different stages, both Black and White students (and, one would assume, students of other racial and ethnic backgrounds) need to feel secure in a sense of their own racial and ethnic identity to move outward into meaningful relationships with others. A focus on affirming identity in elementary schools might, for example, include such activities as family heritage projects in which children are asked to share with the class information they have gathered from interviews with their families. A focus on building community might include class projects in which children of different ethnic backgrounds work together to solve a shared problem such as cleaning up a park near the school that has become unsafe due to drug trafficking. Cultivating student leadership at the elementary level could involve, for example, teaching students democratic leadership skills so that they can form their own student council or serve as conflict managers on the playground. Such leadership opportunities are important for all students even at the elementary level because they foster a sense of social responsibility and empowerment.

These models for the improvement of interethnic relations provide a framework that is useful in analyzing the efforts of particular schools, like Cornell Elementary.

METHOD

As noted earlier, this article is based on data collected in a larger study called Leading for Diversity, in which qualitative case studies were done of 21 schools across the United States to learn how proactive school leaders address racial and ethnic conflicts and how they develop positive interethnic relations in the school community.[2] Cornell was one of the schools in this study. I was the primary researcher responsible for collecting data at this school over a period of three semesters, from Spring 1997 through Spring 1998. Data collection included interviews with people in a variety of role groups, including teachers, administrators, students, other staff, and parents; observations of classes, meetings, assemblies, and other key events at the school; questionnaires for faculty and a group of adult community members who attended classes at the school; and documents and records that were pertinent to the study. Altogether, 40 individuals were interviewed (some of them multiple times), 6 classes and 34 other events were observed, and questionnaires were returned by 16 of 50 faculty members and 24 community members.

I analyzed these data using an agreed-on coding scheme for the larger Leading for Diversity study. We used QSR Nud*ist, a software program for qualitative analysis, to code electronically and retrieve information related to particular topics or from certain sources. I further explored the data to search for salient patterns and themes, using methods described by qualitative researchers such as Erickson (1986), Goetz and LeCompte (1984), and Miles and Huberman (1994). Finally, I compiled a case study report to summarize the findings about this school.

CORNELL AND ITS CONTEXT

Cornell Elementary, like other schools mentioned earlier, is working hard not to blame children for conditions they have no control over, and seeking instead to create a strong learning community that builds on the resources that children, families, community, and staff members bring. However, one of the issues that has perplexed and troubled the school is the tension between providing access for English language learners through native language instruction and creating positive opportunities for interaction between ethnic groups.

Cornell is situated in a low-income area of a large city in northern California. The main entrance to the school is on a quiet, tree-lined street, but another side of the school borders on a major commercial avenue lined with numerous restaurants and stores, many of which have signs in Spanish as well as English.

---

[2]For more information about this study and its findings, see Henze et al. (1999) or visit the project Web site at www.arcassociates.org/leading

Although the neighborhood used to be more African American, at the time of the study (1996–1998) it was predominantly Latino, with smaller numbers of African American, Southeast Asian, and White residents. With approximately 1,400 students, Cornell was the largest elementary school in the district. The physical plant consisted of the main building (built in 1939), two other one-story buildings, and numerous portable units, all linked by a large, concrete yard where students had recess and physical education. The assistant principal commented, "It's almost three different settings even though they're all connected." The large size and the three separate buildings plus the portable units all contributed to a sense of physical isolation that staff members had to work consciously to overcome.

The drabness of the large concrete yard had been brightened to some extent by colorful murals on several portable and building walls. Inside the halls, student work provided color and life for the old buildings. A large bulletin board especially for parent announcements was prominent in the main entrance, with signs in English, Spanish, and sometimes Vietnamese and Cambodian, inviting parents to upcoming events.

A major feature of Cornell's organization was its year-round schedule in which students were assigned to one of four tracks. Each track was "on" for 3 months, and then "off" for 1 month. At any given time, there were approximately 900 to 1,050 students on track and 40 teachers. Students were not tracked randomly; some of the grouping was based on language and the need to provide primary language services in the most efficient manner possible. For example, most of the Cambodian students were on the same track so that Cambodian-speaking aides could go off track at the same time, thus saving the school money. Until a few years ago, Spanish bilingual classes were all in the same two tracks, but this created a segregation problem for the school because other students were not even on site at the same time, let alone in the same classrooms.

The racial and ethnic breakdown of Cornell's student population in 1997 showed that 68% were Hispanic, 14% were Asian, 13% were African American, 2% were Filipino, 2% were Native American, 1% were White, and 1% were Pacific Islander. The majority of certified staff were White, with 26% from other racial and ethnic groups. Cornell students were considered at risk in a number of senses. Eighty-eight percent participated in the free and reduced-price lunch program; 74% had limited English proficiency; and standardized achievement test results on the Terra Nova in English (given only to fluent or native English speakers) were low in all areas. For example, among third graders, only 13% were nearing or above proficiency in reading for their grade level. The community surrounding the school faced serious problems with drugs, gang activity, and violence, making safety and security primary concerns for school staff and parents.

Despite these acknowledged factors that statistics tell us put these children at risk for educational failure (including the idea that early failure in reading begets later school failure), the school was working hard to take a different view of the children it served, one not based on a deficit model, but rather on a view that builds on the resources children and their families bring to school.

Meeting the Need for Access to the Core Curriculum

For immigrant children with limited English proficiency, Cornell provided three types of classes: Spanish bilingual, Vietnamese bilingual, and sheltered. The Spanish bilingual classes, which served the majority of children at Cornell, were designed as a transitional program in which native language instruction was provided in the content areas to allow children to keep up with subject matter while they were acquiring English. Spanish-speaking children were first taught to read in Spanish, and English reading was added after they had begun to read comfortably in Spanish. In Cornell's program, once children made the transition to English, their Spanish literacy skills were not maintained. According to the principal, "We'd like to have maintenance or two-way [bilingual education] in the future, but can't do it all at once. . . . We haven't got our literacy in English together yet." Several teachers also mentioned wishing the school could have a two-way, Spanish–English immersion program, but cited the overwhelming numbers of Spanish speakers compared to the few native or fluent English speakers as a reason why such a program could not work at Cornell.

In addition to the Spanish bilingual classes, there were also two Vietnamese bilingual classes. These classes, unlike the Spanish bilingual classes, included a few African American students. The teacher conducted class in both English and Vietnamese, but she did not teach Vietnamese literacy. All written work was done in English.

For children who were already fluent in English or for whom bilingual classes were not available because there was no credentialed teacher who spoke their language, the school provided sheltered classes. These were the most ethnically mixed of any classrooms at Cornell, typically including Cambodian, Mien, Lao, Latino, and African American students. Instruction was conducted in English by teachers who had received or were working on their Crosscultural, Language and Academic Development certificates, which prepared teachers to make instruction comprehensible by using a variety of techniques including many visuals, hands-on activities, and preorganizers. Instructional assistants who spoke the native languages of the students were available to support the English language learners.

There were only two classrooms at Cornell that were designated as "English only"—that is, neither bilingual nor sheltered. These classes included primarily African Americans and a few other students who were either native speakers of English or proficient enough to be classified as fluent.

The intent behind this array of instructional options was to provide access to the core curriculum for all students, regardless of language background. Consistent with *Lau v. Nichols* (1973), federal law requires that students not be precluded from access to the curriculum, and schools therefore must find ways to provide such access, whether through native language instruction, sheltering strategies, or other combinations. The federal law did not mandate a certain type of program, and states have interpreted the federal law in a variety of ways. California at one time had a law that required transitional bilingual instruction if a school had a certain number of students of similar age who all spoke the same native language. However, that law "sunsetted" in 1987, and from 1987 to 1998, schools had only to follow the federal mandate to provide access, but were free to choose any method of providing access. Since 1998, with the passage of Proposition 227, bilingual instruction has been outlawed in California and can only be offered if a majority of parents at a school sign waivers requesting it. Parents at Cornell did this, and thus bilingual education continues there to date.

Multiple Intentions, Conflicting Means

If the only intent at Cornell were to provide access to the core curriculum, things would be simpler, although not necessarily better for children. However, like most educators, the leadership and staff at Cornell envisioned their school serving multiple goals, only one of which was to provide equal access to curriculum. Another important goal was to teach students to respect others, and within that to value individual, cultural, and other differences. This goal was reflected in the school's motto, "Respect, literacy, and lifelong learning." As the principal explained it,

> Basically, there's sort of different layers about how we're proactive about dealing with different kinds of issues. I think the most broad layer that exists is our mission statement and the philosophy of respect. Our whole school motto is respect, literacy, and lifelong learning. So we basically put respect first as the condition that we like to create around us, that would be like the air we breathe. So that under the issue of respect comes all things that are related to interactions. Of course, a lot of them are overtly or covertly related to issues of ethnicity and culture. When we do that, that becomes a backdrop to refer to if someone makes a [racially stereotyping] comment.

However, developing this respect and the valuing of differences was seen as problematic given the way the school was structured around the delivery of bilingual services.[3] A teacher of a fourth- and fifth-grade sheltered class commented, "We've known for a long time that our kids are basically segregated by language, which ends up being segregated racially or culturally." Another teacher who taught a Spanish bilingual fourth- and fifth-grade class said,

> All my Spanish-speaking kids stay together as one cluster and know nothing about anybody else at the school, even though we're a really rich and diverse school and everything else. To them all the Asians are Chinese, and all the Blacks are scary and that's pretty much the picture they leave here with.

As this bilingual teacher noted, the segregation of her Spanish-speaking students from the rest of the school population contributed to their tendency to stereotype other students. Because they had little day-to-day interaction with Asian and African American students that might lead to a more complicated recognition of their identity, they relied on images they had gathered from home, television, and playground gossip.

In my interviews with several fourth- and fifth-grade students, I heard first-hand evidence of this tendency to stereotype other ethnic groups. For example, one group of students who served as conflict managers were trying to answer my question about the ethnicity of other conflict managers. A student volunteered the information that there was a Chinese conflict manager. A second student countered, "She isn't Chinese." I asked, "What is she then?" The second student replied, "She's, like, Vietnamese." A third student said, "That's just like Chinese." None of the students countered this seemingly authoritative statement. Later in the same interviews, several of the students used the term *chinks* to refer to Asian students. One of the conflict managers, a Cambodian boy, also shared his painful experience of hearing other children on the playground mocking his language by making sounds that were supposed to imitate it.

The principal also recognized the inherent tension between the bilingual program and the goal of integration:

---

[3]It is important to note that bilingual education, in and of itself, does not have to mean segregating children by language. In fact, some of the most successful bilingual programs are those that follow a two-way immersion model, where two groups of students learn each other's languages (Genesee, 1999).

One of the limitations of a bilingual program is that some of the kids aren't as integrated as one might hope, because of the language needs. We've done some things to remedy it, but there's always a sense that it's not enough and sort of a tension between the need to do a bilingual program in the primary language and the need to integrate children. And probably the different people you talk to would line up on bilingual issues differently. And some might see it as a big problem and then it is a catch-22, because not having bilingual education is a racist stand, too. Some people who aren't in favor of it might not perceive it that way, but in my view bilingual education is an equity issue. So those things are juxtaposed.

Her point is well taken. Many people might assume that if segregation results from the way the bilingual program is structured, schools ought to do away with bilingual education. However, not providing children with access to the core curriculum is tantamount to denying them an education, an equally racist stance. Well-implemented bilingual programs allow children who are not yet proficient in the dominant language to have access to the curriculum and to maintain their native language while they are learning English. They also build in opportunities for interaction across language groups.

Building Positive Interethnic Relations: At the Margins, in the Center, and Beyond the School

As the principal noted, the school leadership team had "done some things to remedy" the segregation produced by the particular way the bilingual program was set up. However, given that students spent about 80% of the day in their core classrooms, many of these remedies were relegated to the other 20% of the time. If we think of the center of the school day as being the activity setting in which students spend the bulk of their time, then the core classrooms where students are instructed in reading, math, language arts, science, and social studies form this center, and the other activity settings in which students do electives, after-school activities, lunchtime, recess activities, and assemblies form the margins of the school day. Although these activities are important in students' lives, it is also clear that, from the perspective of those who control education (e.g., district administrators, state legislators), the core curriculum is what really matters. In the next sections, I describe some of the key efforts staff at Cornell were making to develop positive interethnic relations.

At the Margins

Assemblies and Other Special Events with an Ethnic or Multicultural Focus. Cornell staff made a big effort to celebrate all the cultures of the students who attended, although at times culture was still understood in stereotypical and overly generalized ways. Throughout the year, assemblies and special events were held that highlighted one or several cultures or ethnic groups. The intent of these assemblies was to produce positive effects on cross-cultural understanding, tolerance of differences, and respect for one's own and other cultures. The range of assemblies and special events was quite large, including some that were not focused on specific ethnic groups. Those that were observed included National Day of Prevention of Gun Violence, during which students learned a pledge: "If I see a gun, I will not touch it and I will tell an adult about it"; a talent show, in which students from all classes in Grades 3 through 5 performed, most with an ethnic or cultural focus; a fire safety assembly; a Chinese

New Year celebration; an African American Shakespearean group; an oratorical fest for Black History Month; a kite festival; an Asian American assembly; a Native American assembly; and a very large *Cinco de Mayo* fair that took up a whole day and involved the entire community.

Unlike some schools, Cornell's ethnic assemblies were not restricted to a particular ethnic group. Staff members encouraged students of any ethnic group to perform. Thus, in a fourth-grade Cambodian dance performance, several African American students performed alongside Cambodian students. When I asked one of the African American boys later if he had chosen on his own to be part of that performance, he assured me he had and that he did it because it seemed like "it would be fun." This particular performance, it should be noted, was the work of a sheltered classroom with a broad mix of students. The dance performance gave them an opportunity to showcase relationships that had been developed throughout the year.

There was, however, a problematic side to the assemblies and the planning that went into them. Beneath the overt intention of celebrating cultures and appreciating differences lay old animosities among the staff and community. The traditionally large *Cinco de Mayo* event was perceived by some as favoring Latinos. Teachers eventually voted to do away with this celebration and instead have a large multicultural festival on July 4, with shorter celebrations taking place for specific cultures throughout the year. However, several Latino parents later argued against this change, and the issue went up for a vote among the grade-level circuits. Cinco de Mayo was restored, but resentments continued to simmer among those faculty members who had tried to create what they considered a more multicultural and equal-status array of special events. The principal was keenly aware of these tensions and tried hard to mediate and mollify them whenever possible:

> They were saying, "You only care about Latinos and you don't do enough for Asians." When the truth was it had to do with the committee, at least in my perception, and who came forward. So what I did last year, was that the African American parents came forward to do a bunch of special things and Latinos in the community came forward. And so instead of eliminating stuff to keep it balanced, I came and just used resources to bring in an Asian dance group. I think we ended up with an Asian dance group, a Karate demonstration also from Chinese martial arts. . . . My personal goal is to balance the inequities that I see. . . . without having to go through any big committee. . . . No one's going to argue with those activities. It doesn't take anyone's time. The kids have fun things and I'll make those kind of representative. . . . I want to get us out of that hurt feeling.

Another problematic side to the assemblies, mentioned by many staff members, was their tendency to be piecemeal and superficial. There was little follow-up treatment of the assembly topics in classrooms. Sleeter (1991) pointed out that the assembly route is often the first pathway a school takes toward becoming more "multicultural": "Many well-intentioned but superficial school practices parade as multicultural education, such as food fairs, costume shows, and window dressing contributions by people of color" (p. 9). At Cornell, although assemblies were certainly not the only efforts to be multicultural, they were probably among the first, and as such they carried with them the history of tensions around inequality among the different ethnic groups.

After-School Programs and Other Opportunities for Students to Mix.
Recognizing that segregation was a problem during 80% of the school day, Cornell staff had decided to capitalize as much as possible on the remaining 20% of the day as an opportunity for children to engage in mixed-group activities. These included after-school activities such as *Capoeira*, Boy Scouts, Brownies, and *Baile Folklorico*, as well as school-related activities such as serving on student council, being a conflict manager, or being a student assistant. Each year, there was also a week-long trip for the older grades to a nearby national park. Although the focus of these activities was not interethnic relationship building, they did in some cases function as a forum for children of different ethnicities to mix and get to know one another. Those that were not mixed were the result of parent requests that the school wanted to honor (e.g., *Baile Folklorico* and a Vietnamese literacy class).

Physical education and organized sports activities during lunchtime recess were another way in which cross-group relationship building was promoted. The physical education teacher believed that by stressing the need for everyone to share the same set of rules, "you eliminate a lot of the bullying and break up cliques."

Staff members who commented on the impact of these opportunities confirmed much of what Allport's (1954) equal status contact theory suggests. The after-school coordinator reflected, "When kids have opportunities to engage in meaningful stuff with kids of other races—projects, capoeira, student council, working to plan stuff—that's the best way to get them to know each other." A teacher said, "One time when the kids really mix a lot is during the trip to [the national park]. I've seen friendships made in that week because they are with each other 24 hours a day. I've seen people who never mixed before, mixing."

Despite these positive effects, as one teacher noted, "The language issues still tend to separate people because the language you speak will determine who you play with." Thus even when settings are designed to have students of many ethnic groups participating, communication needs may overshadow the integrative desires of the adults who direct the activities. My observations in the school suggest that students were most likely to interact with students of other ethnicities when activities were structured in such a way that they had to communicate across ethnic boundaries to get the task or game done.

In the Center

Several efforts to promote positive interethnic relations were designed to be more in the center of the school day. These included the Tribes and Conflict Resolution (CR) programs, efforts to recruit diverse staff, professional development that focused on equity and intergroup relations, and a unique example of teaming between two classrooms.

Tribes and CR. Tribes is a national program designed for elementary schoolchildren to develop social skills and build positive relationships (Gibbs, 1995). Although it is usually referred to as a program, it is actually curriculum based, with a manual of lessons to be integrated into the classroom on a regular basis. At the time the study began, Tribes had been used at Cornell for 10 years. Thus it had a long history and was well embedded in the practices of the school at all levels. The principal credited Tribes with developing a philosophy of acceptance and intercultural understanding and communication and using "I messages" and listening to each other and appreciation. And all that stuff really makes a big difference, because we have tools to use when stuff comes up.

The Tribes community agreements or norms were posted in the staff lounge and in most classrooms. They were: (a) attentive listening, (b) appreciation/no put downs, (c) the right to pass, and (d) mutual respect. According to the chief executive officer of the company that publishes Tribes materials, "It doesn't address racial conflict directly, but changes the environment in the school so that there isn't any." One of the first Cornell teachers to be trained in Tribes stated, "While Tribes does not explicitly teach about stereotyping or prejudice, the Tribes process should be in place before one attempts to teach this sensitive topic" (Gibbs, 1995, p. 133). At Cornell, Tribes was often cited as the structure within which a racial discussion could take place. During my research at the school, I saw many examples of the Tribes norms in use in staff interactions as well as with students. Many staff members and students told me that conflict and violence had dropped in the past few years due to the combination of Tribes and CR.

Cornell began its CR program (Community Boards of San Francisco, 1987) in 1987. Thus at the time of the study it had been in operation 12 years. Like the Tribes training, every teacher at Cornell had to be trained in CR. There were two components to the program—a curriculum-based program that teachers were supposed to weave into their core classrooms and training for student conflict managers in Grades 3 through 6. The conflict managers checked in with a teacher once a week to discuss any problems they were having, as well as their successes. Parent workshops were held in all the languages spoken by families at the school to tell them about the CR program.

Like Tribes, the CR program was not explicit about racial and ethnic tensions as a potential source of conflict. In other words, it was not built into the training for either adults or children. Several staff members said, "If it comes up, we deal with it" using the CR process. On the other hand, conflict managers were told to go to an adult if certain kinds of conflict came to their attention, including "anything physical, any kind of sexual harassment, anything racial, and anything about money." The staff encouraged a range of students to become conflict managers, including students of different ethnic groups, different English language abilities, different academic achievement levels, and "kids who are troublemakers and leaders among their peers." Thus student conflict managers were able to play roles as leaders that were not dependent on grades or language proficiency.

Although Tribes and CR were viewed very positively by most staff members and students, they were also problematic in a few ways. First, there appeared to be confusion about the expected outcomes of Tribes processes. A parent coordinator said she thought the program was supposed to make kids respectful of others' feelings via "I messages" and other techniques. However, "if it was working, you'd see a better environment." I later checked out this critique with a teacher who used Tribes frequently. He responded that the "I messages" used in Tribes were not intended to change people or make them behave differently. The point is simply to share one's feelings. He felt that, for this purpose, "I messages" were very effective.

Several teachers pointed out that Tribes and CR were limited by a lack of reinforcement in the home and community. In other words, they worked well for some children, but not for those whose parents had different cultural ways of handling discipline:

> Some parents believe in using the standard discipline format as opposed to speaking to their children or taking away a privilege. So the cultural differences are still there, which make it very difficult to build on something like TRIBES. So kids get one idea here and then their home environment does not support it. If anything, it contradicts it.

One teacher also wondered whether Tribes and CR might "mask some underlying tensions—you know, because we have this in place, it tends to be either cover or shadow feelings about other groups that students might have."

Students who were conflict managers said that they were frustrated by the fact that they did not get to deal with "big" conflicts. They felt most of the conflicts they dealt with were "stupid" or "little." The implication was that they felt their work was not important because they were not solving major conflicts. They also explained that sometimes CR was used as an excuse to get out of class, and that at times, conflict managers themselves became jealous of one another and fought. They felt that because they were conflict managers, they should model conflict-free interaction, but this ideal was difficult to achieve.

Efforts to Recruit Diverse Staff.

Cornell had a diverse staff if one looked across all different adult role groups. However, if one only looked at the credentialed teaching staff, it was still mostly White and female (74%), like most schools. The principal, a White woman, explained that, "Even though I've been limited by my possibilities, it's been a goal whenever possible. So I'm aware of it each year, when we're dealing with it." The principal spoke of consciously trying to make the staff as diverse as possible, for example, by hiring bilingual teachers who were actually native speakers of Spanish. However, given the pool of teacher candidates willing to teach in low-income, urban schools, attracting teachers was always an issue.

The instructional assistants mirrored the student population to a much larger extent than the teachers did. Cornell also had a unique program called Academic Mentors. The 10 mentors were paid out of Title VII funds to provide additional support to students at risk. They carried out a variety of reading support activities, as well as lunchtime activities. Three of the mentors were African American and seven were Latina. Several were parents or grandparents of children at the school. Having adult role models who lived in the neighborhood and were from cultural backgrounds similar to those of the students served a variety of purposes related to interethnic relations, not the least of which was encouraging underperforming students to do better academically, as an instructional assistant pointed out:

> When you can relate to the student, they act better and do better . . . Bilingual teachers who are not Latina, they can do a good job, too. But they have to really think and learn a lot about the culture. Where[as] Latino teachers, they know how to get to the kids.

Diverse staff members who worked together on shared projects also modeled positive interethnic relations for students. The two parent coordinators, one Latina and one African American, organized many activities together and in doing so, demonstrated the value and utility of interethnic alliances. In classrooms, non-White teachers and instructional assistants provided feedback to students when racially derogatory comments were made, feedback that was qualitatively different from that provided by White teachers, who also admonished students who made racial slurs. Staff members of color were able to speak personally about the racism they experienced to communicate to students how it feels, as a Korean American teacher explained:

> There's a stereotype among the Spanish-speaking community that all Asians are Chinese. . . . And it really upsets me, and then I think, we could help in that area. . . . If I hear someone saying it, I'll bring it up and say, "you know, I really resent that because . . . all Asians are not Chinese. . . ." I'll say that publicly, "It's very insulting and it's a put down and I would really appreciate your not making that generalization. You know, it's like saying all Spanish speaking students are Mexican." I always pose it that way. Now a lot of where they hear that from is the parents, so we have to educate our parents, too.

A problem in the profile of Cornell's diverse staff was that most of the non-White staff members had lower levels of education and less power and status at the school. Few of the instructional assistants and other noncredentialed staff of color would attend faculty meetings because these meetings were held after their paid time, whereas faculty were paid to attend. A structure that countered this, however, was the Leadership Team, a site-based management team composed of 18 individuals drawn from different role groups in the school, including a classified staff representative, a parent center representative, and others. By specifically including these groups, at least some diversity was ensured within this decision-making body.

Teacher-Driven Professional Development Focused on Equity. A small group of Cornell teachers had developed a monthly forum called SEED—Seeking Educational Equity and Diversity (MacIntosh & Style, 2000). The purpose of SEED was primarily to increase teachers' awareness and to empower teachers to work together on actions they could take to work against racism, sexism, homophobia, classism, and so on. The group originated as a teacher dialogue group in 1990, focusing on Freire's (1970) ideas about critical pedagogy. Sensing a lack of direction and focus in the group, one of the teachers learned of SEED, a model of teacher change disseminated nationally by a group at Wellesley College. She received support from the Leadership Team for herself and another teacher to be trained as SEED facilitators.

The framework used in SEED consists of five stages of inclusion, from being marginal to being in the center. The five stages were related to curriculum, and teachers tried to place what they were doing in terms of what stage it looked most like. "We don't want to do the single group approach," a teacher explained, "because again, if everybody is in the center, there's no need to do these special events to make sure nobody's marginalized." One of the teacher leaders described four of the five phases:

> In Phase 1, the only relevant things that are taught are things that have been done or accomplished by White men. . . . In Phase 3, you have exceptional people that come from outside of the White male thing, so you'll be talking about Harriet Tubman and Martin Luther King, or whatever, but still they're marginalized because they're the exception to the norm, or they act like White men and so they're

now acceptable to bring into the curriculum. In Phase 4—I think every once in a while I see examples of it happening—where, if you look in my classroom, there are things here that would be considered Phase 4, when we're looking at geography and instead of using some textbook we're using where the kids come from. So that would be a Phase 4 type thing. And then her [MacIntosh's] dream is of this Phase 5 that doesn't really exist but where everybody's in the center, where you don't have to have a women's month and you don't have to have an African American month because everyone's included all the time.

The SEED group varied in size and frequency of meetings; they had trouble finding a time to come together. Occasionally, SEED spearheaded a larger event, for example, showing the film *Color of Fear* (Stirfry Productions, 1994). That meeting was very successful, with a turnout of 40 to 50 participants. One of the reasons this meeting was so successful was, according to one teacher, because the film was somewhat known. It also did not require people to commit to coming to the group every time, and the film featured men and therefore drew more men.

For the core group of about 10 teachers who attended regularly, SEED had a powerful impact. Teachers involved with SEED also seemed to take the lead in schoolwide and across-schools change, and in political action within the community (e.g., meeting with teachers at other schools, leading action against Proposition 227). The vision of their roles as educators went beyond the classroom, and SEED had given them tools to implement that bigger vision. But it also had a direct impact on the curriculum they used in class and the way they taught. One teacher said, "SEED was the first place where I could actually seriously think about, become aware of and really start working on, things in my classroom and not just cosmetics. . . . SEED provides the only place to discuss hard issues." Another pointed out, "It helped legitimize what my gut was telling me I wanted to do, so now there were a lot of people out there saying, this is an OK practice, not only OK, but an exemplary type of way to teach, especially in schools like ours that are so multicultural." A third teacher said, "I became aware of prejudices I didn't know I had, and also of power issues and the damage done to minority groups."

Teaming between Two Classrooms. Some teachers had chosen to try to break down the segregation of the students by teaming together, meaning that two classes (usually a bilingual, all-Latino group with a sheltered group that was a mixture of ethnicities) combined their students and did project-based work, with students collaborating in small groups of mixed ethnicities and language backgrounds. The two teachers who had implemented this model most fully were a White teacher named Sylvia and a Korean American teacher named Lenny. They were the only teachers who teamed all day long. Other teams worked together for only 1 hr a day, which was a requirement of the district. Lenny and Sylvia explained,

> One of the reasons why Sylvia and I team is that she has mainly Spanish-speaking students, and I have mainly Cambodian, and we want them to have an opportunity where they're working with other students, so they have to understand each other and know how to problem solve. (Lenny)
>
> Lenny and I do this on a very conscious level. . . . We let the kids know on the first day there are three reasons why we're doing this, and one of them is learning about each other and learning how to get along with each other, learning how to

really respect, develop bonds with each other. And we make it a very explicit part of our curriculum. We don't just say it but we actually act on it. (Sylvia)

Most of Sylvia's students, although still considered limited English proficient, had enough fluency to understand basic English. For those who were still at a beginning level of English, she provided Spanish instruction in small groups or individually. Their model of teaming worked in part because students were at an advanced enough level of English to benefit from a project-based curriculum delivered primarily in English. On one occasion when I observed Sylvia and Lenny's combined class, there were 62 fourth- and fifth-grade students all working in small groups on an immigration project.

The students had interviewed their parents about immigration and now they were starting to pool their information into a matrix. The interview asked parents about their push and pull factors in immigration, and the matrix reflected these questions: Where did they move from and where did they move to? Why did they leave? What were they hoping to find, or do, or accomplish? How did they get there? What were the outcomes (e.g., did they accomplish what they had hoped; was it different from what they had expected)?

As each student shared his or her interview responses with the group, everyone in the group had to write down on his or her matrix what that person was sharing. In one group, an African American girl named Jamila was sharing her interview. She told the other students that her family was African American, that they had moved from a nearby city because they wanted their children to live in the city in which they currently resided, have a car, and have a better life. She felt happy because they had a better life. Other students in the group who were from Cambodia and Bosnia shared their interview results in turn. Jamila was very helpful to the rest of the team, especially helping the Bosnian girl.

Sylvia, Lenny, and other teachers and staff who were familiar with their students all saw impressive results in terms of interethnic relations that they claimed were due to the teaming structure. The after-school coordinator commented, "It's unique at this school. And some of the kids in that combined class are best friends [joined] at the hip." Sylvia herself said,

> I see incredible bonding and friendships and interactions between cultures. And the partnerships, they kind of move around a lot as that are group does, but I see so many cross cultural experiences, real ones, relationships, and hanging out at recess and lunch. I feel on that level it's definitely working.

Unfortunately, although this approach seemed to be among the most powerful in terms of breaking down racial and ethnic barriers, there were few supports for it to happen on a more schoolwide basis, and many constraints. The district did have a requirement that students had to be "integrated" 20% of the day, but this was far less than what Sylvia and Lenny were doing. Legally, they were in suspect territory because, as a teacher pointed out, "You can't [do more] because if you're meeting the bilingual requirement, you have to have primary language 80% of the time." Thus Sylvia, with her bilingual Spanish group, was actually in violation of district policy. Furthermore, even if their model were legally possible, there were not enough nonbilingual classes to have all the classrooms matched, as the principal explained: "If you have two thirds of one ethnicity and one third of the others, you can't match every class one to one."

Beyond the School: Parent Involvement

Cornell staff and leaders were making serious efforts to involve parents of diverse backgrounds in the school. These efforts, particularly when they brought parents of different ethnic groups together in an interactive format, had the potential to change attitudes in the home about other ethnic groups.

Among the various parent involvement efforts at Cornell were the Parent Center, a portable unit in the center of the yard specifically dedicated as a place where parents could come for meetings, or just to chat with a parent coordinator; a Family Resource Center, where parents and other family members could access a wide range of health and social services; translation services that were made available during most meetings and events involving parents; a Parent Education Program that included English as a second language instruction, a Spanish literacy class, a Family Stories class, and general equivalency diploma (GED) classes; a parent accountability event that over 600 parents attended to hear how students at Cornell were doing academically and to discuss ways to improve academic achievement; and responses to parent requests, such as the Vietnamese literacy class after school.

A tension that pervaded many parent involvement efforts was that although there was a sense of striving for equal outreach to all ethnic groups, when one group appeared to be getting more attention, other groups either felt shortchanged or wanted to have the same level of effort directed toward them. Another difficulty arose because of the need to provide services in the language parents could understand. As a result, some meetings were held by language group to facilitate communication and also help parents feel comfortable. This had a dual effect: It increased access for those parents, but also segregated them from other parents who had to meet separately because of their own language needs. This was essentially the same tension that pervaded the bilingual program—the tension between the two goals of providing access and creating an integrated environment. The school tried to get around this tension by doing some of both types of activities—some that were multicultural and others that were unicultural.

Probably the most in-depth cross-cultural sharing among parents took place in the parent education classes, which for the most part involved different ethnic groups and were viewed as a good way for parents to get to know one another across ethnic lines. Attendance was high and the program was well established in the life of the school. The relatively recent addition of the GED classes had helped the school reach out to African American parents, who formerly did not attend because all other classes were designed for nonnative speakers of English. The GED teacher said, "It's one of the most diverse classes I've ever taught. It's wonderful. It truly reflects the school." In the Family Stories class, parents told stories about their own lives and then, with the help of bilingual assistants, wrote the stories in their native language or English. Three books have been published as a result of this effort (Family Stories Group, 1992, 1993, 1995). In this cross-cultural context, parents explored and reflected on universal themes such as love and relationships, raising children, and immigrating to the United States. According to one parent, the classes gave "more chances to talk to each other, to know more about other groups of people. It is really helpful." Another parent, when asked whether these classes help race relations, replied, *"Yo creo que si, porque existe la communicacion entre los groups etnicos"* (I think so, because there is communication among the ethnic groups).

DISCUSSION: CAN SCHOOLS BE VEHICLES FOR IMPROVING INTERETHNIC RELATIONS?

With its rich tapestry of cultural traditions embedded in the student, parent, and staff populations and its rapidly shifting and ever-creative movement toward new forms of school culture, Cornell was struggling to become a place where students and adults of different ethnic and cultural groups could both find strength in their own ethnic identity and also reach out across groups to form alliances and shared community. This is not easy. Rosaldo (1989) described the dilemma facing racial minority groups in what he called "cultural border zones":

> [R]ace relations in North America involve a blend of assimilationist efforts, raw prejudice, and cultural containment that revolves around a concerted effort to keep each culture pure and in its place. Members of racial minority groups receive a peculiar message: either join the mainstream or stay in your ghettos, barrios, and reservations, but don't try to be both mobile and cultural. (p. 212)

Cornell was a site where these static categories were beginning to break down, and where, in their place, I found an energizing sense of motion. The practices and structures I have described have no doubt changed in the 2 years since I last visited, but there appears to be a constant: Cornell is a school seeking to define itself in ways that have not yet been accomplished in other places, making the process both frustrating and highly creative. Having journeyed through many dimensions of Cornell's efforts to promote positive relations among different ethnic groups, I want now to return to the question I posed at the beginning of this article: Can schools be vehicles for improving race relations?

Many would argue that, given the historical inequities that have been created and perpetuated in schools (e.g., segregation, tracking), schools are uniquely unqualified to serve as vehicles for undoing racism and ethnic conflict. When I posed the question recently in a college classroom of about 60 teacher education students, about 10 of them responded that they thought it was impossible for schools to improve race relations for the aforementioned reasons. They felt schools are too much a part of the problem to be really helpful in undoing racism and healing race relations.

In addition, it is clear that schools face "givens" that are part of the larger district, state, and national context and cannot be easily changed from within the school. Cornell faced several of these givens, including the district-imposed structure of the transitional bilingual program, the imbalance in the numbers of students of different ethnic groups attending the school, the lack of available people of color who are credentialed teachers, and the need to provide translation in parent meetings and the resulting tendency to hold those meetings by language-specific groups. Also, a powerful given in any school is the societal racism that exists in every community and filters into the school through parental attitudes, media stereotypes, and differential teacher expectations.

However, it is equally clear that teachers, both individually and in pairs or groups such as Sylvia and Lenny, can do a great deal within their classrooms to "affirm identity, build community, and cultivate student leadership" (Tatum, in press), as well as to model positive intergroup relations among adults (Allport, 1954) and "creatively analyze difference, power, and privilege" (Fine et al., 1998, p. 249). Such classrooms provide students with a "cross cultural and comparative perspective" (Gibson, 1987, p. 310) that is much needed if U.S. schools are to play a role in eliminating racial prejudice. However, these conditions must also be reflected in the larger institutional culture of the school, not in just a few classrooms but in every aspect of the school, including staffing, leadership structures and processes, curriculum and pedagogy, academic and behavioral standards, special programs, celebratory events, professional development of staff, and parent and community involvement. Cornell shows us how one school made determined efforts in all of these realms of school functioning and, as a result, was doing better in terms of ethnic relations than were many neighboring elementary schools. Yet teachers were not satisfied. Several of them, particularly those involved in SEED, thought the school still had a long way to go to become truly antiracist. They felt that multiculturalism was still practiced in largely superficial or "touristy" ways, such as focusing on foods and festivals, rather than, as the SEED framework suggests, placing everyone in the center.

Schools already do have the power to shape race relations in negative ways through sorting, tracking, unequal discipline, and silence about race. The question has to turn to whether or not they will use this power in a positive way. Cornell provides one example of how a school struggled with important priorities that placed integration at odds with bilingual education, but they still managed to work at the margins of the school day, in the center, and beyond the school to create opportunities for positive race relations to develop. To do this required awareness and strong leadership from administrators, teachers, and parent leaders who were committed to developing structures that would countervail the givens that kept people separate. In their creative resistance to racial polarization, members of the Cornell community show us how cultural production in the "borderlands" works, much as Anzaldua (1987) described the individual of mixed ancestry:

> The new *mestiza* copes by developing a tolerance for contradictions, a tolerance for ambiguity. She learns to be Indian in Mexican culture, to be Mexican from an Anglo point of view. She learns to juggle cultures. She has a plural personality, she operates in a pluralistic mode. . . . Not only does she sustain contradictions, she turns the ambivalence into something else. (p. 79)

ACKNOWLEDGMENTS

This study was funded through two grants, one through the Field Initiated Studies program (PR R308F60028), and another through the Center for Research on Education, Diversity and Excellence (PR R306A60001). Both grants are administered by the Office of Educational Research and Improvement (OERI), U.S. Department of Education (USDOE).

I wish to thank the staff, students, and parents at Cornell for sharing with me their efforts to make the school a positive, safe, and respectful place for learning.

The content, findings, and opinions expressed here are those of the author and do not necessarily represent the positions or policies of OERI or USDOE.

References

Allport, G. (1954). *The nature of prejudice*. Cambridge, MA: Addison-Wesley.

Anzaldua, G. (1987). *Borderlands/la frontera: The new mestiza*. San Francisco: Spinsters/Aunt Lute.

Banks. J. (1997). *Teaching strategies for ethnic studies* (6th ed.) Boston: Allyn & Bacon.

Bolman, L., & Deal, T. (1991). *Reframing organizations.* San Francisco: Jossey-Bass.

Braddock, J., Dawkins, M., & Wilson, P. (1995). Intercultural contact and race relations among American youth. In D. W. Hawley & A. W. Jackson (Eds.). *Toward a common destiny: Improving race and ethnic relations in America* (pp. 237–256). San Francisco: Jossey-Bass.

Community Boards of San Francisco. (1987). *Conflict resolution: An elementary school curriculum.* San Francisco: Author.

Cross, W. E. (1978). The Cross and Thomas models of psychological nigrescence. *Journal of Black Psychology, 5*(1), 13–19.

Deal, T., & Peterson, K. (1999). *Shaping school culture: The heart of leadership.* San Francisco: Jossey-Bass.

Erickson, F. (1986). Qualitative methods in research on teaching. In M. Wittrock (Ed.), *Handbook of research on teaching* (3rd ed., p. 119–161). New York: Collier Macmillan.

Family Stories Group. (1992). *Our stories, our lives [Nuestras historias, nuestras vidas]* (Vol. 1). Oakland, CA: ARC Associates.

Family Stories Group. (1993). *Our stories, our lives [Nuestras historias, nuestras vidas]* (Vol. 2). Oakland, CA: ARC Associates.

Family Stories Group. (1995). *Our stories, our lives [Nuestras historias, nuestras vidas]* (Vol. 3). Oakland, CA: ARC Associates.

Fine, M., Weis, L., & Powell, L. (1998). Communities of difference: A critical look at desegregated spaces created for and by youth. *Harvard Educational Review, 67,* 247–284.

Freire, P. (1970). *Pedagogy of the oppressed.* New York: Continuum.

Genesee, F. (Ed.). (1999). *Program alternatives for linguistically diverse students* (CREDE Educational Practice Rep. No. 1). Washington, DC: Center for Applied Linguistics.

Gibbs, J. (1995). *Tribes: A new way of learning and being together.* Sausalito, CA: Center Source Systems.

Gibson, M. (1987). Punjabi immigrants in an American high school. In G. Spindler & L. Spindler (Eds.), *Interpretive ethnography of education at home and abroad* (pp. 281–312). Hillsdale, NJ: Lawrence Erlbaum Associates, Inc.

Goetz, J., & LeCompte, M. (1984). *Ethnography and qualitative design in educational research.* Orlando, FL: Academic.

González, N., Moll, L., Floyd-Tenery, M., Rivera, A., Rendon, P., Gonzales, R., & Amanti, C. (1995). Funds of knowledge for teaching in Latino households. *Urban Education, 29,* 443–470.

Helms, J. E. (Ed). (1990). *Black and White racial identity: Theory, research, and practice.* Westport, CT: Greenwood.

Henze, R., Katz, A., Norte, E., Sather, S., & Walker, E. (1999). *Leading for diversity: A study of how school leaders achieve racial and ethnic harmony* (Final rep.). Oakland, CA: ARC Associates.

Kozol, J. (1991). *Savage inequalities: Children in America's schools.* New York: Crown.

Kreisberg, L. (1998). *Constructive conflicts: From escalation to resolution.* Lanham, MD: Rowman & Littlefield.

Lau v. Nichols, 414 U.S. 563, 566 (1973).

MacIntosh, P., & Style, E. (2000). *The SEED project on inclusive curriculum.* Retrieved May 24, 2000, from the World Wide Web: http://www.wellesley.edu/WCW/projects/seed.html

Maslow, A. (1954). *Motivation and personality.* New York: Harper & Row.

McDermott, R., & Varenne, H. (1995). Culture as disability. *Anthropology and Education Quarterly, 26,* 324–348.

Miles, M., & Huberman, M. (1994). *Qualitative data analysis* (2nd ed.). Thousand Oaks, CA: Sage.

Norte, E. (in press). Structures "beneath the skin": How school leaders use their power and authority to create institutional opportunities for developing positive interethnic communities. *Journal of Negro Education.*

Oakes, J., Wells, A. S., & Associates. (1996). *Beyond the technicalities of school reform: Policy lessons from detracking schools.* Los Angeles: University of California, Los Angeles, Graduate School of Education and Information Studies.

Rosaldo, R. (1989). *Culture and truth: The remaking of social analysis.* Boston: Beacon.

Sleeter, C. (1991). Introduction: Multicultural education and empowerment. In C. Sleeter (Ed.), *Empowerment through multicultural education* (pp. 1–23). Albany: State University of New York Press.

Stirfry Productions. (1994). *The color of fear* [video]. Oakland, CA: Author.

Tatum, B. (in press). Commentary. *Journal of Negro Education.*

Procrastination in College Students

The Role of Self-Efficacy and Anxiety

Appendix C

**Laurel A. Haycock,
Patricia McCarthy,
and Carol L. Skay**

In this study, the authors examined the relationships among procrastination, efficacy expectations, anxiety, gender, and age for 141 university students. Participants were asked to think about a major project and to rate their efficacy regarding the skills needed to accomplish the project. Bivariate correlations showed that efficacy expectations and anxiety had significant, individual relationships with procrastination. When these variables were entered into a regression model, only cumulative efficacy strength was a significant predictor of procrastination. Implications for practice and research suggestions are discussed.

Within United States society, productivity, doing, and accomplishing are highly valued norms (Althen, 1988). Procrastination, or the failure to get things done in a timely manner, directly violates these norms. Procrastination involves delaying responsibilities, decisions, or tasks that need to be done. In addition to the delay inherent in this phenomenon, problematic procrastination is accompanied by an internal, subjective discomfort usually thought to be anxiety (Rothblum, Solomon, & Murakami, 1986; Solomon & Rothblum, 1984). This distress differentiates procrastination from simply deciding to do an activity later.

Procrastination is a common and, at times, serious problem (Burka & Yuen, 1983). Internal consequences may include irritation, regret, despair, and self-blame (Burka & Yuen, 1983). External consequences may be costly and can include impaired academic and work progress, lost opportunities, and strained relationships (Burka & Yuen, 1983). For example, researchers who have studied academic procrastination have found that as many as 50% of undergraduates at

Haycock, L. A., McCarthy, P., & Skay, C. L. (1998). Procrastination in college students: The role of self-efficacy and anxiety. *Journal of Counseling & Development, 76,* 317–324.

one university report a tendency to procrastinate on assignments (Hill, Hill, Chabot, & Barrall, 1978; Solomon & Rothblum, 1984). Furthermore, procrastination may be a significant negative predictor of college grade point average (Wesley, 1994). Doctoral student procrastination may result in failure to finish dissertations (Muszynski & Akamatsu, 1991). Procrastination with respect to scholarly writing may put new faculty members at risk of job loss (Boice, 1989).

Despite these negative effects, procrastination remains a relatively poorly understood phenomenon. According to McCown (1986), behaviorists believe that procrastination is a learned habit developing from a human preference for pleasurable activities and short-term rewards. In contrast, psychodynamic theorists view procrastination as rebellion against overly demanding or overindulgent parents, or as a means of avoiding unconscious death anxiety (Blatt & Quinlan, 1967; McCown, Petzel, & Rupert, 1987). Several cognitive variables have been proposed as predictors of procrastination, including irrational beliefs (Beswick, Rothblum, & Mann, 1988; Solomon & Rothblum, 1984), attribution style (Rothblum et al., 1986), beliefs about time (Lay, 1988; Lay & Schouwenberg, 1993), self-esteem (Beswick et al., 1988), optimism (Lay, 1988; Lay & Burns, 1991), and self-handicapping strategies (Ferrari, 1992). Cognitive variables have been the most frequent subjects of empirical investigations, but the results are equivocal. For example, Beswick et al. (1988) found that irrational beliefs accounted for only 1% of the variance in procrastination for a sample of Australian university students. In contrast, Solomon and Rothblum (1984) found a significant correlation ($r = .30$) between academic procrastination and irrational beliefs for their sample of university students.

A popular theory about the etiology of procrastination is that it is a strategy for protecting a fragile sense of self-esteem (Berry, 1975; Burka & Yuen, 1983). For individuals who base their esteem on high performance, procrastination allows them to avoid complete testing of their abilities, thus maintaining a belief that their abilities are higher than their actual performance might be. Empirical support for a self-esteem—procrastination relationship is modest. For example, in a study of Australian university students, self-esteem accounted for only 5% of the variance in procrastination (Beswick et al., 1988).

Because the empirical support for current explanations of procrastination is so limited, further research is needed, including studies of other variables that may be related to the construct. One promising theory is Bandura's (1986) self-efficacy theory. Although self-efficacy may seem to be similar to self-esteem (e.g., both are components of self-referent thought), Bandura has argued that they are very different constructs. Self-efficacy pertains to an individual's judgment of how well she or he can perform certain behaviors in specific situations. Bandura (1986) defines two related but distinct components of self-efficacy: *efficacy expectations* and *outcome expectations.* Efficacy expectations are beliefs about one's capabilities to accomplish specific tasks. Outcome expectations refer to beliefs about the likelihood that certain behaviors will result in desired outcomes. Bandura argued that if adequate levels of ability and motivation exist, self-efficacy will affect a person's task initiation and persistence. Weak efficacy beliefs can contribute to behavior avoidance, whereas strong efficacy beliefs can promote behavior initiation and persistence.

Given the hypothesized role that self-efficacy plays in initiating and completing behaviors, it is surprising that only a few published studies have attempted to examine the link between self-efficacy and procrastination. Using a global measure of efficacy expectations, Tuckman (1991) found a significant inverse relationship between efficacy beliefs and procrastination for his sample of college students. In a second article, Tuckman and Sexton (1992) reviewed their work and concluded that self-beliefs mediate between external conditions and self-regulated performance, such that a lack of efficacy leads to procrastination. Also using a global measure of efficacy expectations, Ferrari, Parker, and Ware (1992) found a significant negative relationship between efficacy beliefs and academic procrastination, with weak efficacy being related to more frequent procrastination. These studies suggest an efficacy–procrastination relationship, although the use of global efficacy measures is inconsistent with Bandura's (1977) argument that self-efficacy should be measured by items indicative of the behaviors necessary to accomplish a more specific task.

Anxiety is another frequently studied variable, both in research on procrastination (e.g., Rothblum et al., 1986; Solomon & Rothblum, 1984) and in studies of self-efficacy (e.g., Bandura, 1986; Bandura, Adams, & Beyer, 1977). Typically, procrastination researchers have found a significant positive relationship such that individuals with higher anxiety are also more likely to procrastinate. Self-efficacy theory proposes a reciprocal relationship; levels of anxiety arousal can affect the extent to which individuals believe that they are able to handle threatening situations and vice versa (Bandura, 1986). When people experience weak efficacy in potentially threatening situations they also tend to experience increased anxiety. Procrastination may be an avoidance response related to either anxiety or weak efficacy expectations, or perhaps to both variables.

To date, the only demographic variable consistently examined in procrastination studies is gender, and the findings are mixed in this area. Some research indicates no significant gender differences in the incidence of procrastination (e.g., Effert & Ferrari, 1989; Rothblum et al., 1986; Solomon & Rothblum, 1984), whereas other research suggests that women are at greater risk than men (e.g., Paludi & Frankell-Hauser, 1986). Furthermore, women may experience greater levels of anxiety associated with procrastination (Rothblum et al., 1986). More research is needed to clarify the relationship between gender and procrastination. Age might be another significant predictor of procrastination, although no published research has investigated this possibility. For example, it could be argued that younger individuals would report a higher incidence of procrastination given their more limited opportunities to develop efficient work patterns.

As previously stated, little research has been done to examine the role of self-efficacy in procrastination. Furthermore, none of the existing studies assessed domain-specific efficacy expectations and their relationship to anxiety and procrastination. Theoretical considerations suggest that these constructs would be significantly related. Accordingly, this study was designed to assess the amount of variance in procrastination accounted for by a more domain-specific measure of efficacy expectations (defined as beliefs about one's skills for completing a difficult and important task) and state and trait anxiety. Efficacy expectations were chosen as the focus for two reasons. First, Bandura (1986) reported that efficacy expectations tend to be more accurate than outcome expectations in predicting performance. Second, he argued that, because outcome expectations pertain in part to aspects of the external environment, they are not as modifiable as the more internally regulated efficacy expectations. If efficacy expectations are found to be significantly associated with procrastination, then self-efficacy theory may provide a basis for intervention.

The focus of this study concerned the extent to which procrastination can be predicted by variables that are theoretically or empirically tied to the construct.

We hypothesized that efficacy expectations would be the strongest predictors of procrastination and that they would be inversely related to procrastination. It was further hypothesized that anxiety would be the next strongest predictor and that it would be positively related to procrastination. No hypotheses were generated concerning either gender or age, given the equivocal nature of the gender findings and the lack of research on age and procrastination.

METHOD

Participants and Procedure

One hundred and forty-one college student volunteers (87 women, 54 men), enrolled at a major midwestern university, participated in this study. Seventy-nine percent (n = 111) were enrolled in a learning and study skills course, and 21% (n = 30) were in a counseling procedures course for students who were not counseling majors. They ranged in age from 18 to 54 years (M = 24.50, SD = 7.40). The majority, 86%, identified themselves as White, and 14% identified as persons of color, primarily Black (4%) and Hispanic (4%). The sample included both undergraduates (82%) and adult extension and graduate students (18%). A variety of academic majors were represented.

Participation was solicited by one of the researchers during class time. The study was described as an investigation of factors that might be related to procrastination. The participants completed the questionnaires anonymously during the class. Of the 143 possible participants, 141 completed usable questionnaires.

Variables

Self-efficacy.   The Self-Efficacy Inventory (SEI) was created as part of this study to assess behaviors related to the task of "doing an important and difficult project by a specific deadline." Participants were asked to imagine themselves doing a project such as finding a job, writing a paper, or making a big decision, and to respond to the SEI within the context of their imagined project. This approach was used to increase the likelihood that each participant would select a task that was personally meaningful, salient, and challenging. Participants also were asked to list their project.

The SEI items were developed to assess efficacy *level* and *strength* for distinct behaviors generally related to accomplishing tasks. Level is measured by asking respondents to indicate by answering "yes" or "no" whether they think they can do a series of behaviors that vary in difficulty. Strength is measured by asking respondents to indicate their degree of confidence that they can do each behavior (0 = *great uncertainty* to 100 = *complete certainty*). Although Bandura (1986) recommended arranging items in a hierarchy of difficulty, we used a random format as suggested for complex behavior domains such as career self-efficacy (Lent & Hackett, 1987).

A panel of four psychologists with knowledge and expertise in the areas of procrastination and self-efficacy independently rated 45 items, first for their importance to the behavioral domain and next for their difficulty level for a "typical" person. Forty-three items were rated by all four judges as important to the domain; 31 of these had unanimous agreement for difficulty level. These 31 items constituted the final form of the SEI, with 10 items of high difficulty (e.g., "Can you identify target dates for the realistic completion of your work?"), 17 of medium difficulty (e.g., "Can you establish specific goals for your work?"), and four of low difficulty (e.g., "Can you take time-outs as a break from your work?"). The final form was piloted on 12 mental health professionals, and no substantive changes were made as a result of this pilot testing.

Responses to the SEI were scored in three ways. In accordance with Bandura's (1977) guidelines, efficacy level was determined by summing the number of "yes" responses across the 31 items for each participant. Scores can range from 0 to 31, with higher scores indicating higher efficacy expectations. Efficacy strength was scored in two ways. First, based on Bandura et al.'s (1977) procedures, an average score was obtained for each participant by dividing the total strength score by the number of "yes" responses, with a possible range of 0 to 100. In addition, a cumulative strength score was obtained for each participant by summing the confidence ratings for all items with a "yes" response. Cumulative strength scores can range from 0 to 3100, with higher scores indicating stronger efficacy. This latter method was used because we questioned how average strength scores are affected by different efficacy levels. For example, an individual responding "yes" to a small number of items with high confidence would have an artificially high indicator of efficacy if average strength was calculated. A cumulative strength score takes into consideration both the number of "yes" responses and the confidence ratings and may contain more information regarding efficacy beliefs. Cronbach's alpha coefficients, calculated for efficacy level, average efficacy strength, and cumulative efficacy strength, were .81, .60, and .91, respectively, indicating adequate-to-high internal consistency reliability.

Procrastination.   A modified version of Form G of the Procrastination Inventory (PI; Lay, 1986) was used to measure procrastination. The original form of this self-report inventory contains 20 forced-choice items concerning general, everyday behaviors (e.g., paying bills, returning phone calls promptly, putting things off "until tomorrow"). It was modified to include three items from Form A of the PI pertaining to academic tasks, for a total of 23 items. Items were added to increase the breadth of behaviors measured. Responses reflecting procrastination were scored as 2, and those not reflecting procrastination were scored as 1. Scores are summed across items and can range from 23 to 46, with higher scores indicating greater procrastination. In contrast to Lay's (1988) use of a median split procedure to categorize participants into groups of high and low procrastinators, participant scores were treated as continuous variables.

Internal consistency reliability coefficients ranging from .81 to .89 have been reported in three studies (Lay, 1988; Lay & Burns, 1991; Lay, Edwards, Parker, & Endler, 1989). Test-retest reliability for a 9-month interval was .80 (Ferrari, 1989). There is adequate evidence of construct validity for the PI; for example, it has been positively correlated with the Procrastination Assessment Scale, a measure of academic procrastination (Solomon & Rothblum, 1984), and has low correlations with a social desirability scale (Lay, 1986). Cronbach's alpha coefficient for the modified form of the Procrastination Inventory was .84 for the current sample, indicating good internal consistency reliability.

Anxiety.   The Spielberger State-Trait Anxiety Inventory (STAI) (Spielberger, Gorsuch, & Lushene, 1968) was used to measure participant anxiety. The STAI is an anxiety inventory commonly used in procrastination research. It consists of two 20-item scales, the Trait scale and the State scale. The Trait scale is a measure of relatively stable individual differences in anxiety-proneness or a tendency to perceive situations as threatening or dangerous. The State scale measures more transitory anxiety in response to specific stimuli. For this study, participants were instructed to complete the State scale by imagining themselves doing the same important project identified for completion of the SEI. For each STAI item, respondents rate themselves on a 4-point Likert scale (1 = *not at all*, 4 = *very much*). Scores for each scale can range from 20 to 80, with higher scores suggesting greater anxiety. The STAI is a widely researched inventory with substantial evidence of its reliability and validity (Spielberger et al., 1968). For example, test–retest reliability for the Trait scale ranges from .73 to .86 (Rothblum et al., 1986), but it is low, as expected, for the State scale, which measures transient anxiety (range = .16 to .54) (Spielberger et al., 1968).

Demographics. A demographic questionnaire was developed to obtain descriptive information about participants. It consisted of nine questions concerning age, sex, ethnicity, relationship status, student status, educational level, income, and employment status.

RESULTS

Because most of those in the sample were obtained from one university course, and participants from this course were slightly younger and included more men, analyses were performed on all four instruments to investigate any biases related to participant age or sex. None were found. Those in the sample reported experiencing moderate amounts of procrastination (*M* = 33.94, *SD* = 5.13) and high efficacy expectations (*M* = 25.84, *SD* = 4.25 for efficacy level; *M* = 1925.81, *SD* = 480.20, for cumulative strength; and *M* = 73.99, *SD* = 10.81 for average efficacy strength). They reported high state anxiety (*M* = 45.96, *SD* = 12.24) and moderate trait anxiety (*M* = 41.61, *SD* = 10.57).

A series of analyses of variance were conducted to assess differences in procrastination, efficacy, and anxiety as a function of participant demographics. No significant demographic differences were obtained. Zero-order correlations were calculated for scores on the procrastination, self-efficacy, and anxiety measures, and for age and sex. As shown in Table 1, procrastination scores were significantly related to self-efficacy and anxiety. Procrastination was inversely and significantly related to efficacy level (*r* = −.40), cumulative efficacy strength (*r* = −.50), and average efficacy strength (*r* = −.39). Procrastination was also significantly and positively related to both state and trait anxiety (*r* = .31 and .23, respectively) but was not related to either age or sex. Furthermore, there were moderate-

Table 1
Correlations Between Major Study Variables

	SE Cumulative	SE Average	State Anxiety	Trait Anxiety	Procrastination	Age	Sex
SE Level	.81**	.29**	−.38**	−.43**	−.40**	−.03	−.15
SE Cumulative		.80**	−.48**	−.50**	−.50**	−.09	−.07
SE Average			−.40**	−.37**	−.39**	.16	.04
State anxiety				.66**	.31**	.13	−.11
Trait anxiety					.23**	.08	.07
Procrastination						.04	.06
Age							.27*
Sex							—

Note. N = 141. SE = self-efficacy; SE cumulative = efficacy strength cumulative score; SE average = efficacy strength average score.
*p < .05. ***p* < .001.

Table 2
Summary of Simultaneous Multiple Linear Regression Model for Variables Predicting Procrastination

Variable	B	SE B	β	SE β	t	p
Efficacy level	.91	.62	0.75	.52	1.45	.15
Efficacy strength cumulative	−.02	.01	−1.66	.81	−2.05	.04
Efficacy strength average	.34	.24	0.72	.51	1.42	.16
Trait anxiety	−.07	.05	−0.14	.10	−1.35	.18
State anxiety	.08	.04	0.18	.10	1.77	.08
Sex	.85	.84	0.08	.08	1.01	.31
Age	.06	.05	0.09	.08	1.15	.25

Note. $N = 141$. $R^2 = .288$, $F(7, 133) = .771$, $p < .0001$.

to-high levels of multicollinearity between the efficacy, anxiety, and procrastination variables. Each of the efficacy measures was significantly and inversely related to state and trait anxiety. As expected, the three measures of efficacy level and strength were significantly and positively related, as were the state and trait anxiety variables. To examine the relationships between procrastination and all of the predictor variables of interest, a simultaneous multiple linear regression was conducted.

There were two purposes for performing this multiple regression analysis. First, we were interested in determining whether efficacy strength and level continued to be significantly related to procrastination even when the effects of other predictor variables were taken into account. Second, we wanted to identify the efficacy variable that was the strongest predictor of procrastination. The three efficacy measures, both anxiety measures, and the two demographic variables were entered into the regression equation. Although the demographics showed no significant relationship to procrastination in bivariate analyses, they were entered to partial out their influence on the relationships of the other variables. The regression model, summarized in Table 2, accounted for 29% of the variance in procrastination. In reviewing the standardized betas, the coefficient for cumulative efficacy strength is largest, suggesting it is the strongest and only significant predictor of procrastination ($p = .04$). The demographic variables have the smallest standardized betas.

Although efficacy level, average efficacy strength, and anxiety were significant in bivariate analyses, their predictive power was essentially negated by the effect of the cumulative efficacy strength variable due to the high degree of intercorrelations of all of these predictors. Indeed, when cumulative efficacy strength was entered into a regression model by itself, it alone accounted for 25% of the variance.

DISCUSSION

A major theme in the procrastination literature is the search for theoretical explanations of procrastination. Although cognitive constructs such as self-esteem (Beswick et al., 1988), self-handicapping (Ferrari, 1992), optimism (Lay & Burns, 1991), time perception (Lay, 1988), and global efficacy expectations (Tuckman, 1990) have been investigated, to date researchers have not examined the possible role of more domain-specific efficacy expectations. The current study was an investigation of the relationship between efficacy expectations about an important project and procrastination. In addition, anxiety, sex, and age were assessed for their possible connections to procrastination. Anxiety was of particular interest because it is a construct that has been found to be associated with both procrastination and self-efficacy.

The results of a regression analysis indicated that cumulative efficacy strength was a significant and inverse predictor of procrastination. Individuals with strong efficacy expectations tended to report less procrastination. Cumulative efficacy strength was defined as the sum of participant confidence ratings that they could accomplish 31 behaviors necessary to complete a major project.

These findings are consistent with the few studies that have examined global efficacy expectations and procrastination (Ferrari et al., 1992; Tuckman, 1991) and can be explained by Bandura's (1977) self-efficacy theory. Bandura argued that strong efficacy expectations lead to greater task initiation and persistence, whereas weak expectations produce task avoidance and less persistence. Procrastination is one type of behavior avoidance.

Current procrastination interventions emphasize the development of behavioral skills such as self-monitoring and self-reward (Green, 1982), self-control techniques (Ziesat, Rosenthal, & White, 1978), and stress and time management (Brown, 1992). As Solomon and Rothblum (1984) indicated, procrastination encompasses more than poor study habits and a lack of time management. It involves a complex interaction of behaviors, cognitions, and affect. The current results suggest the need for expanding interventions to include the cognitive component of efficacy expectations. An efficacy intervention could be accomplished by first explaining self-efficacy theory to clients. Next, a graduated set of tasks that will produce client success should be identified and executed to increase clients' success experiences and, thus, strengthen efficacy expectations (Bandura, 1986). A common problem for procrastinators is the skill of getting started on a specified task (Burka & Yuen, 1983). The skills necessary to initiate the task often need to be isolated and broken into small, attainable steps.

To illustrate a self-efficacy intervention, we created the following individual counseling example, based on theory and research reported by Bandura (1977, 1986). The hypothetical client is a male undergraduate student who is procrastinating about writing a term paper. Because Bandura (1977) argued that individuals must have adequate motivation and ability, as well as strong efficacy, to engage in behaviors successfully, the counselor should first clarify whether the project is an important one to the client and one that the client is capable of accomplishing. In simple terms, the explanation should involve what completing the paper means to the client. Has he successfully written papers in the past? Next, the counselor should assess outcome expectations by verifying that the project can reasonably be accomplished (e.g., Is there enough time to complete the paper? Does the client have sufficient resources, such as access to a library and word processing equipment?). The third step involves efficacy expectations and consists of helping the client identify the individual behaviors necessary to complete the project. These might include the following behaviors: conduct a literature search, highlight important points in each source, develop an outline, request instructor feedback on the outline, write a rough draft, and revise the paper. If the client's efficacy expectations are quite weak, these behaviors could be further broken down (e.g., "write a rough draft" could be divided into "write an opening paragraph, write 500 more words, write a concluding paragraph").

After the behaviors are specified, the counselor might ask the client whether he can do each behavior (yes/no) and to rate his confidence (0 = complete uncertainty, 100 = great certainty) for each behavior. This exercise would provide an indication of cumulative efficacy strength. The counselor and client could then identify obstacles to completing each behavior, with particular emphasis on those behaviors for which the client has weak efficacy expectations, and determine ways to minimize these obstacles. It is important for clients to successfully complete behaviors between counseling sessions. As Bandura (1986) stated, an individual must experience success to maintain or strengthen efficacy, so the client's "out of session" assignments should not be too ambitious. In subsequent sessions, the counselor would monitor the client's efficacy expectations by asking him to again rate the behavioral steps.

Several of the items from the SEI used in this study suggest the types of obstacles that are common in procrastinating to do a major task. They include failure to do the following: establish specific goals for the project and revise those goals as necessary, set dates for realistic completion of work, reward one's self for progress, establish specific goals for each work session, schedule sufficient blocks of time for working on the project, plan an efficient way to use one's time during each work session, postpone socializing or doing other things during scheduled work sessions, ask others for assistance when one is "stuck," recall past accomplishments to help in doing the current project, and let go of perfectionistic standards. Discussion of how to remove these obstacles may assist the client in writing the paper, while increasing his self-efficacy.

Another important issue concerns identifying individuals at risk for procrastination. We recommend the use of the Procrastination Assessment Scale–Students (PASS; Solomon & Rothblum, 1984) with college students. The PASS can be used by counselors to identify individuals at risk for academic difficulty due to procrastination. These findings suggest that students should also be screened with self-efficacy measures. Self-efficacy theory seems to be a relevant model for higher education settings, given the emphasis on cognitive processes. Furthermore, a significant amount of student procrastination can involve academic tasks (Burka & Yuen, 1983), and these lend themselves well to behavioral hierarchies that are the essence of efficacy expectations. Screening should be done early in a student's academic career so that failures, which weaken efficacy expectations, can be prevented. Identifying students at risk for procrastination on tasks such as term papers and research projects would allow counselors to intervene and thus increase the students' chances of completing their assignments in a timely manner.

Prior research (e.g., Beswick et al., 1988; Solomon & Rothblum, 1984) has demonstrated significant relationships between anxiety and procrastination. In the current study, when the effects due to efficacy were considered, anxiety did not contribute significantly to the variance in procrastination. Anxiety may need to be examined and interpreted in the context of its relationship to other variables. For example, it may be that anxiety has an impact on self-efficacy and that its effects on procrastination are mediated by efficacy expectations. However, given Bandura's (1986) theory of *reciprocal determinism*, it is difficult to distinguish between anxiety as an antecedent or as a consequence of behavior initiation and persistence. Furthermore, correlational analyses do not lend themselves to causal interpretations.

Neither of the demographic variables measured in this study were significant predictors of procrastination. More research is needed to clarify whether any relationships exists, because this is the first study of efficacy and procrastination to examine sex and age. These findings suggest that counselors should not expect procrastination to occur more frequently for either male or female clients. However, they should be sensitive to the possibility that the consequences of procrastination differ due to sex. For instance, there is some evidence that women may experience more anxiety than men because of their procrastination (Rothblum et al., 1986).

Several limits of this study suggest that researchers should be cautious in drawing definitive conclusions from the results. The sample was selected in a nonrandom way and participants were predominantly White and thus may not be representative of university students in general. The data lack behavioral confirmation of participant self-perceptions. Finally, many of the participants identified some type of academic procrastination. It is not known whether the current relationships would be found for other types of procrastination. Nevertheless, the findings suggest several research directions.

Typically, efficacy researchers have defined efficacy level as the number of "yes" responses to items, and efficacy strength as the total confidence ratings divided by the sum of the behaviors receiving positive endorsements (Bandura, 1977, 1986; Bandura et al., 1977). The current results indicate that efficacy strength may be a better predictor than efficacy level for complex processes such as procrastination. From a statistical perspective, a 0 to 100 confidence interval provides a greater range of variability than does the categorical, yes/no format used to measure efficacy level. Indeed, as others have argued (Lent & Hackett, 1987), and as demonstrated by the current results, efficacy level is subsumed by efficacy strength. Furthermore, because an average efficacy strength score is calculated by dividing total confidence by a different number of items for each respondent, there is no way to include information about how many items are positively endorsed. Therefore, a cumulative efficacy score contains information concerning both level and strength. Our results suggest that both efficacy level and average efficacy strength are subsumed by a cumulative strength score. Therefore, researchers and practitioners should use cumulative strength scores.

In this study, although there were no ceiling effects for the SEI (indicating adequate variance), scores tended to cluster near the higher end of the scale. These results are not surprising given that most participants had been in college for a while, suggesting a certain degree of successful behaviors and concomitantly stronger efficacy expectations. Studies that would include samples of at-risk students, larger numbers of new students, or both, would very likely increase response variability. Future research in this area needs to be done with diverse populations.

This study was focused on only one aspect of self-efficacy theory, efficacy expectations. Future procrastination research should also include outcome expectations, which pertain to an individual's judgments about the likelihood that a given behavior will lead to a desired outcome or consequence (Bandura, 1986). For example, does procrastination occur when people have poor outcome expectations because their workloads are impossible to complete? Most of the tasks listed by the participants in this study involved some type of academic procrastination. This study should be replicated with other types of tasks. In addition, although the efficacy measure developed for this study is more task-specific than those measures used in prior research (e.g., Tuckman, 1991), even greater compliance with Bandura's (1977) guideline for specificity could be obtained if research participants were instructed to respond to behavioral items pertaining to the same task.

Although the current results indicate that efficacy expectations are a significant predictor of procrastination, the amount of variance accounted for is modest. One commonly proposed theory about procrastination is that it is a strategy used to protect a fragile sense of self-esteem, especially for individuals who base their esteem on accomplishments (Berry, 1975; Burka & Yuen, 1983). Future studies should assess the unique contributions of self-efficacy and self-esteem to procrastination. Furthermore, Bandura (1986) argued that individuals must have adequate levels of ability for efficacy expectations to be a significant mediator of performance. Future studies of procrastination could include an ability measure such as grade point average.

Finally, there is little research that compares the outcomes of different interventions for procrastination, and there are no studies of efficacy-based treatments. Research is needed to assess the comparative effectiveness of self-efficacy approaches in reducing procrastination. Actual performance should be examined to confirm participant self-reports of procrastination.

This study demonstrated that efficacy expectations were significant predictors of college student procrastination. The findings suggest that interventions designed to reduce procrastination might include a cognitive component such as self-efficacy. We hope that these findings will contribute to theory and practice by highlighting the importance of the social cognitive construct of self-efficacy.

References

Althen, G. (1988). *American ways: A guide for foreigners in the United States.* Yarmouth, ME: Intercultural Press.

Bandura, A. (1977). Self-efficacy: Toward a unifying theory of behavioral change. *Psychological Review, 84.* 191–215.

Bandura, A. (1986). *Social foundations of thought and action: A social cognitive theory.* Upper Saddle River, Prentice Hall.

Bandura, A., Adams, N. E., & Beyer, J. (1977). Cognitive processes mediating behavioral change. *Journal of Personality and Social Psychology, 35,* 125–139.

Berry, R. G. (1975). Fear of failure in the student experience. *The Personnel and Guidance Journal, 54,* 190–203.

Beswick, G., Rothblum, E. D., & Mann, L. (1988). Psychological antecedents of student procrastination. *Australian Psychologist, 23,* 207–217.

Blatt, S. J, & Quinlan, P. (1967). Punctual and procrastinating students: A study of temporal parameters. *Journal of Counseling Psychology, 31,* 169–174.

Boice, R. (1989). Procrastination, busyness and bingeing. *Behavior Research and Therapy, 27,* 605–611.

Brown, R. T. (1992). Helping students confront and deal with stress and procrastination. *Journal of College Student Psychotherapy, 6,* 87–102.

Burka, J. B., & Yuen, L. M. (1983). *Procrastination: Why you do it, what to do about it.* New York: Addison-Wesley.

Effert, B. R., & Ferrari, J. R. (1989). Decisional procrastination: Examining personality correlates. *Journal of Social Behavior and Personality, 4,* 151–156.

Ferrari, J. R. (1989). Reliability of academic and dispositional measures of procrastination. *Psychological Reports, 64,* 1057–1058.

Ferrari, J. R. (1992). Procrastinators and perfect behavior: An exploratory factor analysis of self-presentation, self-awareness and self-handicapping components. *Journal of Research in Personality, 26,* 75–84.

Ferrari, J. R., Parker, J. T., & Ware, C. B. (1992). Academic procrastination: Personality correlates with Myers-Briggs types, self-efficacy, and academic locus of control. *Journal of Social Behavior and Personality, 7,* 495–502.

Green, L. (1982). Minority students' self-control of procrastination. *Journal of Counseling Psychology, 29,* 636–644.

Hill, M. B., Hill, D. A., Chabot, A. E., & Barrall, J. F. (1978). A survey of college faculty and student procrastination. *College Student Journal, 12,* 256–262.

Lay, C. H. (1986). At last, my research article on procrastination. *Journal of Research in Personality, 20,* 474–495.

Lay, C. H. (1988). The relationship of procrastination and optimism to judgments of time to complete an essay and anticipation of setbacks. *Journal of Social Behavior and Personality, 3,* 201–214.

Lay, C. H., & Burns, P. (1991). Intentions and behavior in studying for an exam: The role of trait procrastination and its interaction with optimism. *Journal of Social Behavior and Personality, 6,* 605–617.

Lay, C. H., Edwards, J. M., Parker, J. D., & Endler, N. S. (1989). An assessment of appraisal, anxiety and coping, and procrastination during an examination period. *European Journal of Personality, 3,* 195–208.

Lay, C. H., & Schouwenberg, H. C. (1993). Trait procrastination, time management, and academic behavior. *Journal of Social Behavior and Personality, 8,* 647–662.

Lent, R. W., & Hackett, G. (1987). Career self-efficacy: Empirical status and future directions. *Journal of Vocational Behavior, 30,* 347–382.

McCown, W. (1986). An empirical investigation of the behaviors of procrastinators. *Social and Behavioral Science Documents, 16,* 1–89.

McCown, W., Petzel, T., & Rupert, P. (1987). An experimental study of some hypothesized behaviors and personality variables of college student procrastinators. *Personality and Individual Differences, 8,* 781–786.

Muszynski, S. Y., & Akamatsu, T. J. (1991). Delay in completion of doctoral dissertations in clinical psychology. *Professional Psychology: Research and Practice, 22,* 119–123.

Paludi, M. A., & Frankell-Hauser, J. (1986). An idiographic approach to the study of women's achievement striving. *Psychology of Women Quarterly, 10,* 89–100.

Rothblum, E. D., Solomon, L. J., & Murakami, J. (1986). Affective, cognitive, and behavioral differences between high and low procrastinators. *Journal of Counseling Psychology, 33,* 387–394.

Solomon, L. J., & Rothblum, E. D. (1984). Academic procrastination: Frequency and cognitive-behavioral correlates. *Journal of Counseling Psychology, 31,* 503–509.

Spielberger, C. D., Gorsuch, R. C., & Lushene, R. (1968). *Self-Evaluation Questionnaire.* Palo Alto, CA: Consulting Psychologists Press.

Tuckman, B. W. (1990). Group versus goal-setting effects on the self-regulated performance of students differing in self-efficacy. *Journal of Experimental Education, 58,* 291–298.

Tuckman, B. W. (1991). The development and concurrent validity of the Procrastination Scale. *Educational and Psychological Measurement, 51,* 473–480.

Tuckman, B. W., & Sexton, T. L., (1992). Self-believers are self-motivated; self-doubters are not. *Personality and Individual Differences, 13,* 425–428.

Wesley, J. C. (1994). Effects of ability, high school achievement, and procrastinatory behavior on college performance. *Educational and Psychological Measurement, 54,* 404–408.

Ziesat, H. A., Rosenthal, T. L., & White, G. M. (1978). Behavioral self-control in treating procrastination of studying. *Psychological Reports, 42,* 59–69.

Bibliography

American Psychological Association. (2001). *Publication manual of the American Psychological Association* (5th ed.). Washington, DC: Author.

Ary, D., Jacobs, L. C., & Razavieh, A. (2002). *Introduction to research in education* (6th ed.). Belmont, CA: Wadsworth/Thomson Learning.

Ballard, S. M., & Morris, M. L. (1998). Sources of sexuality information for university students. *Journal of Sex Education & Therapy, 23,* 278–287.

Bloom, M., Fischer, J., & Orme, J. G. (2003). *Evaluating practice: Guidelines for the accountable professional* (4th ed.). Boston: Allyn & Bacon.

Bogdan, R. C., & Biklen, S. K. (2003). *Qualitative research for education: An introduction to theories and methods* (4th ed.). Boston: Allyn & Bacon.

Bracey, G. W. (2003). Tips for readers of research: Seeing through the graphs. *Phi Delta Kappan, 84,* 476–477.

Code of Federal Regulations for the Protection of Human Subjects (2001). Title 45, Public Welfare Department of Health and Human Services, National Institutes of Health, Office for Protection from Research Risks, §46.102d Definitions. Retrieved September 2, 2004, from http://www. hhs.gov/ohrp/humansubjects/guidance/45cfr46.htm#46.102.

D'Cruz, P. (2002, September). Caregivers' experiences of informal support in the context of HIV/AIDS. *The Qualitative Report, 7*(3). Retrieved September 2, 2004, from http://www.nova.edu/ssss/QR/QR7-3/dcruz.html.

Domino, G. (2000). *Psychological testing: An introduction.* Upper Saddle River, NJ: Prentice-Hall.

Donnelly, C., & Glaser, A. (1992). Training in self-supervision skills. *The Clinical Supervisor, 10,* 2–10.

Edyburn, D. L. (1999). *The electronic scholar: Enhancing research productivity with technology.* Upper Saddle River, NJ: Prentice-Hall.

Gay, L. R., & Airasian, P. (2003). *Educational research: Competencies for analysis and applications* (7th ed.). Upper Saddle River, NJ: Prentice-Hall/Merrill.

Haycock, L. A., McCarthy, P., & Skay, C.L. (1998). Procrastination in college students: The role of self-efficacy and anxiety, *Journal of Counseling & Development, 76,* 317–324.

Henze, R. C. (2001). Segregated classrooms, integrated intent: How one school responded to the challenge of developing positive interethnic relations. *Journal of Education for Students Placed At Risk, 6,* 133–155.

Huff, D. (1954). *How to lie with statistics.* New York: W. W. Norton & Company.

Joynson, R. B. (1989). *The Burt affair.* London: Routledge.

Krueger, J. (2001). Null hypothesis significance testing: On the survival of a flawed method. *American Psychologist, 56,* 16–26.

Lemieux, P., McKelvie, S. J., & Stout, D. (2002, December). Self-reported hostile aggression in contact athletes, no-contact athletes, and non-athletes. *Athletic Insight—The Online Journal of Sport Psychology, 4*(3). Retrieved September 2, 2004, from http://www.athleticinsight. com/Vol4Iss3/SelfReportedAggression.htm

Lin, H., Gorrell, J., & Taylor, J. (2002). Influence of culture and education on U.S. and Taiwan preservice teachers' efficacy beliefs. *Journal of Educational Research, 96,* 37–46.

Liss, H. J., Glueckauf, R. L, & Ecklund-Johnson, E. P. (2002). Research on telehealth and chronic medical conditions: Critical review, key issues, and future directions. *Rehabilitation Psychology, 47,* 8–30.

McConnell, J. V. (1962). Memory transfer through cannibalism in planarians. *Journal of Neuropsychiatry, 3,* 42–48.

McLeod, J. (2001). *Qualitative research in counselling and psychotherapy.* London: Sage Publications.

Putney, L.G., & Floriani, A. (1999). Examining transformative process and practices: A cross-case analysis of life in two bilingual classrooms. *Journal of Classroom Interaction, 34,* 17–29.

Redding, N. P., & Dowling, W. D. (1992). Rites of passage among women reentering higher education. *Adult Education Quarterly, 42,* 221–226

Rilling, M. (1996). The mystery of the vanished citations: James McConnell's forgotten 1960s quest for planarian learning, a biochemical engram, and celebrity. *American Psychologist, 51,* 589–598.

Runyon, R. P., Coleman, K. A., & Pittenger, D. (2000). *Fundamentals of behavioral statistics* (9th ed.). Columbus, OH: McGraw-Hill.

Sapp, M. (1995). Teaching ethics to mental health practica students at the master's level: A comparative study. *College Student Journal, 29,* 333–339.

Sebold, A. (2002). *The lovely bones.* New York: Little Brown & Company.

Shank, G.D. (2002). *Qualitative research: A personal skills approach.* Upper Saddle River, NJ: Prentice-Hall/Merrill.

Slavin, R. E. (2003, February). A reader's guide to scientifically based research. *Educational Leadership, 60,* 12–16.

Sprinthall, R. C. (2003). *Basic statistical analysis* (7th ed.). Boston: Allyn & Bacon.

Thompson, B. (1996). AERA editorial policies regarding statistical significance testing: Three suggested reforms. *EducationalResearcher, 25,* 26–30.

Thorndike, E. L. (1914). *Educational psychology: Briefer course.* New York: Teachers College, Columbia University.

Index